Living Memory

Blackwell Studies in Discourse and Culture

Linguistic anthropology evolved in the 20th century in an environment that tended to reify language and culture. A recognition of the dynamics of discourse as a sociocultural process has since emerged as researchers have used new methods and theories to examine the reproduction and transformation of people, institutions, and communities through linguistic practices. This transformation of linguistic anthropology itself heralds a new era for publishing as well. *Blackwell Studies in Discourse and Culture* aims to represent and foster this new approach to discourse and culture by producing books that focus on the dynamics that can be obscured by such broad and diffuse terms as "language." This series is committed to the ethnographic approach to language and discourse: ethnographic works deeply informed by theory, as well as more theoretical works that are deeply grounded in ethnography. The books are aimed at scholars in the sociology and anthropology of language, anthropological linguistics, sociolinguistics and socioculturally informed psycholinguistics. It is our hope that all books in the series will be widely adopted for a variety of courses.

Series Editor

James M. Wilce (PhD University of California, Los Angeles) is Professor of Anthropology at Northern Arizona University. He serves on the editorial board of *American Anthropologist* and the *Journal of Linguistic Anthropology*. He has published a number of articles and is the author of *Eloquence in Trouble: The Poetics and Politics of Complaint in Rural Bangladesh* (1998) and *Language and Emotion* (forthcoming) and the editor of *Social and Cultural Lives of Immune Systems* (2003).

Editorial Board:

Richard Bauman – Indiana University
Eve Danziger – University of Virginia
Patrick Eisenlohr – University of Chicago
Per-Anders Forstorp – Royal Institute of Technology, Stockholm
Elizabeth Keating – UT Austin
Paul Kroskrity – UCLA
Norma Mendoza-Denton – University of Arizona
Susan Philips – University of Arizona
Bambi Schieffelin – NYU

In the Series:

1. *The Hidden Life of Girls*, by Marjorie Harness Goodwin
2. *We Share Walls: Language, Land, and Gender in Berber Morocco*, by Katherine E. Hoffman
3. *The Everyday Language of White Racism*, by Jane H. Hill
4. *Living Memory: The Social Aesthetics of Language*, by Jillian R. Cavanaugh

Living Memory

The Social Aesthetics of Language in a Northern Italian Town

Jillian R. Cavanaugh

WILEY-BLACKWELL

A John Wiley & Sons, Ltd., Publication

This paperback edition first published 2012
© 2012 Jillian R. Cavanaugh

Edition History: Blackwell Publishing Ltd (hardback, 2009)

Blackwell Publishing was acquired by John Wiley & Sons in February 2007. Blackwell's publishing program has been merged with Wiley's global Scientific, Technical, and Medical business to form Wiley-Blackwell.

Registered Office
John Wiley & Sons Ltd, The Atrium, Southern Gate, Chichester, West Sussex, PO19 8SQ, UK

Editorial Offices
350 Main Street, Malden, MA 02148-5020, USA
9600 Garsington Road, Oxford, OX4 2DQ, UK
The Atrium, Southern Gate, Chichester, West Sussex, PO19 8SQ, UK

For details of our global editorial offices, for customer services, and for information about how to apply for permission to reuse the copyright material in this book please see our website at www.wiley.com/wiley-blackwell.

The right of Jillian R. Cavanaugh to be identified as the author of this work has been asserted in accordance with the UK Copyright, Designs and Patents Act 1988.

Library of Congress Cataloging-in-Publication Data

Cavanaugh, Jillian R.
  Living Memory : The social aesthetics of language in a northern Italian town/ Jillian R. Cavanaugh.
      p. cm. – (Blackwell studies in discourse and culture)
  Includes bibliographical references and index.
  ISBN 978-1-4051-6882-3 (hardcover: alk. paper) ISBN 978-1-118-27743-0 (paperback: alk. paper) 1. Sociolinguistics–Italy–Bergamo. 2. Language and culture–Italy–Bergamo. 3. Italian language–Dialects–Italy–Bergamo. 4. Bergamo (Italy)–Intellectual life–21st century. I. Title.

  P40.45.I8C38 2009
  306.440945′24–dc22

                                                                    2008048207

A catalogue record for this book is available from the British Library.

Cover image: Photograph by Scott Collard.
Cover design by Design Deluxe.

Set in 11.5/13.5 pt Bembo by Toppan Best-set Premedia Limited
Printed in Malaysia by Ho Printing (M) Sdn Bhd

1   2012

Contents

Series Editor's Preface

Blackwell Studies in Discourse and Culture was launched in 2005, committed to publishing books whose ethnographic approach to language and discourse contributes to linguistic–anthropological theory. Jillian Cavanaugh's *Living Memory* is just such a work. Cavanaugh's profoundly engaging account illuminates precisely the issues outlined in the goals of the series: namely, to address issues such as:

- the global and local dynamics of the production, reception, circulation, and contextualization of discourse;
- the discursive production of social collectivities;
- the dynamic relation of speech acts to agents, social roles, and identities;
- the emergent relation of ideologies to linguistic structure and the social life of linguistic forms; and
- the dialectical relations of local speech events to larger social formations and centers of power.

This book stands out as a remarkable contribution to our understanding of "the social aesthetics of language," as the subtitle promises. It demonstrates the profound links between sentiment and structures of power, between feelings and the forces shaping social practice in general and speaking in particular. Few if any ethnographies so effectively map the intersection of emotion, practice, ideology, and history. The uniqueness of Cavanaugh's accomplishment involves her success at each of the following, and offering a breathtaking synthesis: 1) conveying the *feel* of speaking Bergamasco (a sense acquired through the intimacies of participant observation in, for example, performances of Bergamasco plays) and Italian, 2) analyzing contemporary tensions between the imagining of "pure" forms of Italian and Bergamasco (each purged of the other's influence) and the actual practice of speaking in mixed forms, and 3) recounting the social history of ideologies – particularly ideologies of language, such as purism.

Thus, this work establishes Cavanaugh as a leading figure illuminating the social aesthetics of language, and particularly the triadic relationship of speaking and feeling in which language is recruited as a medium of emotional expression, an index of affectively valenced gender performance, and an object of emotional identification. The first is exemplified in local enthusiasts' assertion that particular Bergamasco words are more "immediately expressive" than their Italian counterparts. The complexities of the second link desirability in the heterosexual marketplace to speaking Italian in the case of women, and Bergamasco in the case of men. The third involves nostalgia for the local code itself – and its presumed impending loss. Paolo Frér, the poet/performer whose life and passing Cavanaugh movingly describes, could recruit Bergamasco as the perfect tool for expressing emotional attachment to place (Bergamo's Città Alta), while his audience shouted their appreciation of the poet, his particular idiom, and the Bergamasco language more generally. Paolo exemplifies men's duty to do what they can to "save Bergamasco." His audience's appreciation, and widely circulating nostalgic assertions of the impending loss of Bergamasco, have – Cavanaugh shows us – arisen out of the history of Italian politics since the 1920s. National policy since the Fascist period has not simply adopted various means of suppressing "dialects" but has in effect contributed to their decline precisely, if paradoxically, through representing them as dying.

Happily, Cavanaugh exemplifies the complex relation of language(s) to feeling that is her subject. Hers is that rare work that combines careful and convincing intellectual argument *about* the double-faceted aesthetics of language described above with a style that helps readers – like Paolo's audience – *feel* the place, the people, and what is at stake in the unfolding history. Cavanaugh's accomplishment reflects the richness of data collected through diverse methods, effectively synthesized. The stories she tells seethe with feeling, but it is just as important that her writing brings this home to us so powerfully.

Thus *Living Memory* takes its place alongside its esteemed predecessors. To Cavanaugh, our thanks. To the reader, an invitation to encounter Bergamo with as much empathy as you can muster. Welcome to the world of discourse and culture as they meet in lived experience.

Preface

The year I was 15, my family moved to Florence for a year. We moved there so that my sister and I would learn about another culture; I came home with a widened perspective on the world, fluent in Italian, and with a fascination of language in general and Italian ways of speaking in particular that endures. Perhaps it began the day that my classmates in the Italian high school I attended that year taught me a Florentine tongue twister: *una Coca-Cola con la conuncia corta-corta* (a Coke with a very short straw). It's obviously not what the phrase means that matters, but how it is properly said by Florentines: *una Hoha-Hola hon la honunsha horta-horta.* My friends hooted with laughter as they coached me, and then made me say it to everyone we met when I had learned it correctly. These performances always made the recipients laugh, pronounce me '*brava!*' (good, smart), and then comment on how very Florentine I had become in so short a time. Not Italian, but Florentine – that's what mattered to those who heard me say this short phrase. Later in the year, as my Florentine accent flourished, when I told people I met that I was an "*ameri-Hana*" (not an "*ameri-Cana*", as it would have been in a standard Italian accent), I received the same set of evaluations. By dropping my 'c's just like other Florentines, I became local, leap-frogging the national boundaries that separated me from my friends there.

It became resoundingly clear how very locally anchored in Florence I had become when my family and I visited Pisa, mere kilometers away, and my Florentine-accented Italian was met with cold shoulders and rude comments, while my parents' hesitant, American-accented Italian was appreciated and welcomed. When I told my Florentine friends about it when we returned to Florence, they laughed and told me a Florentine proverb: "it's better to have a death in the family, than a Pisan at the door." Pisans evidently have the same saying about Florentines; their mutual animosity dates back centuries to when they were independent, warring city-states. While I was amused to be an American teenager caught up in a centuries-old feud between Italian cities, this incident sparked a recognition of how deep connections to local places are in Italy, how these connections are expressed through bits of language like accents, and how Italians use local identities and ways of speaking to define themselves vis-à-vis each other, the Italian nation-state, and others from abroad.

Later during my graduate studies in the late 1990s and fieldwork in the early 2000s in another part of Italy, I learned that the different ways of speaking I had experienced as a teenager in Italy were common across the peninsula. While these linguistic varieties are considered to be in the process of being lost, many Italians continue to use them and value them. In Italy, the *questione della lingua* – language question – has always been a socioeconomic, political, and cultural issue. When I was a teenager in the 1980s, local ways of speaking primarily set localities apart from one another, as well as helped orient their speakers to the centralized nation-state. In the 1990s, increasing immigration and Europeanization meant that locality was increasingly called on to help Florentines, Pisans, and all Italians orient themselves within larger contexts as well. This is not to say that Italians have not long looked beyond their own boundaries – extensive emigration to the Americas, Australia, and Northern Europe since the middle of the nineteenth century; participation in two World Wars; and decades of consumption of media forms from abroad, for instance, have connected the particular places of Italy to other places further afield. However, the 1990s and then early 2000s have posed their own sets of challenges, and language – and how it is used, felt, and reflected upon – can be a valuable tool for helping to understand these challenges.

Indeed, so many of the pressing issues that Italians – as well as other Europeans, and people around the globe – face today can be productively viewed through the lens of language: who are we in relation to our neighbors, near and far? How should we bring up our children? What is the best way to pursue a livelihood? What does our past mean? What should we leave behind and what do we need to bring with us in order to make the present and the future meaningful? This book aims to use language to begin to answer these questions for one small community in northern Italy.

Acknowledgments

In Bergamo, I have been fortunate to meet many generous people to help me formulate and begin to answer these questions. So many Bergamaschi welcomed me into their busy lives and homes, and I am honored to call them friends. I give my thanks and gratitude to the families and friends who welcomed us and made us feel at home: the Zoppetti, the Scuri, and the Pizzigalli-Fazio, as well as Maria Stefania, Franco, Giorgio Paolo, Mariuccia and everyone at *Passemezzo*, and everyone in my *compagnia teattrale*, especially Rosella and Elia. A debt of gratitude goes to Roberta, Erika, Elena, Elisa, and Daniele without whom the transcriptions would have been impossible, and much less fun. Vittorio Mora shared his expertise, and many Bergamasco poets shared their work and inspirations with me. At the *Ducato di Piazza Pontida*, I thank the Duke, my classmates, and especially Carmelo Francia, for helping me understand the value of Bergamasco. Thanks also go to the *Ateneo*, and to the *Biblioteca Civica*, for their help, as well as to Chris Carlsmith for introducing me to Bergamo in the first place. My appreciation to the **sciure** at the *Scuola della Nonna* and the *Centro Sociale della Città Alta*, and to Paola Schellenbaum, whose ongoing interest and conversation has enlivened this project since that first rainy day.

A number of individuals and organizations have supported this work since its inception. Research and write-up support has been generously provided by a number of organizations: the International Dissertation Research Fellowship Program at the Social Science Research Council; the Wenner-Gren Foundation for Anthropological Research; the National Science Foundation, Linguistics Program (Dr. Bambi B. Schieffelin, PI); the National Endowment for the Humanities; the Council for European Studies' Pre-Dissertation Fellowship Program; and New York University's Dean's Summer

Fellowship for Preliminary PhD Research at the Graduate School of Arts and Sciences Program. Brooklyn College and the City University of New York Research Foundation have been generous in their support of this project, awarding me a Tow Faculty Research Fellowship, several PSC-CUNY Research Awards, and a Whiting Fellowship.

This book and the dissertation that preceded it have benefited from a number of readers who have provided important comments, insights, and questions. The biggest thanks go to Bambi Schieffelin, advisor, mentor, and friend, without whom none of this would have been possible. Her insight, generosity with her time and energy, patience, and ability to see to the heart of the matter are truly an inspiration. I am grateful to Don Kulick for many close readings and conversations before, during, and after fieldwork, and to Susan Rogers, Alessandro Duranti and Jane Schneider, for sharing their expertise and insightful comments. The text is incalculably richer due to the close reading and astute commentary of all these readers.

A number of other scholars have helped this text find shape in a number of ways throughout the years. I am indebted to Fred Myers, Ron Kassimir, Miyako Inoue, Judith Irvine, Alexandra Jaffe, Kathryn Woolard, Rob Moore, Steve Feld, Glauco Sanga, Franco Luràa, Franco Brevini, Cristina Grasseni, Stefano Coveri, Antonio Marazzi, and Giuliano Bernini. Emily McEwan-Fujita, Dan Suslak, and Suzanne Wertheim have been helpful interlocutors, and Shalini Shankar and Katherine Hoffman have contributed at more points than I can count; this text would be immeasurably poorer without them. Thanks also go to everyone at Wiley-Blackwell, including my editor, Rosalie Robertson, Julia Kirk, Deirdre Ilkson, and Paul Stringer. I'm grateful to Jim Wilce, Blackwell Studies in Discourse and Culture series editor, for asking hard questions, and giving such good feedback.

None of this would ever have happened, of course, if my parents had not taken us to Italy in the first place; nor could those initial interests have been developed without their ongoing love and support. Thanks to my whole family for their love and support, and especially Mom and Doug, who thought it was so important their daughters experience how other people live. Finally, thanks to Scott Collard, who has provided loving support, numerous delicious meals, generous copy-editing, an ongoing soundtrack, and kept me grounded in what it is really all about; and Rawlins, who has made it all the more fun.

Earlier formulations of some of the material in Chapter 3 appeared in Journal of Linguistic Anthropology (2006) 16(2):194–210.

Constructing Transcripts: Orthographic Conventions and Transcription Processes

Nearly all of the transcripts in this work came out of my collaborative efforts with native-speaker transcription consultants. In these transcribing contexts, there were no pre-established rules for how the Bergamasco language was written, as my consultants were unfamiliar with the current (or any other) orthographic conventions for writing it.[1] This process produced complex, multilayered transcripts, with each transcriber's interests shaping how the transcript was produced. There were five of them: Anna, Rina, Ella, Elsa, and Daniele, all between 23 and 40 years old.[2] Anna, in her late thirties, and Rina, in her early thirties, were both *"laureata"* (had college degrees), and had taken linguistics degrees.[3] Ella and Elsa, both in their mid-twenties, were working on their *laurea* degrees in languages (*Lingue*). Although he was older (mid-thirties), Daniele was also working on his laurea in literature, having entered the workforce at an early age and then later gone back to school. Rina, Ella, Elsa, and Daniele are Bergamaschi (pl. Bergamasco) and spoke and/or heard the Bergamasco language on a daily or nearly daily basis. Anna was born in the nearby town of Lecco (the local vernacular of which is very similar to Bergamasco), but had lived in Bergamo for several years and was married to a Bergamasco man. All professed an interest in the local language and said it would be a shame if it were lost. However, only Daniele was involved in any type of language activism. As an active member of the political party the Northern League, Daniele was explicit about his pro-Bergamasco stance, and often organized local language-related events, such as poetry readings, in his small hometown in the province of Bergamo on the plains south of Bergamo.

We worked together in two different ways. Anna, Elsa, and Daniele made their own initial transcriptions of various events, which we subsequently discussed line-by-line, often word-by-word. With Ella and Rina, we transcribed together, sitting side-by-side with two pairs of headphones. I listened and they wrote, and we stopped often to discuss both the content and structure of what we were hearing: the meaning of a particular word or phrase as well as which speaker had said what, for example. Both methods are time-consuming and render richly layered transcripts for analysis, but the second method was particularly painstaking. Occasionally, we would be able to transcribe only a few pages in a two or three hour session, either because of the difficulty of the recording – Ella and I transcribed sections of a recording made over a long meal with 12 participants, for instance, which took several transcribing sessions – or because we ran into something particularly interesting that we wanted to discuss, such as why a particular vowel sound made a speaker sound so very Bergamasco. Wherever possible, I wrote down their comments on the transcripts we produced; I have retained these traces of our interactions in some of the transcripts used in this book.

When we first began transcribing, I framed it as a project with two aims. First, I wanted them, as native speakers, to help me understand and correctly represent the speech on my tapes. Second, I also hoped for them to help me understand when speakers spoke one language or the other, and formulate reasons why this happened. For this reason, I asked them to give me their opinions and evaluations about what was happening in the recordings, and what they thought of when they heard people speak. None of my transcription consultants were present at these recordings, or knew the speakers who were, which helped to keep their comments on a general, not personal, level. Instead of "insider" knowledge about the dynamics of a particular group or conversation, what I desired – and got – was commentary on what people were doing with language, and potential reasons why.[4] I looked for patterns in how they evaluated when and why speakers used each language, as well as what these choices meant to them as Bergamaschi.

One of the first tasks I set out was to indicate whether an utterance or a word was in Italian or Bergamasco, so that I could track on a basic level how much of each language was being used. I did not initially anticipate what a complex task this occasionally was, however, involving extensive discussions of whether to categorize a particular word or element as Italian or Bergamasco. These discussions often took up a good deal of the transcription sessions, providing extensive metalinguistic commentary on bivalent moments, when an utterance displayed lexical, morphosyntactic, and/or phonological elements of both Italian and Bergamasco. In many ways, these discussions became investigations into what it was that made speakers sound "Bergamasco" to the transcribers, progressing from a transcriber's judgment that an utterance or a word "sounded Bergamasco" or "wasn't good Italian" to a closer look at exactly what it was that produced this perception. Transcribers also offered negative or positive evaluations of different examples of speech, and Anna and Rina paid special attention to what they saw as deviations from standard Italian and notated them accordingly due to their training in sociolinguistics. This type of attention often evolved into discussions of whether to define instances of non-standard Italian as "Regional" (variation linked to locality) or as "Popular" (variation linked to class), demonstrating how interconnected these categorizations are when they are applied to actual examples of speech (for discussions, see, among others, Berruto 1989, Cortelazzo 1977, and Pei 1941). Throughout, it was obvious that we were producing much more than a transparent or objective representation of the recordings we were listening to; indeed, the choices that we arrived at demonstrated how the process of transcription is anything but transparent or objective (Haviland 1996; Ochs 1979). Our own intellectual and social interests informed what we found, represented, and highlighted in our transcripts.

Such interests were not unique to us. While transcribing sessions evoked a level of commentary that would be unusual in everyday conversation, these ways of attending to language were not out of the ordinary in particular contexts. Audience members at poetry readings and dialect theater performances often favorably commented on the use of particular Bergamasco words or phrases, noting that there are certain things that just cannot be said in Italian.[5] Likewise, in highly formal contexts where standard Italian was the expected language, such as television or radio newscasts or speeches by public officials, Bergamaschi (like all Italians) displayed an incredible delicacy in detecting regional and local accents, which act as phonological traces of a speaker's origin. Speakers sometimes offered their own examples of "bad Italian" or pointed to others as speakers of "real Bergamasco." So while the precision with which a transcriber pinpointed a specific element as what made an utterance sound particularly Bergamasco was perhaps exceptional to the transcribing sessions, the types of linguistic phenomena they paid attention to were similar to phenomena that elicited comment in everyday life when language itself became the focus. The transcribers' comments often provided acute crystallizations of viewpoints I heard across other contexts in everyday life.

Discussions with Daniele about transcriptions were different than discussions with the other transcription consultants because of his political beliefs. With the other transcribers, politics only occasionally entered into our discussions, making it clear to me that their pride of place or recognition of certain structural inequalities in Italy did not translate to any form of political support for Bergamasco or other dialects. With Daniele, however, our interactions tended to be less linguistically oriented and more politically oriented. Daniele transcribed several one-on-one interviews in which the speakers used mostly Italian, and while he expressed pleasure when Bergamasco occurred, seeing it as a sign of a positive local attitude that he applauded, he had little interest in discussing the whys and mechanics of those occurrences. Instead of wanting to explore what code-switches between Bergamasco and Italian or using a Bergamasco accent might signify, he knew already: they were signs of local-ness, that the speaker was inherently and justly attached to Bergamasco, despite the force of Italian and the Italian nation-state. Eventually, I let him take the lead in our discussions, recognizing him as a different type of local analyst. Observations about language often led to Daniele telling me about various Northern League initiatives or events in support of the dialect or Bergamasco culture, which then led to general discussions of politics, the genius as well as failing health of Umberto Bossi (the charismatic leader of the Northern League), the Celtic origin of so many Bergamasco words, the odious dealings of politicians in Rome – in short, all of the topics and viewpoints that were common to nearly all the *leghisti* (Northern Leaguers, pl. of *leghista*) I interacted with. The rhetoric became familiar to me as I spent time with a number of leghisti, and Daniele provided a clear window onto this position (see Chapter 6 for a more complete discussion of the Northern League).

What is Bergamasco?

Bergamasco differs from Italian lexically, morphosyntactically, and phonologically (Sanga 1987, 1997). Lexical differences tend to cluster in particular domains, especially those most related to domestic tasks and the types of work that Bergamaschi traditionally participated in. So, for example, there are a number of specifically Bergamasco lexical items associated with silkworm husbandry, once an important way for many Bergamasco agriculturalists to earn cash. Morphosyntactic differences primarily involve the presence of compulsory subject clitic verb forms, postverbal negation, definite article forms (masc. sing. 'ol'; fem. pl. 'i'), and some verbal forms (such as pres. ind. 1sing. ending –[e]). Phonologically, Bergamasco differs from Italian primarily through the tendency towards degemination, the presence of two front rounded vowels ([ø] and [Y]), the occurrence of [s + tʃ], and the loss of word final vowels.[6]

There have been no studies on the mutual intelligibility of Italian and Bergamasco, although anecdotal evidence and my own research suggest that attitudes impact monolingual Italian speakers' ability to understand Bergamasco (there are presently extremely few monolingual Bergamasco speakers). Some Italian speakers, for example, deny understanding a word of it, while others might claim that they understand it, though it sounds "odd" (*strano*) or "hard" (*duro*) to their ears.[7]

Current Bergamasco orthography primarily follows that of Italian, but diverges in its extensive use of diacritics to indicate vowel sounds. The two front vowel sounds that occur in Bergamasco and not in Italian are represented by **ö** and **ü** ([ø] and [Y], respectively pronounced 'eu' and 'u' as in French); otherwise, acute and grave accents indicate closed or open qualities of [e] and [o]. The diacritic system is complicated and depends on a number of non-phonological requirements (for example, 'e' and 'o' in prepositions will never receive accents, no matter what they sound like). Another divergence from Italian orthography is the representation of [s + tʃ] (a combination not present in Italian) as s–c, as in **s–cèta** (girl [stʃɛta]).

In the transcripts that occur in this book and when Bergamasco appears in the text, I have sought as much as possible to follow the orthographic rules laid down by Vittorio Mora (1966) and taught by Carmelo Francia at the *Ducato di Piazza Pontida*. I have referred to the 19th-century Bergamasco–Italian dictionary written by Antonio Tiraboschi in addition to the more recent Italian–Bergamasco and Bergamasco–Italian dictionaries produced by Carmelo Francia and Emanuele Gamberini and printed by the *Ducato di Piazza Pontida*, as well as the one written by Carlo De Sanctis. All translations from Italian and Bergamasco are my own. Whenever possible, I have consulted with Bergamaschi who know more than I about these issues. Any remaining mistakes, of course, are mine.

I adhere to the following conventions in transcripts and in the text:

- **Bold** = Bergamasco
- *Italics* = Italian
- **Bold and underlined** = bivalent (could be either/both Bergamasco and Italian)

When Bergamasco and Italian words appear in the text, they are glossed into English (often in parentheses) and in bold or italics only the first time they appear, unless they are quotes, in which case they stay in their original form. Additionally, when attention is paid to particular elements of language, in addition to using IPA symbols when relevant, I apply the following rules:

- 'a' refers to the grapheme, or how the letter or word is written.
- [a] is a phonemic representation.
- /a/ is a phoneme.
- : indicates lengthening of the sound that precedes it.
- [ ] Brackets around non-IPA symbols frame transcriber commentary on an utterance, word, sound, which may be in Italian, Bergamasco, or English, or a combination of any of the three.

1

Introduction

I stood at the blackboard, sweating through my shirt, chalk in hand, sounding out vowel sounds under my breath, trying to hear the difference: "**Có-mò. Có-mò? Có-mò.**" The small room, full to overflowing with local art and knick-knacks, felt close and stuffy; traffic noises outside punctuated the buzz of the fluorescent lights. Behind me, the rest of the class chimed encouragement and aid in Italian: "*forza, Americanina!*" (go on, little American!), "*Dai, lo saprai già!*" (Come on, you know this one!). The teacher, who we called Maestro, told me that it was open (the sound of the 'o' in the word I was stuck on), which helped, a little. I plunged ahead, writing down the words in Bergamasco, the local language in this northern Italian town, that Maestro had dictated earlier. I got through two, long sentences, receiving lots of hints and corrections as I went along from both Maestro and the rest of the class. It seemed to take forever, but at the end Maestro said, "*va* **bé!**" – it was fine, especially since I didn't really understand what I was writing. Everyone laughed, leaving me completely flustered by the time I sat down. The tall middle-aged woman who sat to my left stood up and took the chalk from me, ready to continue the dictation at the board. She was faster and much better than I was, hardly making any mistakes or needing assistance, sounding out the words with confidence as she wrote. The young man who sat next to her, an ardent supporter of the regional separatist movement, the Northern League, followed her to the board and had nearly as many problems as I had. The young woman on the other side of him – with whom he frequently argued politics – did slightly better, though she queried Maestro on a number of points as she wrote. She, like the woman next to me, was a *ripetente* – an Italian colloquialism for "flunker" (literally, "repeater"), although they had taken the course repeatedly because they wanted to, not because they had to – and so was more familiar with the myriad rules governing how to write their local language. As the rest of the class went up to the board to write, comments and encouragement in Italian and Bergamasco filled the air, demonstrating that just because you knew how to speak Bergamasco did not necessarily mean you knew how to write it. One older Bergamasco man in particular, who spoke Bergamasco nearly exclusively and had taken the course several times, made numerous mistakes, in spite of Maestro's repeated corrections. His good-natured Bergamasco curses made the rest of the class laugh; our suggestions joined the Maestro's to create a chorus of shared effort.

Why make these efforts? Why dedicate an hour and a half every Friday night from October to May, sometimes year after year, to the task of learning how to read and write this – their own – language? The dozen participants that year cited various reasons: because they were aspiring Bergamasco poets, because they wanted to be able to speak it better, because they wanted a good reason to get out of the house and their regular routine once a week, or simply because, **"l'è gran bèl, ol bergamàsch"** (it's very beautiful, Bergamasco). They agreed that Italian, which they all spoke, was necessary and ubiquitous during these modern times. But Bergamasco, the language of their ancestors, was the sound that meant "home" to them, and doubly precious as many people perceived it as slipping irrevocably into the past. They saw it also as a direct link to that past, and to many of the cultural practices and values they explicitly valued: hard work, social closeness, honesty, straightforwardness, humor.

Within living memory, Bergamo has been transformed from one of Italy's poorest provinces into one of Europe's most prosperous. These changes have in turn altered nearly everything about how Bergamaschi live, eat, work, and play, as well as how they speak. For most people these are not existential issues, but practical ones, which play out in multiple arenas of their everyday lives, from classrooms to dining room tables. They face such transformations as they grapple with how to live in a modern, global world – to look toward the future, meaningfully inhabit the present, but not leave the past behind entirely. People's everyday lives, the activities they undertake, the places they choose to live, and the ways in which they choose to speak connect them to specific local histories. At the same time, Bergamaschi and Italians from other small communities think of themselves as Italians and Europeans, working in modern jobs that may involve extensive interaction with colleagues across the nation, continent and world; spending euros on their everyday expenses; reading local and national newspapers in order to discuss politics over lunch. Balancing local, national, and international orientations and activities, as well as the influences of tradition and modernity, are concerns that Bergamaschi share with people around the globe. Language, as an everyday practice and symbolic resource, is an essential site for trying to achieve and express this balance.

A Local Place in the Heart of the Periphery

The town of Bergamo, divided between the *Città Alta* (Upper City) and the *Città Bassa* (Lower City), had a population of roughly 117,000 in 2006; the province added approximately 800,000 more.[1]

The province is distributed across three geographical areas: the mountains in the north, the plains in the south, and a hilly zone in between. The town of Bergamo, where I focused my research, lies

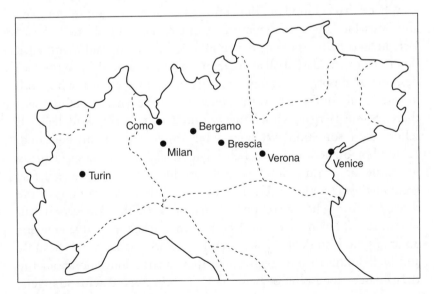

Figure 1.1 Map of northern Italy.

right in the middle, and is the commercial, administrative, and social center of the province, as well as its largest urban area. Multiple suburbs, most of which were once small towns in their own right, surround the town, swallowed up by the urban sprawl that characterizes so much of central northern Italy.

I was drawn to Bergamo by its linguistically, culturally, socioeconomically, and politically dynamic situation. I was told by Italians in other places, such as Venice, Bologna, and Milan, that Bergamo had a local dialect, Bergamasco – an ugly, crude-sounding dialect, many of them commented – that was still in use, although it, like all dialects in Italy, was fading in favor of increasing use of Italian. I heard that Bergamaschi, the local people, were rough, uncultured, hard workers whose economic efforts had led them into recent prosperity, although modern values, such as education, had not really caught on there, as Bergamaschi tended to leave school as soon as they could in order to get into the workforce. I was warned that the Northern League, which many Italians regarded as a reactionary and extremist right-wing political party, enjoyed strong support there, and that most Bergamaschi shared the League's xenophobic views toward Southerners and immigrants. I was told to get ready to eat a lot of polenta, the traditional staple of Bergamasco cuisine.

What I have found in Bergamo, of course, was more complex and variable than the picture painted by outsiders. I heard Bergamasco being spoken in a number of contexts, and although it differs from standard Italian in many ways, it would be wrong to describe it simply as "rough" or "ugly." I met people who both violated and conformed to the stereotypes I had heard before I got there. Some Bergamaschi I met worked in factories, and had left school at 14, sometimes younger, while others were highly educated. A number owned and ran their own small businesses, specializing in textile or construction materials production, while quite a few were *impiegati* (clerks or office workers), white-collar workers in the service sector who make up the majority of the modern Italian workforce (Martinelli et al. 1999). I met teachers and engineers, librarians and students, bakers and bankers. Most were friendly and welcoming to me, even while they were telling me about the Bergamasco stereotype of being closed and reserved with strangers. Some Bergamaschi were indeed supporters of the Northern League, and many others thought that certain of the Northern League's ideas made sense. Many, however, disapproved of much of the League's platform: secession of the north from Italy (since put aside, at least officially), opposition to immigrants, and at-times xenophobic views on southern Italians. And while polenta was still on the menu of every *trattoria*, most families ate a wide variety of Italian foods.

I went to Bergamo to undertake a project on language ideology; to study, in other words, the ways in which Bergamaschi viewed and used language – what they thought about Italian and Bergamasco and did to them, as well as how they spoke them. To date, no researcher had undertaken such a project in Northern Italy, and I quickly found that Bergamaschi themselves talked about their sociolinguistic situation in terms of shift and change, and, very often, outright loss, even when they admitted that they themselves spoke their vernacular regularly. They nearly always talked about Bergamasco in relation to Italian, and often not in flattering terms. There were also a number of people who demonstrated their support of the dialect and local ways of living through engaging in various types of cultural production activities, such as writing poetry in the dialect, participating in dialect theater, writing dictionaries in the dialect, or taking classes in how to write it.

At poetry readings and play practices, during interviews and everyday conversations, I often observed Bergamaschi react to and evaluate their own and others' use of language. This was as true for those who spoke Bergamasco and explicitly valued it, as for those who rarely thought about it and claimed not to speak a word of it. "What a beautiful word," someone might whisper under their breath to another audience member. Someone else might laugh about a particularly strong accent, while a director might correct an actor's pronunciation of certain phrases, implicitly reacting to and putting into motion linguistic ideological frames of evaluation. "I hope they didn't hear my accent," "my Bergamasco isn't very good because I only use it to speak to my grandparents," "that's not a real Bergamasco word," "her Italian isn't really very good," were all metalinguistic statements I heard in various contexts from diverse speakers: that is, talk about talk. These types of implicit and explicit cues illustrated that for Bergamaschi, as for many people, the form of their language use often mattered as much as the content.[2]

The Local Social Aesthetics of Language

I consider these Bergamasco linguistic and metalinguistic activities as discursive positionings within an ideological frame in which Bergamasco and Italian were associated with certain types of selves, time periods (past, future, present), activities, and values. Scholarship on the relationship of power and language in particular has recently been considered through the lens of language ideologies, dynamic sets of beliefs about language that are enacted and reproduced in everyday linguistic practice and interaction. Language ideologies are "the cultural conceptions of the nature, form, and purpose of language, and of communicative behavior as an enactment of a collective order" (Gal and Woolard 1995:130), and include large-scale sociohistorical processes that shape and are shaped by language. The study of language ideologies evolved out of linguistic anthropologists' increasing interest in the points of articulation between language use and political economies and other hierarchical social structures (for overviews, see Gal 1989; Kroskrity 2000; Schieffelin et al. 1998; Woolard 1998). In Bergamo, language ideologies generally coalesced in debates about the roles of Bergamasco and Italian, and reflections on how local speech played an active part in the ways various types of power were distributed, struggled over, contested, and reinforced.

Bergamasco language ideologies drew on, but were not reducible to, social distributions of value that contrasted notions of social solidarity with conceptualizations of status, power, and dominance long familiar to linguistic and cultural anthropologists (see, for example, Brown and Gilman 1972). Analysts have categorized speakers' affective orientations towards languages according to these two axes of social differentiation, based on the concepts of power or prestige and solidarity or in-group authenticity in order to explore how speakers value their languages. The relative social value of language may be linked to the higher social position of a language's speakers, indexing socioeconomic advancement, or based on the association of that language with particular literary genres or traditions which are valued as "high" culture with a social group (Dorian 1982; Gal 1979; Morford 1997). Value may also be built on the institutional support a language receives from national, regional, and local forms of government, including efforts to standardize and circulate written forms of the language, ensuring its use in official contexts of use such as schools and government offices, as has been true for Italian (De Mauro 1972; Kramer 1983; Lepschy et al. 1996). Bringing a language such as Bergamasco into a classroom setting, where it has not been used previously, may be a bid to tap into this type of prestige and value.

Alternately, value may be based on speakers' association of the language with intimate contexts such as in the home or among family or friends. This is what Trudgill (1972) and others have called "covert prestige" or solidarity (Heller 1995; Labov 1966a; Milroy 1987), valuing a language variety precisely because it lacks those other institutional and literary bases for prestige, but is the language of social bonding. Solidarity is often the most important – and sometimes only – form of value attributed to many minority languages like Bergamasco. Dorian's observation about Scottish Gaelic that "in the case of a strictly local-currency language of low prestige, lacking any institutional support whatever, the home domain is clearly crucial to the continuity of the language" (Dorian 1981:82) highlights the high value placed on the role of solidarity in maintaining a minority language. Bergamasco was, indeed, often described as the language of "*confidenza*" (social intimacy and emotional connection), the language of friendship and family, so much so that it was rare to hear anyone addressed in anything but its informal forms.[3]

Stressing such differences between Bergamasco and Italian paints a picture in which the languages were neatly distributed across diverse roles, values, speakers, and appropriate contexts of use. In this way, it is tempting to define Bergamo as a diglossic situation, in which the two languages are hierarchically ranked into a High language (H) of status and a Low language (L) of solidarity (Eckert 1980; Ferguson 1959; Jaffe 1999). Diglossia, however, describes a strict distribution of the H and L languages across speaking contexts, and so cannot fully depict the fluidity with which Italian and Bergamasco were used in most everyday life. In an effort to describe the Italian context more precisely, Berruto has used the term "dilalia," in which the H language can be appropriately used across all social contexts, while use of the L language is restricted to more informal, intimate contexts (1989, 1994).[4] This simple binary of H vs. L, however, still fails to account for the variability of language use across speakers and contexts or the extensive mixing of Italian and Bergamasco that often occurred in everyday conversation. There was a wide range of variation between standard Italian and pure Bergamasco that fell outside of this framework and called for analysis.

A defining characteristic of the Bergamasco sociolinguistic situation in the early 2000s was that it involved multiple languages and multiple language ideologies. In this sense it was what Bakhtin has called "heteroglossic." Bakhtin recognizes that in essence all language situations involve heteroglossia, "the social diversity of speech types" (1981:263); in talking about Bergamo, the concept is particularly fruitful due to its attention not just to multiplicity, but to the specific local meanings of multiplicity. Bakhtin asserts that "all languages of heteroglossia, whatever the principle underlying them and making each unique, are specific points of view on the world, forms for conceptualizing the world in words, specific world views, each characterized by its own objects, meanings and values" (1981: 291–292). Different heteroglossic languages are motivated, in other words, by different ideas about the world and language's place in that world, which exist in dynamic tension with one another.[5]

As Kathryn Woolard has recently noted, Bakhtin's conceptions can be difficult to pin down ethnographically (2004). For Bakhtin, heteroglossia is the environment of every instance of language use, such that every utterance resounds with the various histories – or voices – associated with the words involved. Within this environment of heteroglossia, voices animate language varieties, such that using a particular language variety may be tantamount to an expression of a certain "conceptualization of the world in words." However, Bakhtin posits that voices circulate within a community and are not the property of individuals, making it difficult to apply this concept to real live speakers, especially when, as was true in the Bergamasco situation, linguistic and ideological planes were not so tightly or unequivocally aligned. The continuum of mixed or bivalent language use between Italian and Bergamasco reflected, but was not easily reducible to, a wide array of social meanings.

The concept of indexicality engenders an analysis that captures this variability and tracks the heteroglossic deployment of linguistic varieties and ideologies of language across contexts and speakers.[6]

Indexicality is the capacity of language to signify non-referentially (referential meaning being the semantic sense of words), through causality or contiguity. As a smoke indexes – or points to – fire, so can language index contextual factors about speakers, settings, attitudes, orientations, stances, etc. Indexicals both presuppose certain features of context, and entail others. When an accent is indexically deployed, for instance, its use presupposes that participants in an interaction recognize the accent and the social values and stereotypes with which it is associated (otherwise it would be meaningless). Such use also reinforces or may act to alter – but, in any event, acts on in some fashion – these values and stereotypes and their links to the accent. Indexes are like delicate anchors that connect the non-referential forms of language and the context, both the immediate micro-context of speakers' relationships and unfolding histories, and the larger macro-context of politics, economics, and institutional power. Such anchors are never static, but instead are constantly being recast and reset.[7]

In Bergamo, speaking in a Bergamasco way indexed values such as home, family, and intimacy, but also peasant-ness, lack of education, and backwardness, while speaking Italian pointed to values such as personal refinement, educational achievement, and formality. The fluidity of the heteroglossic deployment of different ways of speaking, however, meant that the indexical potentials of any particular utterance were always multiple. Following Woolard, who argues for analysis that acknowledges "opposed values as simultaneously and equally present in many bilingual phenomena" (1999:6), I foreground instances in which languages and meanings overlapped, as speakers could speak bivalently, drawing simultaneously on the linguistic and symbolic resources of both languages. This possibility of simultaneity ensured that, however starkly the binaries might be described, in practice, divisions or categories were rarely so simple.

The form of language in Bergamo dynamically resonated with multiple voices; orientations towards that form, such as the metalinguistic commentary I mentioned above, were similarly various as well as remarkably common. Pervasive attention to the form or shape of language as well as to its function (what it does or means) indicates the utility of the concept of aesthetics in analyzing the Bergamasco language situation. For Bourdieu in his work on taste and distinction, perceiving aesthetically means attending to form over function (1984). Bourdieu and others (Clifford 1988; Myers 1994, 2002; Shusterman 2000) have demonstrated how culturally specific aesthetic sensibilities are. Indeed, Sharman has argued that culture itself is "an aesthetic system, whereby meaning is produced and reproduced through the attachment of value to experience" (2006:842), while Coote maintains that all "human activity has an aesthetic aspect" (1992:246).

While aesthetics has a long, tangled history of focusing specifically on art and form, I use the term here in a more applied, quotidian sense, coupling it with "social" to emphasize this approach. Brenneis used the concept *social aesthetics* to describe a process that "fuses intellectual sense-making activity with local aesthetic criteria for coherence and beauty . . . and with ethnopsychological notions of personhood, emotion, expression and experience" (1987:237). He explored how, in the rural Fijian Indian village of Bhatgaon, local ways of thinking about certain verbal and musical genres and their performance went hand in hand with particular ways of feeling about these practices, which were in turn linked to ideas of the self and others. He emphasized that, "[i]t is indeed very difficult to separate ethnopsychological from aesthetic notions; in articulating the bases of their enjoyment or appreciation of particular events, villagers also articulate their sense of self and experience" (Brenneis 1987:238). Villagers' ideas about themselves were intimately linked to how they felt about what they aesthetically responded to, such that there was an explicit link between linguistic and musical performance, ideas about these performances, and emotion.

People nearly always feel what they speak, not just during performances in which the right lines must be spoken or the alliteration of a phrase deliciously falls from the lips, but also in making choices about what and how to speak, speakers know when something feels right or wrong, beautiful or ugly. In linguistic anthropology and related fields, focusing on the form and performance of language has often occurred under the auspices of looking at poetics, another non-referential function of language (Banti and Giannattasio 2004; Bauman 1983, 2000, 2004; Bauman and Briggs 1990; Caton 1990). Jakobson (1960) stressed that the poetic function – in which there is a focus on the shape or sound of language – is always present in language, even when it is backgrounded. Here I want to push this observation to the heart of my analysis.

In order to do so, I introduce and explore the concept of the social aesthetics of language. A social aesthetics of language is the interweaving of culturally shaped and emotionally felt dimensions of language use and the extra-linguistic factors that rank people and their groups into hierarchies. The concept of the social aesthetics of language is meant to capture the texture of the discourses, practices, ideologies, sentiments, and socioeconomic and political constraints that produce and inform speaking and living. This texture is produced at the intersection of power and emotion. For many Bergamaschi, for example, feeling attached to Bergamasco and feeling like you should speak Italian to your children balanced the prestige and socioeconomic advantages of Italian with the socially valued privilege of sounding local in certain contexts. One of the central conundrums for those who study and ponder the aesthetic has been to describe the link between person and object; the social aesthetics of language describes how implicit and explicit metalinguistic activity can be analyzed to reveal exactly these links between people and what they speak.

Issues of power are always implicated in aesthetic systems. Wolf, discussing Sufism in Pakistan, has observed that, "the link between poetics and politics is strong" (2006:247), while Eagleton (1990) has stressed the intrinsic connections between aesthetics and power. Bourdieu's conceptualization of distinction demonstrates that aesthetic systems are hierarchically ranked, implying the presence of differentially distributed socioeconomic power across classes (1984). In France, displaying one's taste in art, food, and clothing, for example, is an embodied act that situates one within the class hierarchy. Without the necessary education and what Bourdieu calls "social origin," one cannot simply walk into the Louvre and properly appreciate the art; this is a learned aesthetic activity. Similarly, in Bergamo, enjoyment of Bergamasco cultural productions – such as poetry readings or play performances – the satisfaction found in hearing a well-turned phrase in Bergamasco conversation, even the cringe evoked by a Bergamasco word spoken out of place in an Italian setting, hinged on the hierarchical positioning of Italian as the language of power and Bergamasco as the language of intimacy and *confidenza*. For most Bergamaschi, speaking anything but Italian in school or in a similarly formal, public setting was unthinkable and unpalatable; to do so would have been to make the speaker sound old-fashioned and backward, unable to control the forms of speech that made one modern and economically successful. At the same time, speaking without some Bergamasco elements was equally unlikely and was met with varying degrees of censure from other speakers for sounding too formal and overly elaborate.

Such feelings are socialized and learned from childhood on. The field of language socialization (Fader 2000, 2001; Garrett and Baquedano-López 2002; Kulick and Schieffelin 2004; Ochs and Schieffelin 1984; Schieffelin 1990, 2000) has extensively demonstrated how "linguistic and sociocultural knowledge are acquired simultaneously and are inextricably bound up with one another" (Garrett 2005:335). Clearly, aesthetic sensibilities and practices are part of what is learned in and through language as novice speakers, such as children, are socialized into culturally appropriate speaking practices, ideas, and subjectivities. Language socialization studies of bi- and multilingual communities have demonstrated that novices learn what languages mean together with how to speak them (Fader 2007; Kulick 1992; Paugh 2001). As a novice learner of Bergamasco, I was often the subject of instructive judgments about Bergamasco and Italian. For example, my tortured attempts at the blackboard in class were deemed extraordinary, implying that being an outsider – as well as a young female – made my efforts appear unusual but admirable to my Bergamasco classmates. At the same time, my frequent attempts to speak Bergamasco in everyday life were met with such extensive corrections and laughter that achieving verbal fluency through practice was essentially impossible. Such implicit resistances to my speaking it made it difficult for me to speak it; similar gatekeeping practices frequently prevented younger Bergamaschi from speaking it, as well.

Kulick and Schieffelin have noted that any theory of socialization or "becoming," whether it is local or scholarly, includes affect, or "emotions, feelings, moods, dispositions, and attitudes associated with persons and/or situations" (2004:352). What Bergamaschi felt about and through language was constrained by the sociohistorical hierarchy in which Italian dominated Bergamasco and other local languages.[8] To capture this dynamic, I use the terms emotion, affect, and sentiment in discussing Bergamaschi's intimate, lived relationships with their languages. Emotion is a broad term to encompass the culturally defined categories of feeling that speakers claimed and attributed to one another. Affect as I use it is the practice of emotion, a broader term without sentiment or emotion's implications of the interiorization of feeling (Besnier 1990). Focusing on affect directs attention to how emotions are constructed discursively, often co-constructed through interaction. In this way, the use of certain affective practices may involve constructing the self as a culturally appropriate feeling being. Sentiment is the hardest to define and most immediately intuitively understood of these terms. I shape my usage of sentiment on Steven Feld's use of the term (1990) as the expressive, embodied, shared, and practiced experience of emotions, expressed through song and weeping, shared through gesture and verbal comments, connected to cultural ideas about death, sadness, birds, landscape, and sociality among the Kaluli people in Papua New Guinea (see also Abu-Lughod 1999 and Yanagisako 2002 on sentiment). Sentiments such as nostalgia often overcame Bergamaschi, linking them immediately to past experiences and images, and rendering language practices such as code choice and code mixing sentimentally informed. Speakers' metalinguistic observations demonstrated that affective concerns shaped how language was produced and responded to. Emotions such as embarrassment (*vergogna*) or humorous engagement (**fà quàter grignà**, lit. "do/ have four laughs") could dynamically frame language use such that a sound or word or code choice could feel good or bad, right or wrong, beautiful or ugly (Sapir 1949[1927]). These sentimental frames were also aesthetic judgments, which in turn were linked to hierarchies of status and value.

Feld (1988, 1990) has demonstrated how aesthetics are emotionally and bodily experienced (see also, for example, Arno 2003), such that learning to speak and feel is bound up with cultural conceptualizations of aesthetic values and experiences. Power and emotion are also often intricately interconnected, for example, in terms of the appropriate distribution of emotion across a group, or in the role played by emotional display in achieving – or being shut out – of power (Irvine 1989, 1990; Kulick 1993, 1998). Abu-Lughod and Lutz have argued that emotional discourses are "implicated in the play of power and the operation of a historically changing system of social hierarchy" (1990:15) (see also Rosaldo 1984; Scheper-Hughes 1985, 1992). Affect and power intersected in the social aesthetics of language in Bergamo, shaping how people related to Italian and Bergamasco, constructing a position of power through correct Italian, or building a sense of social closeness through using Bergamasco words or sounds.

A Modern *Questione della Lingua*

The modern social aesthetics of language in Bergamo is rooted in specific local, national, and European histories, and Bergamaschi were not alone in having complex relationships to their languages. Across Italy, the *questione della lingua* – language question – has been a vexed socioeconomic, political, and cultural issue since the time of Dante (Alighieri 1996). Some of the most potent obstacles faced by those who sought to unite European nation-states in the 18th and 19th centuries were internal divisions: regional and local minorities whose loyalties lay first with their own towns, provinces, or regions, and only then with larger, more distant and abstract political entities like the state. Language was one way in which these difficulties were expressed, for modern concepts of the nation-state included a shared national language, while most people spoke smaller local languages (Anderson 1991; Inglehart and Woodward 1972). From England to Spain, France to Greece, creating a modern nation-state meant establishing a suitably modern language which could then unite the masses – and then making that process seem natural and unforced (Grillo 1989; Judge 2007; Tsitsipis 1998). Most often, the language of the rulers became the language of the state: French is the language spoken in Paris, from which the French kings and Revolutionaries ruled (Crowley 1996; Weber 1976); Spanish (known as Castilian) is the language spoken in Madrid in the Castile region, still the Spanish national capital (Urla 1993b; Woolard 1989). These language varieties generally needed to be codified through dictionaries and grammars in order to demonstrate that they were suitable to be national languages, and then spread throughout the state via national institutions such as education and the mass media (Anderson 1991; Cameron 1995; Jaffe 1996; Swiggers 1990). Local languages were often depicted by governments and in schools and mass media as divisive and provincial, limiting individuals' participation in the nation both politically and economically (Eckert 1980; Jaffe 1999; Kabatek 1997). Many European local languages became tarnished with the image of the backward peasant who had failed to modernize with the rest of his or her neighbors due to these efforts (Drysdale 2001; Kuter 1989; Timm 2001).

When Italy was united as a nation-state in the 1860s, less than two percent of Italians spoke Italian (De Mauro 1972, 1994). For centuries previous, educated elites read and wrote various lingua francae, including Latin, French, and the variety of the Florentine dialect that was eventually chosen to be Italian, and everyone spoke their local languages during the course of everyday life. Although efforts were made to increase the number of Italian speakers after unification, through education and other means (Kramer 1983; Leoni 1980; Migliorini and Griffith 1984),[9] the *questione della lingua* remained a national problem for many decades, taken up in various ways by different governing forces. National leaders blamed local languages for dividing citizens from one another and preventing their full participation in the nation-state; Fascists especially legislated heavily against local languages. Over the 20th century, Italy nonetheless slowly became more unified through a number of political and economic shifts. Foremost among these were the so-called economic miracle years that followed World War II, in which rapid industrialization, particularly in the north, led to increases in wages, improved living conditions and access to consumer goods, rural to urban and south to north migration, and greater than before participation in education (Besana 1997; Duggan 2007; Ginsborg 1990; Mack Smith 1997). Such changes contributed to a rapid increase in speaking Italian over the generations that participated in and followed these shifts. Over the past hundred years, massive linguistic transformation has occurred: according to the latest available statistics, 98 percent of Italians currently speak their national language (ISTAT 1997, 2007).

Bergamo's language situation must be understood vis-à-vis this politics of the *questione della lingua*, which has long set the interests of the national language in opposition to those of the many regional and minority languages spoken by Italians, helping to create and solidify these divides in the process. Since unification, Italian has consistently been promoted over and above local languages in the

educational system, in the media, and in national bureaucracies, such
as civil services. Local pride of place has often been pitted against
participation in the nation, and language is one of the most tena-
cious symbols for this conflict. As of 2006, roughly half of Italians
spoke another language in addition to Italian, most a dialect (ISTAT
1997, 2007).

Italian local languages that, like Bergamasco, are descendents of
Vulgar Latin are referred to as "*dialetti*" (dialects) or even just the
generalized "*dialetto*" (dialect) in Italian, terms that automatically
position such languages beneath the national language – itself a
descendent of the Florentine dialect – in terms of prestige and
status (Maiden and Parry 1997). Numerous language scholars have
emphasized the social dimensions of distinguishing languages from
dialects, sometimes turning to the old adage that a language is a
dialect with an army and a navy to illustrate this (Auer and
di Luzio 1988; Blommaert and Verschueren 1998; De Mauro 1994;
Gal 1995; Gal and Woolard 1995; Haugen 1966). This is certainly
true of the Italian situation, where the only Italian "language" is
Italian, while the other Italo-Romance linguistic varieties that
share its territory – including a number that have long histories of
being written and used for numerous linguistic functions, such as
Venetian, Milanese, and Sicilian (Beretta 1998; Burke 1987; Kramer
1983; Steinberg 1987) – are demoted to being "dialects" and have
no legal protections (Dal Negro 2005; Orioles 2002). I refer to
Bergamasco at times as a dialect because this term reflects Italian
usage, for although Bergamasco is not a linguistic dialect of Italian,
its position relative to Italian is an essential element in the meaning
of Bergamasco to those who spoke it when I did my research. I
also refer to Bergamasco and other local varieties as "local languages" or vernaculars when discussing them more generally to
contest this positioning.[10]

Across Italy at the start of the new millennium, the so-called
dialects were most often talked about as practices consigned to
obsolescence, fast becoming things of the past. In Bergamo, people
often pointed to how infrequently younger people seemed to speak
it, especially when contrasted with their grandparents. Young people,
indeed, often claimed to not speak it at all. My research, however,
showed that it was too soon to tell, for patterns of use were varied
and multiple. Ideas of loss, however, persisted.

My Place in Bergamo

Elizabeth Krause has argued that ethnography is "a mutually constituted 'space of encounter'," built on "a foundation of competence,
practice, and sensibility" (2005:594), involving "structured spontaneity" (595). The following excerpt from my field notes demonstrates
some of the structured spontaneity that occurred during my research,
as well as how it was often a dynamic, interactional process. The
excerpt describes part of an evening that my American *moroso* (boy-
friend), who joined me in Bergamo in 1999–2000 to do his own
research at the civic library, and I spent with two research consultants who also became friends. Federico was Bergamasco,
Sara was from a small town in the south; he was an engineer,
she a teacher. This was the first in what became a regular, frequent
type of outing for the four of us. They had just met and become
"*fidanzati*" (seriously dating, but not formally engaged), and we got
to know them as they got to know each other.

> *Field notes December 2, 1999:* The conversation became Federico
> telling us various typical Bergamasco words (like "**pòta**," which
> means, "ahh, shit happens") and phrases, which were proverbs and
> funny sayings, and mostly little word games. One meant, "look at
> that cow there go into that house there," but was something like
> "**A! la ka al a a ka la**" – equivalent, in some ways, perhaps, to
> the *coca-cola con la conuncia corta corta* in Florence,[11] which I told them
> about. Sara told us how to say different things in her dialect, and it
> turned into a game: Federico would tell us how to say something
> in Bergamasco, Sara would give it in her dialect and we would give
> it in English.

Many of our early interactions involved comparisons between our
cultures. As the ethnographer, I paid close attention to the examples
and comparisons that Federico and Sara offered as "data"; as a new
friend, I offered my own examples and comparisons. As my research
progressed, I was also able to contextualize them as exemplars of
many things about Bergamo. For instance, many southerners have
come to Bergamo to find work and many of these have married
Bergamaschi. Such unions generated questions about, among other
things, what the children would or would not speak. As a young

couple starting their lives together (for they married soon after), Federico and Sara faced questions about how to afford setting up a household, where to buy a home, what types of relationships to maintain with family and friends as they became a couple, what activities to spend their free time on – all common concerns for people their age in Bergamo and elsewhere. I eventually heard Federico's tongue twister again and learned how it and many of the other sayings he told us that night were properly written and translated in Maestro's class (**Ah! Chèla aca là l'à a la cà!** or Ah! That cow there is going in the house!). Federico and I had ongoing discussions about politics, especially the challenges and appeal of the Northern League; Sara's brother, deeply engaged with local politics, often joined these discussions. Sara offered an insider's view of Bergamasco schools, as well as her perspective on what it was like as an outsider in Bergamo. Our "mutually constituted 'space of encounter'" was one in which cultural and personal interactions and understandings were constantly unfolding.

At the same time, I strove to build my research on "a foundation of competence, practice, and sensibility." When I began fieldwork in Bergamo in the fall of 1999, I chose the Città Alta as the center of my ethnographic research, drawn by its role as the "old city" and symbolic heart of Bergamo. Although it used to be more crowded, at that time fewer than three thousand people lived there, most of them well-off. Whenever I told people in Bergamo that we lived in the Città Alta, they took it as a given: of course, foreigners would want to live in the most scenic and well-preserved – and touristy – neighborhood in town.

We rented an apartment there from a family – a prosperous and well-educated couple, Davide and Tullia, and their daughter, Marina, who was in college – who quickly became a second family to us. They fed us elaborate Sunday *pranzi* (lunches, the most important meal in Italy), taught us to play Bergamasco and Italian card games, and answered my endless questions about their town and way of life. The Città Alta became our neighborhood, the place where we bought bread, vegetables and meat, went for strolls, and ran into the same people day after day, slowly getting to know them. Many of the people who owned and ran businesses in the Città Alta also lived there, slightly apart from the wealthy more recently arrived residents. There was Maria, who owned and ran the bakery; Mariana, who worked in the grand Civic Library and had recently married; and Giuseppe, who sold me newspapers every day and with whom I had long discussions about the complexities of Italian politics, to name just a few. Most were people who had lived in the Città Alta for decades, if not generations, so we got to know many working- and middle-class merchants and their families, whose children attended school with the children of the elite.

In addition to Sara and Federico and Davide, Tullia and Marina, there were a number of individuals and families with whom I spent more extensive and intimate time, most of whom you will meet on these pages. One of the most important was an iron-smithing family, who had a **butiga** (workshop; in this case, a forge) in the Città Alta. Father Paolo and son Roberto worked in and ran the butiga; their wives, Carla and Franca, were both extraordinary seamstresses. Both couples lived across the square from the butiga in apartments connected by a balcony. A sister of Paolo lived upstairs with her family; a son-in-law had his glass-blowing studio on the ground floor (and often used the butiga for various soldering jobs, etc.); Franca's brother worked with Paolo and Roberto in the butiga; and the whole family shared a *cantina*, or socializing room, with a

Figure 1.2 Paolo in his family's cantina (photograph by Karen Evenson).

full kitchen and long dining table, which was filled with Paolo's collection of Bergamasco puppets and other items.

Paolo, a well-known Bergamasco poet, was my self-appointed guide to a number of Bergamasco cultural events, and introduced me to numerous people who shared his enthusiasm for Bergamasco culture, the Città Alta, and the pleasures of good food, wine, and friends.

I also attended and participated in a number of explicitly linguistic and cultural activities, such as poetry readings, theater performances, and anything else that pertained to the dialect. In addition to Paolo, I met and spent time with a number of poets who wrote in Bergamasco, many of whom I interviewed, and attended multiple poetry readings that they conducted. The *Ducato di Piazza Pontida*, a social organization that promotes Bergamasco culture and language,[12] sponsors the majority of such events in Bergamo, and I soon got to know many of its members and leaders. The Ducato offered the yearly course in Bergamasco that I introduced at the beginning of this chapter, in which I participated for the entire "school year" in 1999–2000 and for the first half of the 2000–2001 school year. During the fall of 2000, I also attended another course on Bergamasco, taught by a former attendee of Maestro's course, and sponsored by the *comune* (city administration) of a small town on Bergamo's southeast periphery. Both of these courses took place during the evening after the end of the workday, were relatively small (10–20 participants), and focused nearly exclusively on writing Bergamasco.

I also joined up with a local dialect theater troupe (*compagnia teatrale del dialetto*), called "*Tradizione e Novità*" (Tradition and Novelty). There were at least 20 such troupes in the province of Bergamo in 2000, each attached to a particular town, neighborhood, or parish. Tradizione e Novità came from the *Borgo Santa Caterina* (Santa Caterina neighborhood), which lies just below the Città Alta to the west. I attended most of their rehearsals and performances during 2000, tape-recording extensively, and, in October 2000, I even played a small part in one of their productions.

I met regularly with local experts on the dialect, history, and culture of the area, some of them repeatedly. In the local library, I read extensively about local modern history, language, and culture. Through routinely reading several newspapers and tuning in to local and national radio and television newscasts, I attended to local and national media, keeping up with local issues and tracking media treatment of dialect and culture.

The Northern League was particularly active in the news and Bergamasco politics that year, and I attended a number of their rallies to get a sense of who participated, how large a crowd they consistently drew, and what language such rallies were conducted in (nearly exclusively Italian). I also attended the meetings of the *Associazione Linguistica Padana* (Padanian Linguistic Association), whose members were explicitly Northern League, although the group itself was not formally associated with the League. ALP, as they called themselves, was founded in 1999 and met several times over the next year and a half; I attended all of their meetings during this time, in which they discussed their goals to record as many northern dialects as possible, salvage whatever linguistic practices (such as story-telling) as possible, and linguistically analyze the similarities and differences among these dialects so that they could eventually produce a northern Italian *koinè*, or common language.[13]

I balanced my participation in dialect-oriented activities with others less explicitly concerned with the local. Bergamaschi, like most Italians, tend to participate in various types of social organizations or group activities, from bicycling troupes to amateur intellectual societies to formula car racing fan clubs. Eager to take advantage of these common forms of public sociality, I joined various groups, such as an organization that promoted and performed Renaissance and Medieval dance. The people with whom I danced, including Sara and later Federico, were mostly well-educated and interested in history and culture, but not necessarily in language per se. As such, their perspectives, comments, and attitudes provided good counterpoints to those of the many people with whom I spent time who were explicitly engaged in language issues. I also attended a women's knitting circle and helped out at a neighborhood center for the elderly. Both of these met in the Città Alta, and were attended by women (the knitting circle) or older people (the neighborhood center) from the lower as well as upper city. In both of these contexts, I got to know older people, mostly women from working- or middle-class backgrounds, who spoke primarily in Bergamasco and told me about how Bergamo used to be, or how their own lives had progressed. These life experiences and stories enriched my perspective on the town, its social history, and the changing roles of women as mothers, grandmothers, and participants in the workforce.

I systematically interviewed people from all of these groups and contexts about their lives and linguistic abilities, viewpoints, and backgrounds, tape-recording them. I also conducted a number of informal, tape-recorded interviews with workers at a small family-run factory just outside of Bergamo, as well as several group interviews with high school students at a scientific high school in the lower city that drew students from all over the province. In all these interviews, I asked participants about their own and others' language skills, their views and attitudes about the dialect and related cultural productions (such as poetry and theater), as well as various current events and popular culture happenings.[14]

In all contexts, I tape-recorded and took notes whenever people let me – during play rehearsals, Bergamasco courses, public events, and everyday conversations. Some of these recordings were in Bergamasco; some in Italian; the majority in a mix of both.

Transcribing

As I discuss in more detail in Constructing Transcripts: Orthographic Conventions and Transcription Processes, I subsequently transcribed several of these recordings with native Bergamasco-speakers, which provided me with a few different advantages. First, as my Bergamasco was at variable stages during my time there, it enabled me to have native speakers listen to what was recorded and help me "get it right" in our transcripts. One of the most central and vexing issues about "getting it right" was being able to tell what was Bergamasco and what was Italian. Although some things were obvious to me, and most were clear to them, often there was no definitive answer for what language a word or phrase belonged to. These instances were always informative, because at each one we would be forced to be incredibly specific in offering reasons for why, when there were words or phrases that contained both Italian and Bergamasco elements, a word belonged to one or the other code. This process emphasized that transcription is always a process of selection (Edwards 1989; Ochs 1979), and transcribers need to be explicit about the conceptions of and expectations about language that they bring to their task (Haviland 1996).

Second, as native speakers, these assistants often had metalinguistic information about interactions that helped me to understand what was going on beyond code choice and the referential meaning of the words. Besides decoding idioms and contextualizing certain expressions, these assistants provided constant commentary on the value and meaning of how things were being said, helping me begin to sketch the indexical frames within which such talk could be understood. "That woman's Bergamasco accent is so strong it makes me laugh," one of them would say, or "this is a common way to say that across northern Italy, not just in Bergamo," another would say. Such observations demonstrated the indexical links between accents and humor, for example, as well as similarities and connections between Bergamasco ways of speaking and neighboring local varieties. Together, we could speculate as to why someone had used Bergamasco to say one thing and Italian to say something else, or what using a particular proverb had meant. Through these speculations, I learned a lot about what speaking *sounds like* to Bergamaschi themselves, as well as how it feels. As will become clear throughout this book, I treat transcribers' comments as essential data in their own right, which in turn helped me make connections between linguistic patterns of use, language ideologies, and local conceptualizations of place, time, and self.

Outline of Chapters

In the chapters that follow, I investigate several topics to explore the social aesthetics of language in Bergamo. I begin with the small details of everyday life, slowly widening the scope of my discussion to include larger contexts such as the national and international. Through gradually widening the analytical lens from the micro to the macro, I aim to create an intimate sense of the social aesthetics of language for the reader across various contexts as a foundation for understanding how this aesthetics is embedded within and informed by institutions and processes of power, such as the national government and increasing Europeanization.

In Chapter 2, "Bergamasco in Use: The Feel of Everyday Speaking," I look at everyday language practices. I concentrate on a range of contexts and speakers, when speakers explicitly reflected on language but also when their attitudes and orientations were more implicitly expressed. Most everyday speaking involved use of Italian and Bergamasco, as speakers drew from both languages to orient themselves towards different types of speakers and contexts, express diverse selves and values, and align themselves with tradition and modernity, prestige and solidarity. Chapter 3 considers the role gender played in ideas about and practices of language use in Bergamo, as it aligned with conceptualizations of tradition and modernity, prestige and solidarity, roughness and refinement. Through the close examination of a number of transcripts in both these chapters, I explore what it felt like to speak as a Bergamasco person.

One of the places linguistic hierarchies become evident is through an examination of literary and performative genres, as certain genres mattered more than others within the social aesthetics of language of Bergamo. Chapter 4, "Bergamasco on Stage: Poetry and Theater," focuses on Bergamasco poetry and theater, the most important genres in the dialect, demonstrating the intersection of power and emotion in Bergamasco language practices on stage. Bauman defines genre as "a speech style oriented to the production and reception of a particular kind of text," which is "a constellation of systematically related, co-occurrent formal features and structures that serves as a conventionalized orienting framework for the production and reception of discourse" (2000:84). Hierarchies of genres are often tied to hierarchies of taste and values as well as to social hierarchies (Caton 1990). As the most common forms of local cultural and linguistic production, poetry and plays played a central role in *Bergamaschità* (Bergamasco-ness), or local conceptions about what makes the place, people, and community unique. Bergamasco enjoyment of these genres, as well as the role they attributed to them as bulwarks against the loss of Bergamasco language and culture, meant that poetry and plays had power within the sociolinguistic landscape as well as evoked myriad emotional responses. Even those who did not participate in them recognized these activities as central to Bergamaschità, and an important site for its − and the dialect's − reproduction.

Chapter 5, "Modern *Campanilisimo*: The Value of Place," connects language to another valuable symbolic resource in Bergamo: the place itself, and the Citta Altà, or Upper City, in particular. Just as the dialect on stage stood for Bergamaschità, a notion which combines contemporary and nostalgic ideas about local identity, so too did this place, whether as a distant silhouette glimpsed during a daily commute from below, as a destination for socializing on Saturday nights, or through its invocation in multiple poems about what it meant to be Bergamasco. By looking at the ways in which people talked about the Citta Altà, how it was represented in the media, as well as language used in the homes of several of its residents, this chapter scrutinizes connections between language and place, illustrating the parallels between Bergamasco and the Citta Altà, as well as how they were different types of symbolic resources.

Chapter 6, "Bergamo, Italy, Europe: Speaking Contextualized," widens the lens to discuss the historical relationship between language and power in Italy and Bergamo and beyond. It briefly sketches the *questione della lingua* – language question – at the national level and then contextualizes local language politics in the events of the 20th century. These include local responses to Fascism's anti-vernacular policies and contemporary debates involving the Northern League. I turn to broader political debates about language, in which Bergamasco and Italian stood as emblems of local and national communities, respectively, although the sets of values they pointed to varied across political contexts. I explore how, during the Fascist period, supporting Bergamasco was one allegedly non-political way to assert the importance of local ways of living against the totalitizing vision of a united state pushed by the national government. More recently, due to the Northern League's strident defense of Bergamasco, supporting local cultural traditions, including the dialect, sounded to many Bergamaschi like de facto support for the League and its right-wing positions on immigration and other topics.

Bergamo was not alone in facing complicated political, economic, and social challenges at the start of the new millennium, and Chapter 6 also links the language politics of Bergamo to larger currents in Europe. Explicitly nationalistic political parties like the Northern League had gained strength across the continent over the past several decades, even as nation-states were being economically and politically integrated into the European Union. Increasing numbers of immigrants from North Africa and Asia were filling demographic gaps, but providing new cultural and political challenges. By scrutinizing these large-scale political and economic phenomena from the perspective of Bergamo, this chapter grounds these sometimes amorphous phenomena in the detail of everyday life.

The final chapter brings together the multiple strands of meaning that make up the social aesthetics of language. The politics of language, the socioeconomics of linguistic choice, the meaning of poetry, the appropriate flow of everyday conversation, nostalgia for the Bergamasco past, anticipation for the Italian and European future, the beauty of linguistic purity, the authenticity of conversational multivalency, the meaning of place – all play a part in what it meant and how it felt to speak in Bergamo. The social aesthetics of language has implications for Bergamasco and perceptions of its impending loss, and I argue that while there were multiple shifts in action, loss was not yet a foregone conclusion. Such an approach has broader application than just the Bergamasco, Italian, or European situations, as it brings together rich lines of inquiry to better understand speakers' everyday experience, the choices they make, and the results of these choices.

2

Bergamasco in Use:
The Feel of Everyday Speaking

Late on a Sunday afternoon, the sounds of cursing ricocheted off the frescoed walls and heavy, wood-beamed ceilings of the dining room where a group of us were playing cards. The aromas of the large, multi-course lunch we'd eaten earlier lingered in the air, and empty cups of espresso, which followed the meal, were scattered at the edges of the table. Davide, our host, had just won another hand of **cotècc**, a Bergamasco card game, and declared himself the victor in loud Bergamasco. The rest of us were equally loud in our protests, but each in a slightly different way. Giana, an old family friend, called Davide a number of inventive names in Bergamasco. Giana's two teenage sons laughed as they switched between Italian and Bergamasco, telling their mother to calm down. Davide's wife, Tullia, who was not Bergamasca but had lived in Bergamo for many years, used Italian to question Davide's so-called run of luck. Marina, their daughter, protested in Italian, with the hint of a Bergamasco accent, that she didn't really like cards anyway. After protests in Italian that it's not fair to take advantage of beginners, I tried out a tentative Bergamasco curse, just to see if I could pull it off. Davide turned to me in surprise and guffawed. He pronounced me "**bràa**" (good, clever in Bergamasco) for the attempt, but then told me – in Italian – that I had better work on my pronunciation some more.

This afternoon of card playing was typical in many ways of how people speak in everyday life in Bergamo. Most strikingly, nearly everyone was speaking in a different way: in Bergamasco, in Italian, and in ways that utilize elements of both languages, whether switching between them, as Giana's sons and Davide did, or combining elements of both, as with Marina's Bergamasco accented Italian. These differences are linked to a number of factors, such as where one was born, age, gender, family habits, and personal preferences. Although they were not in play here since everyone was well-educated and upper middle class, class differences also mattered in the course of everyday interactions. In general, the higher the socioeconomic position of a speaker, the less likely they were to speak Bergamasco. This group was an obvious exception to this rule, a point to which I will return below. In addition, although everyone spoke in a different way, everyone else in the room understood what the others were saying, for the most part. Tullia and I may have been the exceptions to this, but we both could at least follow the conversation, even if we could not interpret Giana's innovative Bergamasco curses at Davide down to the last detail. The fact that the only utterance that drew attention and evaluation was my own attempted curse in Bergamasco, which elicited surprise and amusement from Davide, only made the normalcy of this conversation even plainer. I experienced his reaction as an implicit gate-keeping strategy, as well – keep trying, he seemed to say, but you will probably never quite get there.

Speaking in these multiple, diverse ways added up to a locally distinctive way of speaking, a Bergamasco social aesthetics of language. The texture of language in Bergamo contained both languages, even as Italian and Bergamasco had their own specific symbolic associations and contexts of use. In this chapter, I explore why "speaking Bergamasco" did not simply mean speaking the vernacular, but also meant speaking in distinctively Bergamasco ways. This included speaking Italian with Bergamasco elements, such as accent, syntactic forms, words, and idioms. Speakers chose among the various ways to speak, and had gut feelings about what sounded "right" and "wrong," what sounded "good" and "bad." These evaluations were never purely linguistic, but depended on the complex interplay of what the languages meant. To explore these judgments and attitudes, I draw on transcripts of Bergamasco use of language, speakers' commentary on language, as well as some of the insights provided by the transcription consultants with whom I worked.

Heteroglossia, Bivalency, and the Feel of Language

Heteroglossia is an apt concept to describe the language situation in Bergamo. The notion has been used to describe many situations in which there are a multitude of "voices," such as when people use more than one language in the same interaction, as they do here, as well as to describe the variation that characterizes almost all everyday speaking. Bakhtin describes heteroglossia as "the internal stratification of any single national language into social dialects, characteristic group behavior, professional jargons, generic languages, languages of generations and age groups, tendentious languages, languages of the authorities, of various circles and of passing fashions, languages that serve the specific sociopolitical purposes of the day, even of the hour" (1981:263). Tension between these varieties, which exist in dynamic relation to one another, is inherent to heteroglossia. If we consider that all language use is heteroglossic – full of different styles, dialects, accents, tones – then the Bergamasco conversation above does not seem nearly so strange. What is particular about it, however, is that all that variation is distributed across two languages, Italian and Bergamasco.

Speakers in Bergamo did not simply choose between Italian and Bergamasco as two static codes. They could, as Woolard puts it, "thrive in their tense intersection" (1999:5). Even people who explicitly did not speak Bergamasco – such as Tullia and Sara, who moved there as adults, or Marina, who did not learn much of it growing up – participated in this dynamic linguistic world through their own language use, and their evaluations and reactions to others' language use. Many of the people with whom I interacted spoke both to a certain degree, so that in the course of everyday conversation it was not uncommon to hear speech that moved between the two languages. Italian words with a Bergamasco accent, Bergamasco sentences with Italian words in them, Italian utterances structured around Bergamasco syntax – these were common occurrences in Bergamo that can be classified as bivalent (Woolard 1999). Bivalency means that utterances draw on both languages. Like Marina's Bergamasco accented Italian or Giana's sons' interspersing of Bergamasco and Italian phrases as they tried to calm their mother down, it is clear that both languages were being utilized at the same time (if not always in the same breath). This is one reason why when Bergamaschi travel outside of Bergamo, other Italians recognize them as Bergamaschi as soon as they open their mouths to speak: they sound like where they come from. This is true for virtually all Italians, most of whom carry some trace of their origins in their manner of speech.[1]

Analyzing bivalent speech creates a number of challenges during transcription and analysis. As will be explored below, individual words can be clearly bivalent, or may just as clearly be Italian or Bergamasco, but occur combined in ways that make a phrase or utterance – perhaps an entire interaction – bivalent. Attention to the lexical level, then, may produce one perspective on bivalency, while attention to the level of the phrase or utterance or discourse in general may produce another. Here, I have attempted to represent as closely as I can the bivalent feel of language use in Bergamo, leading me to analyze certain stretches of speech as bivalent through an examination of how the various Italian and Bergamasco elements add up to mixing. Wherever possible, I have followed my research and transcription consultants' views on what sounded mixed to them as they focused on particular sounds, words, and phrases.

In spite of how bivalent so much speech was in Bergamo, when most people talked about language in Bergamo they maintained that speaking Italian and Bergamasco together was undesirable. Speakers understood Italian and Bergamasco to be two distinct codes, and mixing them up was a sign that one did not know any better. The many forms of bivalent speech were usually described in one of two ways: as "bad" Italian (when Bergamasco interfered[2]), or as "inauthentic" Bergamasco (when Italian interfered).

Notice that the terms of evaluation were different for each language, and that there were thus *different* right ways to speak them: for Italian, speakers were judged to be speaking good versus bad Italian; for Bergamasco, speakers were judged to be speaking real versus inauthentic Bergamasco. These are language ideologies, the types of judgments speakers make about languages and speakers that are rooted in their ideas about morality, cultural similarity and difference, and aesthetics. The first type of judgment is an implicit ranking of Italian over Bergamasco, for good Italian is characterized by not having any Bergamasco elements in it. Good Italian is learned and practiced in contexts of power and prestige, such as schools (especially high school and college), government bureaucracy, politics, and media. The second type of judgment is built on participants' links to their community and place, as demonstrated through their speech; "real" Bergamasco demonstrates speakers' close connections to their place, culture, and traditions (remember that Davide seemed to me to be suggesting that Bergamasco was just not for me, an outsider). Real Bergamasco is learned in the home, with family, and spoken to those with whom you are closest. It is often judged in terms of its "authenticity." So, speaking could give you power (over other speakers who do not speak Italian as well as you do) and/or could make you socially and emotionally close or distant from your local community (in relation to others who speak Bergamasco). Italian and Bergamasco were valued differently, in other words, due to what they were associated with and what they indexed, or pointed to, in the world outside of language.

Why Bergamasco

Focusing on what indexing involved in practice, we find that Bergamaschi valued their own language for many reasons: it was the language their ancestors spoke, the language their mother and father or grandparents spoke or continued to speak, the language they spoke with close friends and family, or simply, as was true for some participants in the writing course, because it was "**gran bèl**," very beautiful. They also valued it in and of itself. In everyday conversations that focused on language, the value of Bergamasco as a language with unique semantic resources – what its words mean and evoke – was a common and popular topic. Example 2.1, which took place during an informal group interview over glasses of wine and extensive socializing in a family cantina (or recreation room), illustrates this. Present were Paolo, dialect poet and ironsmith; his wife, Carla; their son, Roberto, also an ironsmith; and their friend, Daniele, a newly retired accountant in his late fifties, who directed and ran a dialect theater company. Daniele was very interested in Bergamasco, an interest he shared with Paolo. His paternal grandfather came from the south and he grew up speaking that vernacular as well as Bergamasco. His comments here were typical of this focus on the referential richness of Bergamasco, as he defined for me the Bergamasco word "**malfât**" that Paolo had just used:

Example 2.1

1   DANIELE: *Ci sono espressioni bergamasche che hanno la difficoltà della traduzione italiana.* "**Malfât**": *'poco agevole da fare,' sarebbe la traduzione italiana.*

1   DANIELE: There are Bergamasco expressions that are difficult to translate into Italian. "**Malfât**": 'not so easily accomplished,' would be the Italian translation.

2   JC (researcher): *Sì.*

2   JC: Yes.

3   DANIELE: *'Poco agevole da farsi,' ma in bergamasco è immediato.*

3   DANIELE: 'Not so easy to get accomplished,' but in Bergamasco it's immediate.[3]

Daniele pointed to **malfât** as an example of a Bergamasco expression that cannot be easily translated into Italian. He also used malfât to illustrate how Bergamasco is sometimes more efficient and to the point than Italian. The longer Italian phrase *poco agevole da farsi* is less "immediate" than the Bergamasco word, which conveys its meaning simply and more directly, without having to rely on so many words.[4] This was a common view of Bergamasco, valuing its perceived economy of words, especially for terms that Bergamaschi felt were intimately related to their local values: straightforwardness and the ability to express oneself simply and without elaboration. Malfât, as an expression that gets straight to the point about whether something is easily or well done, was portrayed here as reflecting something basic about Bergamasco values of sincerity, simplicity of expression, and the importance of a job well done (or not, as may be the case). The cultural value of "real" Bergamasco words like malfât is drawn, then, not only from the semantic richness of the word itself, but also for its connections to authentic Bergamasco values and traditions of straightforwardness.

This point is further illustrated by considering words that sound Bergamasco but were seen as having been influenced by Italian, or what my transcription consultants referred to as *bergamasco italianiz-zato* (Italianized Bergamasco).[5] Example 2.2 is taken from a poem recited during a poetry reading in Castagneta, a neighborhood in the Citta Altà. Giorgio, a retired accountant in his mid–seventies and one of the two poets reading that evening (Paolo was the other) recited his poem in which St. Peter sorts out souls as they arrive at the pearly gates.

Example 2.2

Con d'**öna lista in mà**   With a list in hand
Smistàa fò *le anime*   He sorted out the souls
De chela *grande* **confussiù**   Of that great disorder

When we transcribed this recording together, Rina attended to certain bivalent elements over others in instructive ways. "**Con**" is the same in both languages, and did not elicit comment. Similarly, the integrated borrowing "**confussiù**" (from Italian *confusione*) drew no comment. We both wondered why "*grande*" was in Italian (not the Bergamasco **gran**), and speculated that it was perhaps to add a syllable to the line, as the metric structure of the poem changed in the following line. Rina immediately pointed to "**smistàa fò**," however, as mixed up, drawing on Italian and Bergamasco simulta-neously, and we discussed it extensively. In spite of her linguistic training, she was not immediately sure which parts of it were Italian and which Bergamasco, because although the verb is conjugated like a Bergamasco verb (in the third person singular imperfect form) and has a Bergamasco spatial adverb following it, "**fò**" (out; *fuori* in Italian), the word itself, **smistàa**, sounded too much like the Italian word *smistare* (to sort out) to be the real Bergamasco form. During our next transcribing session, Rina returned to "**smistàa fò**," having consulted with her grandmother in the meantime. According to her grandmother, the real Bergamasco verb for "to sort out" should be **desmescià fò**, making **smistàa fò** a partial back-translation from the Italian *smistare*.

Bergamaschi often portrayed the relationship of Italian and Bergamasco as mutually informing, ongoing, and pervasive. An illus-trative example of this that I have heard more times than I can count is the way to say "fork." In old or "real" Bergamasco, the word for fork is **pirù**; today this form has fallen into disuse in favor of **forchéta**, which is the same as the Italian word (*forchetta*) in all but pronunciation (the quality of the second vowel sound and a shortening of the /t/).[6] Likewise, the example of how the Italian word for television, *televisione*, has been translated into **televissiù** in Bergamasco was often held up as another example of how, through assimilated borrowings like these, Bergamasco is becoming increasingly Italianized.

These examples demonstrate how some Bergamaschi placed great value on the "authenticity" of words in Bergamasco, and we see that one of the hallmarks of an "authentic" word or phrase was the lack of elements – or perceived influence – from the other language. We must regard the concept of "authenticity," then, as contextually and relationally defined, not a simple equation of "pure" dialectal forms with an imagined "pure" cultural identity (Coupland 2001). These examples also show, however, the difficulties faced when purist tendencies like these, which favor archaic forms that have often dropped out of popular use, went up against the realities of the spoken word. Although words like "**malfàt**" may have been valued as exquisitely Bergamasco, numerous expressions, words, phrases, and sounds have been imported across linguistic lines and integrated into the other language, as **pirù**/**forchéta**, *televisione*/**televissiù** and countless other examples demonstrate. **Smistàa fò** may have drawn Rina's scrutiny during transcription as problematically bivalent, but it elicited no commentary during the performance of that poem. Similarly, even during transcription, other bivalent forms, such as **con** and **confussiù** passed without comment – perhaps as more integrated borrowings, or acknowledged sites where the two languages have perhaps always overlapped. Social and linguistic judgments aligned to make these types of evaluations, and the tension of heteroglossia emerged at some moments and was backgrounded at others. That these examples occurred in a poem perhaps meant that they received more attention than they would in the course of everyday conversation, as poetry in Bergamasco is supposed to be written in the purest forms possible (a point to which I will return in Chapter 4).

Many Bergamaschi, including Rina, viewed their vernacular as the vehicle of the Bergamasco past and the mode of expression for the true Bergamasco self. But, as we see here, not just any

Bergamasco will do. When speakers like Rina and her grandmother undertook their own processes of "sorting out" Bergamasco and Italian in order to distinguish "authentic" Bergamasco words and phrases, the value of how Bergamasco "should be" was contrasted with how Bergamasco often "is." The latter was often deemed lacking in authenticity due to being Italianized.

Purism may represent, as Hill (1987) characterizes it, a "losing battle," or an opportunity for speakers to attempt to "break the cycle of dependence on the dominant language" (Hoffman 2008:225). For Bergamaschi, ideologies of purism weighed against contemporary everyday bivalencies. As we will see repeatedly, Bergamaschi often held up examples of their own and others' speech for scrutiny, finding bivalent moments amusing or using them as fodder for discussions about what has changed in Bergamo. Purism for them was a strategy for negotiating the complexity of bivalency in practice, trying to make sense of it according to ideas of how language should be used and how it was used. Instances such as Rina's reaction to **smistàa fò** and Daniele's discussion of **malfàt** linked purity to the past, and depict present practices as potentially problematic. At other times, the pure linguistic practices of the past were portrayed quite differently.

Why NOT Bergamasco

If Bergamaschi valued their language because of its richness and links to their values and traditions, why would Bergamasco have been in danger, as they perceived it to be? Why didn't this semantic richness lead them to embrace it whole-heartedly? Why did Rina have to consult her grandmother in order to figure out the "real" Bergamasco? The next transcript suggests what the use of Italian indexes for Bergamaschi. This segment occurred in an informal interview with a locally well-known architect, Stefano. During the interview, Maria, a woman in her early forties, was cataloguing Stefano's immense library and had been in and out of the room during our conversation about Bergamo and its vernacular. Although she had not until this time joined the conversation, she suddenly asked if she could say something:

Example 2.3

1 MARIA: *Posso dire la mia sull'argomento?*

2 JC (researcher): *Sì, sì certo.*

3 MARIA: *Perché è molto diversa l'attenzione che voi persone colte avete nei confronti del dialetto, possedendo però una lingua nazionale, che vi consente di argomentare, di rapportarvi a un mondo più vasto di quello che è il rione. Ma lei pensi alla gente che per secoli ha avuto solo per secoli il dialetto e quindi vede nell'abbandonare del dialetto . . . le faccio l'esempio la mia mamma mi ha . . . io sono cresciuta con lei che lavorava in paese, e quando dovevo iniziare la prima elementare mi ha mandato in collegio perché se no avrei parlato dialetto a scuola con i bambini del paese, e lei lo vedeva come una grossa limitazione del mio avvenire . . .*

4 STEFANO: *Si limitava il futuro.*

5 MARIA: *Esatto.*

6 STEFANO: *Non si sarebbe sposata piu`.*

1 MARIA: May I give mine [my view] on this topic?

2 JC: Yes, yes, of course.

3 MARIA: Because it's very different the attention that you cultivated people have in regards to the dialect. Possessing already a national language, that gives you the ability to think about, to relate yourself to a larger world than that of the neighborhood. But think about the people that for centuries, had only for centuries [sic] the dialect, and then see in the abandonment of the dialect . . . I'll give you an example, my mom made me . . . I grew up with her, she worked in a small village, and when I was supposed to start first grade she sent me to boarding school because if not I would have spoken the dialect in school with the kids from the village, and she saw that as a huge limitation on what I could become.

4 STEFANO: It limited the [your] future.

5 MARIA: Exactly.

6 STEFANO: You wouldn't have been able to move [anywhere else].

7 MARIA: *Lei scherza Architetto,*
   ma c'è questa [idea] . . .
   probabilmente sbagliata. Però
   noi non dobbiamo vederla dal
   nostro punto di vista, no, in
   cui valutiamo questa ricchezza
   (. . .) ma dal punto di vista
   di chi il dialetto l'ha vissuto
   come . . . come dire, come segno
   della sua inferiorità sociale,
   economica. Quindi non
   vedeva l'ora di, non dico di
   abbandonarlo, però di metterci
   possibilmente vicino
   all'italiano a livello scolastico
   magari, però di mettercelo;
   secondo me c'era
   quest'impulso.

7 MARIA: You joke, Architect,[7]
   but there is this [idea] . . .
   probably wrong. However, we
   have to see it not just from
   our point of view, no, in
   which we value this treasure
   (. . .) but from the point of
   view of who lived the dialect
   as . . . how to say it, as a
   sign of social, economic
   inferiority. Therefore, one
   couldn't wait, I'm not saying
   to abandon it, but to put
   oneself as close as possible to
   Italian at the educational
   level, I guess, but to put
   oneself there. I think that
   there was this impulse.

For Maria, it was impossible simply to treasure Bergamasco for how culturally authentic or semantically rich it sounded, unlike the architect and myself. Right away she pointed out that this is due to a difference in class: we, as "cultivated" people, have the luxury to view only the advantages of Bergamasco, because we already "possess" our national languages, and the privileges (educational and socio-economic) that this incurs. Raised in a working-class family, Maria and others like her tended to regard Bergamasco as limiting their future. Maria grew up in a small village in the province of Bergamo, with a working mother who aspired to a better life for her daughter and saw Bergamasco as an obstacle to getting ahead socially and economically. For her and others like her, it was a "sign of social inferiority." Her mother sent Maria away to school so that she would be able, as the architect put it, "to move" – both out of the small world of the village and out of the working-class world in which only Bergamasco was spoken.

Perhaps because of the conversation that she had overheard earlier as the architect and I discussed Bergamasco's richness, Maria softened her stance a little towards the end of her remarks, saying that it was not about abandoning Bergamasco, which was "*probabilmente sbagliata*" ("probably wrong"), but rather getting closer to Italian,

especially scholastically. She also implicitly switched to our point of
view that the vernacular is a "*richezza*" ("treasure") by using the
inclusive "we" soon after she accused the architect of joking: "we
have to see it not just from our point of view" ("*Però noi non dobbiamo vederla dal nostro punto di vista*"). When she emphasized that
the dialect was a sign of social inferiority, she used the impersonal
(like "one" in English), perhaps pointing to how far she – and others
like her, whose parents made similar choices – had come. She was
well-educated, well-employed, and spoke Italian well, having successfully traveled the distance between her working-class childhood
as Bergamasco-dominant and her middle-class adulthood as Italian-
dominant. She very precisely and astutely identified what caused
people like her to stop speaking the dialect: its connections to a
small, limited local world, one that was not just geographically
bound but also anchored in the working class. This was the impulse
that underwrote a shift away from Bergamasco and toward Italian,
she asserted, a claim that I heard again and again, and is supported
by sociolinguistic and archival evidence.

For people Maria's age, growing up speaking only Bergamasco
and not Italian was tantamount to growing up living in what De
Mauro calls a "linguistic ghetto" (1972). Before World War II, most
Bergamaschi were poor, either peasant share-croppers who worked
in the fields (*contadini*, plural of *contadino*), transhumant shepherds
(*pastori*, plural of *pastore*), or manual laborers who worked in the few
large industries in the province of Bergamo, the majority of which
were textile mills (Brusco 1986, Cento Bull et al. 1993, Cento Bull
1981; Cofini 2000; Della Valentina 1984).[8] They also spoke Bergamasco almost exclusively. Only the elite spoke Italian regularly
and educated their children in it. Many Bergamasco parents depended
on their children's labor for much of the year, and although five
years of education was officially obligatory after the end of the 19th
century, few children actually attended for that long. What little
Italian they did learn was seldom necessary in their everyday lives
and its use was confined to a few public activities and contexts, so
they rarely spoke it.

In spite of widespread efforts to eradicate Italian vernaculars
before and during the Fascist period, nearly all scholars agree that
it was not until the post-World War II period that the majority of

Italians began to learn and speak Italian, instead of or alongside their vernaculars (De Mauro 1972, 1994; Kramer 1983; Leoni 1980; Migliorini and Griffith 1984). This was the case in Bergamo, where the 1950s and 1960s heralded unprecedented economic prosperity, as well as expansion of and increased access to Italian-language media forms (Besana 1997). Extended and universalized schooling, where only Italian was and is permitted, allowed greater numbers of Bergamaschi access to well-paying white-collar employment. Parents no longer depended on their children's labor to make ends meet, and this, coupled with the employment opportunities the economic boom offered, meant that nearly all families had the means and the desire to send their children to school and keep them there long enough to learn Italian well.

Survey and interview data from the 1970s suggests that the majority of speakers used both Bergamasco and Italian, often inter- changeably, with the highest percentages of speakers who claimed to speak Bergamasco "frequently" in the lower-middle (34 percent) and working classes (95 percent) (Berruto 1978). In these data, speakers in lower class positions claimed to use more Bergamasco, while speakers in higher class positions stated they used more Italian. Younger speakers, especially those with the highest levels of educa- tion, claimed to speak less Bergamasco and more Italian than their elders, a pattern replicated across other unpublished studies in the 1970s and 1980s (Mora 1975, 1982, 1983). These data are primarily based on self-report, which may be unreliable for tracking speaking practices because speakers may under- or over-report use of a lan- guage depending on extra-linguistic factors or because such knowl- edge is often beyond speakers' consciousness (Gumperz 1982). Nonetheless, consistent patterns of class-differentiated language use over 30 years as well as the decrease in overall percentages of speak- ers during that time-span suggests the relative accuracy of these data. At the end of the 1990s, I found monolingual vernacular speakers only among the oldest Bergamaschi, whereas monolingual Italian speakers were common under the age of 30 (see also ISTAT 1997, 2007). Speakers between 40 and 60 were generally bilingual, and could have been dominant in either language.

The image of social mobility and progression from Bergamasco to Italian is more complex when examined closely. Equal access to education did not always equate with equal participation in educational opportunities. In Bergamo, educational levels have not risen at the same rate across all classes, as early entry into the job market was sometimes valorized above education in the lower and low-middle classes (Carra 2000) (see also Bertacchi 2000). Bergamo's healthy economy still depended in large part on manual laborers, most of whom were Bergamasco, although a percentage was also made up of immigrants from around the world and southern Italy. Additionally, the predominance of small and medium-sized closely knit family firms in Bergamo's economy encouraged many Bergamasco youth, especially but not exclusively males, to leave school as soon as possible in order to enter the job market (either in their own family firms or those of others) and earn money. These youth effectively chose jobs in manual labor over continuing education toward accessing white-collar careers later. This was true for people Maria's age who grew up during the time of economic expansion, and there is evidence to suggest that it had continued for younger Bergamaschi as well (Bertacchi 1981; Carra 2000). Local and national education statistics showed that Bergamo tended to have lower rates of participation in secondary education than other parts of the country. Although there were signs that the percentage of Bergamasco youth participating in secondary and post-secondary education had expanded,[9] there was still a gap between the economic and educational status of many Bergamaschi. Not all Bergamaschi, then, participated in the upward movement from rural agriculturalist/pastoralist or working-class status into the middle classes, and a large working class persisted at the time of my research, whose members spoke both Italian and Bergamasco.

So while virtually all Bergamaschi were materially better off than they once were in terms of their access to education, wage earning, participation in consumer markets, and residential comforts,[10] and the middle class had grown over the previous four decades, many Bergamaschi were still members of the lower classes in the early 2000s. Their class positions relative to other Bergamaschi and Italians had not changed. For those who left school early for manual labor jobs, striking the balance between the Italian and Bergamasco may have been complicated by their limited access to the national language through education (still the most common way to achieve the standard) and their continued use of Bergamasco in the workplace and at home. Their language use diverged from that of others with more education and a more thorough knowledge of Italian.

In the early 2000s, Bergamasco mattered because of its indexical links to local traditions, values, and ways of life. Italian mattered because it allowed its speakers to rise above these local conditions, which often included hardship and poverty. The balance between these opposing value systems was dynamic, depending on the context, the relationships among speakers, and the type of activity in which one was engaged. It was more likely, for instance, to find Bergamasco spoken or valued in the ways that Daniele, the architect and myself did if one was in the home or among friends, or if one was taking part in an event explicitly aimed at the vernacular, such as talking about it in an interview or discussing it during a poetry reading. It was also more likely that those who explicitly valued it had a certain distance from it and what Maria described as the limitations it imposed on one's future. Speakers in the upper or middle classes who were socioeconomically and linguistically secure – that is, able to speak Italian well, either alone or in addition to the vernacular, like the card players who began this chapter, Daniele, and the architect – could afford to value the language for its richness. For a speaker like Maria, whose mother actively pursued ways for her to move beyond these restraints, the vernacular was not just a *richezza*, but also a potential liability.

Being Bergamasco

For all speakers, Italian was valuable for the mobility it afforded and the prestige it endowed. At the same time, to get rid of one's Bergamasco accent altogether would have been to hyper-correct, which would make one sound arrogant (Labov 1966b, Milroy 1987). To many ears, it sounded inauthentic and insincere to speak with no accent, as people relied on these cues in order to position a speaker within the sociolinguistic landscape. Roberta, who as a director of dialect theater was ever attentive to speech and its delivery, asserted during an interview that:

Example 2.4

Da noi qui a Bergamo quando qualcuno parla correttamente, correttaménte [exaggerated correct pronunciation of the '*e*'] – *perché si chiude, correttaménte* – *dicono* **"Té, te parlèt ricamàt incö?"** *"Tu, parli ricamato, oggi?" Cioè con un ricamo, vuol dire che parli bene oggi. E allora noi parliamo tutti così come ci viene.*

Here in our Bergamo when someone speaks correctly, correctly – because it's closed [the 'e'], correctly – they say, **"You, you're speaking fancy today?"** [lit. "embroidered"] *"You, you're speaking fancy today?"* That is, with a flourish [lit. "an embroidery"], which means that you're speaking well today. And so we all speak just as it comes to us.

As Anna pointed out while transcribing, Roberta produced a hypercorrect form of the /e/ in her pronunciation of "*correttamente*" [korɛtamente] (correctly) instead of the more Bergamasco pronunciation [korɛtamɛnte], thereby demonstrating how the /e/ should sound in standard Italian and how it never did in Bergamo unless someone was putting on airs. She supplied the local mode of condemnation for such an act of snobbery – that the speaker was guilty of "fanciness" or unnecessary labor or frills (recall the Bergamasco value of straightforwardness and simplicity of expression about **malfàt** discussed above). She did this in Bergamasco initially, suggesting that such a display of hyper-Italian-ness would be met with its opposite: a fully Bergamasco phrase, which she then repeated in Italian (perhaps for my benefit). Roberta made it clear that this type of censure works – that "we" just talk as we do, so speaking without local markers like this locally pronounced /e/ is relatively rare. She also presented Bergamasco and local forms of Italian as more "natural" than standard Italian; as being that which was "just as it comes," without monitoring.

But compare Roberta's image of the censure that hypercorrection could receive with the anxiety that Marina, Davide and Tullia's daughter, experienced about her pronunciation in one particular social context. One day in late November 2000, I went with a group of her family and friends to hear her defend her *tesi di laurea* (similar to a master's thesis), a sophisticated analysis of modern

German philosophy, at a prominent university in Milan. A jury of several professors, including her advisors, probed her knowledge with a wide-ranging and daunting series of questions. She answered authoritatively, with aplomb, poise, and wit, and was subsequently awarded the highest honors. Later, however, she worried to the group that the panel might have heard her Bergamasco accent, and presumed she was stupid. So although in many in-group contexts, Bergamaschi spoke "just as it comes," as Roberta said, in others they monitored their speech to try to weed out as many Bergamasco elements as possible so as to not appear provincial. Marina was certainly not worried about her accent when she complained that she was not enjoying the card game, for in this private context, in the home and among family and friends, speaking in a Bergamasco way sounded "natural" (i.e., it elicited no comments or feelings of anxiety). Only in a more formal, public context would she have worried about outsiders' potentially negative judgments based on how she spoke. This was especially true given Italian's role as the language of education and intellectual sophistication.

Fine-tuned attention to location in geographical and social space meant balancing speaking "authentically" (i.e. sufficiently connected to your local place) with speaking "correctly" (sounding upper class and educated). Such balancing acts were achieved through bivalency, which could bring heteroglossic tensions to the fore in speakers' evaluations of their own and others' speech. These evaluations and choices of code varied across speakers, according to age, social class, occupation, linguistic repertoire, and gender (which I will discuss more at length in the following chapter). An older person might have received more censure for speaking Italian and a younger person less, a construction worker would be expected to speak more Bergamasco and a lawyer more Italian, and so on. There is a local theory of self-operating here, based on indexical presuppositions: who you are (young or old, rich or poor, rural or urban, male or female) should line up with how you speak and how you sound to others. What was appropriate speaking varied across speakers, contexts, and activities, although rarely did speaking not involve at least a shadow of a Bergamasco accent, even among upper-class speakers. To speak otherwise would have been to demonstrate one was untethered to place, linguistically homeless.

Turning to an example of a Bergamasco conversation, we can see this bivalency in action. Example 2.5 is drawn from an interaction that took place after a Bergamasco play rehearsal. Several of the cast members and the director, Roberta, and her husband, Ennio, stood around after the rehearsal, discussing an ongoing and vexing problem: appropriate footwear. While talking about shoes is common in Italy, it is rarely about how to find ugly, old-fashioned shoes, as this conversation was. The play that the company was working on was set at the turn of the last century, and they were having difficulty finding the right kind of *zoccoli* (**sàcoi** in Bergamasco) – the type of wooden clogs that most Bergamaschi wore during this period. The clogs that they had found up to this point had just not been right. Participants in this conversation included cast members Linda, an administrator for the city in her mid-thirties, Vanessa, a homemaker in her sixties, and Silvano, a retired bank manager also in his sixties, as well as Roberta and Ennio, who were in their mid-fifties and ran a travel agency, when they weren't putting on plays. The comments in brackets are Ella's commentary during transcription and my translations of these.

Example 2.5

1   ENNIO: **Eh va beh. A èt a tö cos'è.** [Bergamasco *"stretto."* Italian translation: *"Vai a comprare qualcosa"*]

1   ENNIO: Okay, fine. Get something. ["Narrow" Bergamasco. Italian translation: "Go and buy something"]

2   ROBERTA: *Hanno sempre un po' di tacchettino.*

2   ROBERTA: They always have a bit of a heel.

3   ENNIO: **Eèt a tö cosa?** [Bergamasco less *stretto* than first phrasing above]

3   ENNIO: Get what? [Bergamasco less narrow than first phrasing above]

4   ROBERTA: **Eh l'so mia . . . Negòt.**

4   ROBERTA: Oh, I don't know . . . Nothing.

5   VANESSA: **Adah!** [*bergamasco inciso* – like "**scolta**"]

5   VANESSA: Look! [incisive Bergamasco – like "listen!"]

6   ROBERTA: *Piuttosto fai un paio di scarpe brutte e le taglio. Eh!*

6   ROBERTA: It would be better to do a pair of ugly shoes and cut them. Ah!

7 ENNIO: **Eh, fa ü laùr del gèner**.

7 ENNIO: Right, do something like that.

8 LINDA: *Perché neanche quelli che* **dicea** *lui non van mica* [*"mica" è del nord Italia*] *bene* [*italiano, ma verso il dialetto, un'italiano molto bergamaschizzato*]. *Sono quelli da ospedale, quelli "Dr. Schulz."*

8 LINDA: Because not even those that he was saying would go that well [*mica* ("not that") is a northern Italian word] [Italian, but towards the dialect, a very Bergamasco-ized Italian]. There are those of the hospital, those "Dr. Schulz."

9 ENNIO: **Pèr de scarpe bröte, eh . . .**

9 ENNIO A pair of ugly shoes, huh . . .

10 SILVANO: **A m' gh'è nò a ca de laùre.** [*bergamasco stretto*.]

10 SILVANO: We don't have anything like that at home. [Narrow Bergamasco]

Within this single conversation, we can see the various types of language being used, from extremely *"stretto"* (narrow or strict) Bergamasco (Ennio's first utterance in line 1 and Silvano's in line 10) to conversational Italian (Roberta's utterance on line 6). Also evident is the variation in sequential patterning of language choice. Italian could follow Bergamasco, Bergamasco could follow Italian, or a single language could be maintained. Ennio, Vanessa, and Silvano spoke only Bergamasco in this conversation, Linda only Italian – although Ella, the transcription consultant with whom I transcribed this interaction, noted that it was a very Bergamasco-ized Italian – and Roberta spoke both. In this section of the interaction, speakers spoke the same language throughout an utterance, a pattern that was not always the case. It is clear, however, that everyone was participating and following the discussion. Multiple competencies and preferences characterize this interaction, like the one that followed the **cotècc** game discussed above, and so many others in Bergamo.[11]

We also see a second layer of information in this transcript: the bracketed commentary of Ella, which demonstrated that "speaking Italian" and "speaking Bergamasco" were more complicated to define than appears at first glance. At my request, while we were transcribing, Ella noted when participants spoke Italian and when they spoke Bergamasco, and pointed out when she thought that people sounded more or less Italian or Bergamasco, most often focusing on utterances in which a speaker sounded particularly Bergamasco. Ella did not comment on utterances that were in Italian and apparently did not sound Bergamasco at all, such as Roberta's utterance on line 6: "*Piuttosto fai un paio di scarpe brutte e le taglio. Eh!*" ("It would be better to do a pair of ugly shoes and cut them. Ah!") Some utterances, however, sounded dialectal to Ella, although they were technically in Italian, such as when she commented "[Italian, but towards the dialect, a very Bergamasco-ized Italian]" on line 8. At these moments, it became clear that there was a continuum from the most Bergamasco-sounding utterances to the least. Bergamaschi use the (Italian) terms *stretto* (narrow, strict) or *duro* (hard, difficult) to indicate varieties of Bergamasco they deem "very" Bergamasco. This is a relative assessment: the Bergamasco of town is generally considered less stretto than that of the mountains, even if an utterance is entirely in Bergamasco. Being more stretto involves a lexicon and phonology that differs more from Italian than other varieties deemed less stretto.[12] This is illustrated in how Ella distinguished between two varieties of Bergamasco as more or less stretto when she had me write "[Bergamasco less narrow than first phrasing of question]" next to line 3. Ella also indicated specific items that sounded regional to her, but not necessarily Bergamasco, such as "[*mica* ('not that') is a northern Italian word]" in line 8 (see Chapter 3 for a more extensive discussion of *mica*).

Sounding Bergamasco

Ella's commentary on the interaction in Example 2.5 demonstrates that there were specific ways in which utterances sounded more or less Bergamasco or Italian. These examples illustrate an attention to two parts of speech: lexicon and phonology. Ella focused on the first through comments such as in line 8 – "[*mica* ('not that') is a northern Italian word]" – and line 5 – "**Adah!** [*bergamasco inciso*, like '**scolta**' (listen!)]" – and on the second when she attended to how speakers sounded, such as through her characterization of Linda's pronunciation as part of what made her utterance in line 8 sound like "Bergamasco-ized Italian." In particular, she pointed to her use of the bivalent form "**dicea**" ("said": *diceva* in Italian, **disìa** in Bergamasco). This is a common form in Bergamasco-ized Italian (I have several examples of it in my data), modeled on the tendency in Bergamasco to drop intervocalic /v/, as seen in examples such as **caàl** (*cavallo* in Italian; "horse") (Sanga 1997).

The use of certain grammatical structures could also make speakers sound Bergamasco. The use of calques, in particular – borrowed items in which the parts are translated separately or literally into the other language – stood out as a Bergamasco way of speaking, both to my transcribers, and to other Bergamaschi in their everyday lives. These calques appeared as words or phrases in Italian modeled on either idiomatic Bergamasco phrases or Bergamasco syntactic patterns. Example 2.6 was taken from a recording made during a Bergamasco writing class. It was an exchange between two men in their twenties. In response to the teacher's request for volunteers to come up to the front of the room to write on the blackboard, Francesco told his friend, Ernaldo, to do it:

Example 2.6

FRANCESCO: **Vai su** *te*!   FRANCESCO: Go up you!

ERNALDO: **Vado su** *io*.   ERNALDO: I am going up!

Bergamasco has numerous phrasal and prepositional verbs, which pair a verb with a particle that is either a spatial adverb or a preposition. In this it differs from standard Italian, which has fewer phrasal verbs.[13] In English, either form is permitted and equally "correct": one says "I go up the stairs" as well as "I ascend," and "you go in" is just as correct as "you enter." For instance, in Italian one would use the verb *versare* (to pour), while in Bergamasco the equivalent would be **fà dét** (to put/make in).[14] To translate this exactly and say **faccio dentro** (I put/make in) in Italian rather than the more standard *verso* (I pour) sounded very Bergamasco to Bergamaschi (although this phrase may be used by other Italians) because it imports the Bergamasco two-word phrasal structure into Italian. Example 2.6 contains a relatively set calque, for "**vado su**" was a common phrase in Bergamo. My point is not that only Bergamaschi may have said these phrases, but that such ways of speaking sounded particularly Bergamasco to local ears. Indeed, when Anna heard Francesco and Ernaldo use this phrase while transcribing, she burst out laughing. She observed that they sounded simple-minded, like typical Bergamaschi. In other words, their use of this Bergamasco calque in Italian indexed a rough, uneducated speaker, who perhaps did not know that this was not correct Italian.

I suggest that there is something else behind Anna's laughter, too. Whenever I listen to this part of the recording, I laugh as well. Francesco and Ernaldo sound like they were joking around, playing up sounding like this stereotype in order to be funny. Ernaldo, even more than Francesco, sounded like he was aiming for a laugh, as he slightly mimicked Francesco, echoing back his phrase. Perhaps they were drawing out the contrast between the cultural image indexed through such language use and the scholarly setting of the classroom that they were in, making a joke out of sounding rough and unedu-cated in school.

Bergamasco is indeed frequently described as the appropriate language in which to *fare le battute* (make jokes), and exchanges such as this one reinforce Bergamasco ways of speaking as inherently humorous. Minority languages often index humor, due to their common associations with naturalness and in-group solidarity.[15] For example, Fenigsen has observed that Bajan, the minority language in Barbados, like many creole languages, is considered better suited to humor and intimacy than the standard language. In more formal environments, such as the classroom, which require the standard, Bajan may occasionally be used as a humorous "sideline" (Fenigsen 1999:63).

Bivalent forms such as those in Example 2.6 do more than just sound humorous through indexing solidarity and authenticity, however. By drawing on both languages simultaneously, the use of these bivalent forms allows Ernaldo and Francesco to avoid the frills of sounding too Italian, and simultaneously – though implicitly – comment on the cultural stereotypes which depict Bergamaschi as more appropriately herding animals than writing on a chalkboard. Such joking foregrounds the tensions of heteroglossia, contrasting how one should sound in a particular setting with how one shouldn't, as well as which types of speaking selves are more appropriate to certain settings.

Being Italian "in a Bergamasco way"

Trying to achieve a balance between Bergamasco and Italian often required more extended effort on the part of speakers. The next transcript, which addresses this endeavor, is doubly informative: in it, Bergamaschi talk about attitudes towards the two languages, and they do so using both languages. It is drawn from the same conversation I had with Paolo, Carla, Roberto, and Daniele in which Daniele commented on the value of **malfàt**, discussed above (Example 2.1). This transcript is taken from a section of the discussion that focused on how mothers taught their children Italian:

Example 2.7

1   DANIELE: *E glielo insegnavano alla bergamasca* . . .

1   DANIELE: *And they taught it in the Bergamasco way* . . .

2   CARLA: **Mesciando sö 'l bergamàsch e** *italiano.*

2   CARLA: **Mixing up Bergamasco** *and Italian.*

3   DANIELE: *Mischiando un po' di bergamasco e un po' di italiano.*

3   DANIELE: *Mixing a little Bergamasco and a little Italian.*

4   JC: *Un po' d'italiano.*

4   JC: *A little Italian.*

5   DANIELE: *Non solo.*

5   DANIELE: *Not only.*

6   CARLA: *Questo è capitato all'epoca,* **nò**? **Al'època di mé s-cècc. Che l'éra lé 'l momentì, ch'i disìa** . . .

6   CARLA: *This happened during that time,* **no**? **At the time of my children. It was then, in that little moment, that was said** . . .

7   ROBERTO: *Allora, c'era un momento che dice* . . .

7   ROBERTO: *Well, that was a moment that you said* . . .

8   CARLA: **Nóter a m' parlàa bergamàsch** . . .

8   CARLA: **We who spoke Bergamasco** . . .

9   ROBERTO: *Vai a prendermi quella* **braga di sabbione** *lì.*

9   ROBERTO: *Go and get me that* **pile of sand** [means "bucket of sand"] *there.*

This transcript shows us what it meant to speak in the Bergamasco way, which these speakers described as not simply speaking the vernacular, but as speaking in ways that drew on both languages. They achieve this bivalency individually and jointly, through their various choices of code (Italian, Bergamasco or some-times both within the same utterance), switching codes (as Carla did), and maintaining the same code no matter what one's interlocu-tor speaks (as with Daniele, who maintains Italian here, although he spoke both). Carla and Roberto in particular show us what it meant to speak in this mixed or bivalent way, each in their own manner.

This segment begins with Roberto observing that mothers taught their children (to speak) "*alla bergamasca*" ("in the Bergamasco way"). Carla's utterance in line 2 not only described but also iconically depicted what he meant by alla bergamasca: "**Mesciando sö '1 bergamàsch e** *italiano*" ("Mixing up Bergamasco and Italian"). The phrase is mixed in complicated ways. Lexically, "**sö '1 bergamàsch**" is in Bergamasco and "*italiano*" is in Italian, while "**e**" (and) is identi-cal in both varieties and so could be either or both simultaneously (see Berruto 1978, 1987 for discussions of Italian/dialect homo-phones). The phrase "**Mesciando sö**" (mixing up)[16] is the most complicated, for it is both a back-translation of a Bergamasco con-struction and morphologically embedded Italian in a Bergamasco word. "**Mescià**" is "to mix"; adding the spatial adverb **sö** (up) makes it "to mix up." The suffix -*ando* is the Italian progressive gerund suffix, similar to -ing in English. There is no progressive form in Bergamasco historically, but it has become increasingly common to add -*ando* to a Bergamasco verb stem in order to express an ongoing action (Mora 1966). "**Mesciando sö,**" then, is a Bergamasco verb with an Italian verb ending, followed by a Bergamasco adverb, all fitted into a Bergamasco phrasal structure. Carla's deft mixing of Italian and Bergamasco elements gives us an illustrative example of what mixing up Bergamasco and Italian can look like when one speaks in a Bergamasco way.

In line 3, Daniele translated Carla's phrase into Italian, but altered it as well, adding "a little" before each type of language – "*Mischiando un po' di bergamasco e un po' di italiano*" ("Mixing a little Bergamasco and a little Italian") – making it sound almost like a recipe, tying this task to other domestic duties. Like cooking, one threw in a little of this and a little of that when speaking to their children.

Then, by saying *"Non solo"* ("Not only"), he stressed (line 5) that this was not the only thing that these mothers did. On line 6, Carla asserted that this happened during the time when her children were growing up, not that long ago: *"Questo è capitato all'epoca,* **nò**? **Al'època di mé s-cècc"** (*"This happened during that time,* **no**? **At the time of my children**.") Again, her utterance contained both Italian and Bergamasco, with certain elements ambiguous in terms of whether they were Italian or Bergamasco. Notice especially the two iterations of "at the time of," which is lexically identical in the two languages, and which lie between the clearly Italian beginning of the utterance and Bergamasco end of the utterance. When Elsa transcribed this recording, she marked only the second occurrence of the phrase as sounding Bergamasco, implicitly indicating that the first occurrence was in Italian. Listening to the recording, however, the two are essentially identical phonologically. Elsa's efforts to delineate for me when each language occurred seem here to have been influenced by the order of how the words occurred, or by what Saussure would have called the "syntagmatic relations" among them (1986). Occurring in close association with non-bivalent words seems to make bivalent words less obvious or visible as such to those listening. This process perhaps helps to explain how certain instances of bivalent speech may pass without comment or notice, even when the form of speech matters (as during transcribing).

Roberto echoed and translated the last part of Carla's utterance into Italian in line 7 (*"Allora, c'era un momento che dice . . ."*), perhaps for my benefit, as my abilities in Bergamasco were still doubted by the speakers.[17] Carla then essentially continued her previous utterance on line 8, in Bergamasco, saying that that was the time when we, who spoke Bergamasco, said things in a certain way (**"Che l'éra lé 'l momentì, ch'i disìa . . . Nóter a m' parlàa bergamàsch"**). She describes the category of people who spoke like this as potentially all Bergamaschi. Carla and Roberto both indicated that this was a particular time in the past, a specific moment, when Bergamaschi spoke this way.

Roberto then gave an example of the type of thing that "we who spoke Bergamasco back then" said: *"Vai a prendermi quella* **'braga di sabbione'** *lì."* ("*Go and get me that* **'pile of sand'** *there*"), in which **braga di sabbione** is a mix, starting in Bergamasco (**braga**) and ending in Italian (*di sabbione*). Using the word **braga**, which literally means "all that one can carry with both hands cupped together" in Bergamasco, makes the phrase informal and plays on translating between the varieties, and the difficulties that this may cause. Braga is similar to malfàt, for it is a particularly Bergamasco word that expresses an idea simply and economically, whereas it would require much more effort and explanation in Italian. When I subsequently asked what **braga di sabbione** meant, Roberto told me it stood for "bucket of sand," but was "a little in Bergamasco, [but] wrong" ("*Un po' in bergamasco, sbagliato*"), laughing while he explained. I only learned the full definition of braga when I looked it up later in a Bergamasco–Italian dictionary.

"**Braga di sabbione**" is an absurd phrase, which made everyone who heard Roberto say it laugh (except me, who needed that later explanation to get the joke). Roberto said it as one would a punch-line, directly quoting some unnamed Bergamasco, pausing for comedic effort before "braga" and following the phrase with loud laughter, in which he was joined by everyone else present. He physically leaned into the phrase as he said it, making us see from his movement that this phrase was set apart from the rest of his utterance. He essentially adopted a more Bergamasco voice than usual (and Roberto usually had a strong Bergamasco accent, although his Italian was good), so that we heard the voice of these other Bergamaschi who did not know any better and mixed the two languages, even as they perhaps tried to use as much Italian as possible. This kind of semi-self-mocking was common among Bergamaschi, especially for comedic effect, as they simultaneously embraced the rough characteristics of the Bergamasco stereotype and distanced themselves from them. This type of joking indexed a persona who was at once like Roberto and his audience, but also distant enough to laugh at, though with affection. The peals of laughter that followed it indicated the pleasure this phrase gave to the rest of the participants in this conversation.

The past Carla, Daniele, and Roberto were describing was not so far away. Roberto's joke indicated that this happened at a time when many Bergamaschi did not know better, implicitly comparing it to the present, when they do. He certainly did, as he deftly used his knowledge of both languages to create a verbal image of this mixed up past. But Carla's heteroglossic phrase about

"**Mesciando sö 'l bergamàsch e** *italiano*" resonated with how many Bergamaschi still speak. She did not seem to be joking when she said it; perhaps, as a Bergamasco-dominant speaker, she was still doing the best she could with the Italian she had. This conversation, the argument at the card table, the clogs discussion, and many other interactions like them in which I participated indicated that at least some speakers speak alla bergamasca. At the same time, Roberta's and Marina's concerns about sounding the right amount of Bergamasco (too little or too much) at the right time and place demonstrate the tensions surrounding how Bergamaschi thought they should and did speak when they reflected on their language use, both past and present. Speaking itself demonstrated how these tensions were played out in everyday conversation, with various speakers making different choices, often drawing on both the power and prestige of Italian and the local authenticity, self-deprecating humor, and warm sentiment afforded by and in Bergamasco, sometimes within the same utterance.

Indexicality in Action

So far, we have mostly considered examples in which speakers have, for the most part, used bivalency to their own effect, in order to make a point or get a laugh. The indexical associations of Italian and Bergamasco were not always so easily corralled by speakers' intentions and efforts. Indeed, Bakhtin maintains that no single speaker can control all of the variation that makes up heteroglossia (1981), and various studies of language minorities have demon-strated that speakers' linguistic understandings and abilities may not perfectly line up with their intentions and/or desires (see, for example, Dorian 1982, Kulick 1992, and Urciuoli 1995). Humor, honesty, and the social intimacy of confidenza reverberated in speak-ing alla bergamasca, but also the tendency to leave school early, work hard, and implicitly put local ties above what Stefano and Maria depicted as moving up and out of the small Bergamasco world of the tightly knit neighborhood and small town. Along with the posi-tive associations people may have had about the value of Bergamasco due to its semantic richness or cultural uniqueness, these less positive associations contributed to the social aesthetics of language in Bergamo; what it felt like and sounded like to speak.

Let's return to calques to illustrate this. As well as constructions that pair spatial adverbs with verbs of motion (such to go + up, for instance, which occurred in Example 2.6), calques also include metaphoric uses of this phrasal construction, as in Example 2.8. This was taken from an interview I conducted at a metal mechanics factory in one of the provincial valleys just north of the town of Bergamo. Marco, in his mid-twenties and a recently hired worker there, was telling me about how he spoke Bergamasco to some people, like his male friends and family members, but Italian to other people.

Example 2.8

MARCO: *Come adesso* **sono dietro a parlare** *in italiano con te.*

MARCO: *Like now,* **I'm getting on with speaking** *in Italian with you.*

To be "**de dré a . . .** [an act]" in Bergamasco means that someone is in the middle of doing it, is undertaking it, although it literally means to be behind it, a form which perhaps emerges out of Bergamasco's aforementioned historical lack of a progressive verb form. To import this form into Italian and state that one is "*dietro a . . .* [an act]" is a word-for-word translation of a Bergamasco idiom, which is not standard Italian. It sounded Bergamasco because of this, but also because of the phrasal construction of the verb and because it did not employ the Italian progressive verb form (which would have been *sto parlando con te*, I'm talking to you). When Anna and I went over this example, she pointed to this construction in particular as making Marco sound very Bergamasco to her. As before with Francesco and Ernaldo, she also observed that it made Marco sound uneducated and ignorant, speaking in the voice of a stereotypical Bergamasco. In fact, Marco and I spoke about how he had left school when he finished middle school in order to enter the workforce, and sometimes worried that his *italiano bergamaschizzato* might hurt his chances of getting a better job. In the factories where he had worked, the workers all spoke Bergamasco or both Italian and Bergamasco to each other, while the bosses spoke mostly Italian. Marco wondered aloud if he would ever attain a managerial position given his non-standard Italian.

Marco's fears were not unfounded, given the close ideological association of Italian, education, and socioeconomic success. This is not to say that his language skills alone could ensure that he never rose into management. Rather, his language use indexed his lack of education and lowered chances of rising above manual laborer. So while Marco expressed to me how important he thought the vernacular was, and how often he spoke it with family and friends (and since I had told him at the start of the interview that I was interested in the dialect, it is not surprising that he told me this), the advantages associated with Italian also clearly had an impact on his feelings about speaking.

Who Is the Joke On?

We have already seen how the uneasy tension between Italian and Bergamasco often produced laughter when speakers highlighted it in explicit or implicit ways. The next transcript, taken from the same recording as the **smistàa fò** segment discussed above, demonstrates this point acutely. I recorded it during a poetry reading that took place one Sunday evening in a church social center in a neighborhood in the Città Alta in 2000. Two local poets had been invited to speak, Paolo and Giorgio. The two were old friends and had grown up together in the Città Alta, though they had later taken different paths: while Paolo had followed his father into iron working, Giorgio had run a bank. They continued to share their interest in the vernacular, however. There were roughly 40 people in attendance that night, most of them from the neighborhood, nearly all of them over the age of 50. It was a casual, festive affair, with audience members responding with laughter and encouragement during the poetry, and calling out poems they knew and wanted recited in between. The poetry recital was followed by an hour or so when everyone mingled, drank wine, and tucked into platters of *pan'e salami* (bread and salami), the quintessential Bergamasco snack.

The following took place at the beginning of the evening, as Giorgio introduced himself and Paolo and talked a little about the importance of having an evening like this, dedicated to dialect poetry.

Example 2.9

GIORGIO: *Molto importante sapere parlare il dialetto,* **'ncö i s-cècc i la l' parle piö!**

GIORGIO: [It's] *Very important to know how to speak the dialect,* **today, the kids don't speak it anymore!**

AUDIENCE: **No** [agreeing with him].

AUDIENCE: **No** [agreeing with him].

GIORGIO: *Però, effettivamente è importante. Vi racconto un aneddotto e poi ho chiuso: mi raccontava un assicuratore –* **quei** *che fanno le assicurazioni – che quando venivan giù dalla montagna* **chi póer bortulì chi gh'éra de spiegà chi gh'éra it ön'incidènt che gh'éra de ciapà i sólcc de l'asigürassiù** *parlavano in bergamasco:* **"alura, cià, me, pòta." Chès-ce chè chi gh'éra de pagà** *capivano che aveva ragione* **ghe disìa***: "non ho capito. Può ripetere in italiano?" Farli parlare in italiano* **l'éra töt ol cuntrare l'éra perdìt** *la causa.*

GIORGIO: *However, effectively it's important. I'll tell you an anecdote and then I'm done: An insurance man was telling me –* **one of** *those who does insurance – that when they came down from the mountain* **those poor bortulì who had to explain that there had been an accident and they needed money from the insurance,** *they spoke in Bergamasco:* **"Well then, right, me, who knows." These here, who had to pay,** *understood that they* [the poor bortulì] *were in the right* **asked them***: "I don't understand. Could you repeat it in Italian?" Making them speak in Italian* **it came out all the contrary and they lost** *the case.*

AUDIENCE: [laughter]

AUDIENCE: [laughter]

GIORGIO: *Questo per dire, questo per dire, quanto importante è il dialetto, quanta sicurezza e quanto piacere dà. Perché* **gh'è di parole che** *in italiano* **s' pöl mia fale, troale, i gh'à mia la tradüssiù i è adoma 'n dialèt** *e il dialetto è un qualchecosa di nostro, che abbiamo sentito da quando* **a m' séra s-cècc e che nóter, nóter e i nóter** poeti, **töcc chei chi scrif,** e *anche* **chei chi la parla** *cerchiamo di manterlo vivo.*

GIORGIO: *This is to say, this is to say, how important the dialect is, how much security and how much pleasure it gives. Because* **there are** words that *in Italian* **you can't do, find them, there's no translation from the dialect** *and the dialect is something of ours, that we have felt from when* **we were kids and that we, we and our** poets, **all those who write** and *also* **those** who speak it *search to keep alive.*

Giorgio explicitly described this heteroglossic anecdote as evidence of "how much security and how much pleasure" the dialect gives, and indeed, the audience laughed and found his story amusing. But looked at just a little more closely, this story seems to illustrate exactly how much *insecurity* speaking the dialect can bring. The insurance men, who spoke Italian and appeared to understand Bergamasco, recognized that these **póer bortulì** (essentially, poor Joe Shmos, or country bumpkins) brought legitimate claims to them, for which they should be financially compensated. They also, however, suspected that these póer bortulì were limited linguistically, and asked them to repeat their stories in Italian. Notice that it is not that they could not speak Italian, but just that they spoke it so poorly that the sense of their stories came out "**töt ol cuntrare**" ("all the contrary"), exactly the opposite of what they meant (and successfully expressed in Bergamasco) so that their case was lost and they did not receive the compensation they justly deserved.

On the face of it, this does not appear to be a funny story – and yet the audience laughed, as Giorgio clearly expected them to. Did they laugh because they felt distance from such events, that such things could never happen to them or would not have happened to them in the past? I believe it is because the anecdote highlighted the linguistic and social tensions that characterized their own experience. They laughed because the story was so potentially close to their own experience, or the experience of their not-so-distant predecessors, while at the same time they were able to think of themselves as *not* póer bortulì. Giorgio recounted that an insurance man told him this story, presumably as a funny anecdote at which Giorgio was supposed to laugh. In finding it funny, Giorgio (and later the audience) established themselves as different from the hapless Bergamasco-only speakers in the story. Implicitly, they would have all known better, have been better able to express themselves in Italian when they needed to. This story drew out exactly why mothers needed to teach their children Italian in the days of Maria and Carla's children, and why they continued to do so: money and power, or, more precisely, the possibility of participating in socio-economic opportunities and state-level institutions and activities conducted in Italian, such as schooling, interacting with government or private bureaucracy (like insurance companies), voting, etc. That is, Italian afforded the ability to interact within a larger sphere than Bergamasco made possible. As the architect put it to Maria and me, knowing Italian, and knowing it well enough to avoid these types of linguistic mistakes, allows one to "move" – up and out of what was considered the small, intimate circle of Bergamasco poverty and ignorance.

In addition to the content of what Giorgio said, there is another layer of data available to us in this transcript: its form, specifically Giorgio's extensive switching between Italian and Bergamasco. This switching demonstrates first and foremost the thorough bilingualism of Giorgio and his audience: his through his utterances; them through their apparent comprehension of what he said. Next, we can observe where he switched, what he said in each respective language, and the effects that these choices generate. He began by using Italian to state that it is important to speak the dialect and immediately switched to Bergamasco to lament that, today, kids don't speak it anymore. By saying this in Bergamasco he positioned himself and his listeners on one side of a generational divide – they are not the kids who don't speak it anymore (since they all at least understand it). They are the ones who recognize how important the dialect is and think that children not speaking it is a problem. After the audience agreed, Giorgio continued in Italian, returning to his theme of the importance of Bergamasco, and introducing his anecdote to illustrate this importance.

Giorgio effectively used Italian and Bergamasco to give voice to the speakers associated with each language. He began in Italian, establishing that he heard this story from an Italian-speaking insurance man, and gave an initial description of the póer bortulì in Italian: they had to come down from the mountains. The stereotypical Bergamasco was often portrayed as a poor shepherd who stayed up in the mountains with his flocks, forgoing nearly all modern experiences and conveniences. He (and this stereotype is essentially always male – see the next chapter for a more complete discussion of this) is poor, uneducated, rough, and speaks the most stretto forms of Bergamasco.[18] By beginning this description in Italian, Giorgio positioned himself alongside the insurance men, to whom the bortulì came to make their applications. He switched quickly to Bergamasco when he named the póer bortulì and described the actions they took (explaining what had happened accurately in Bergamasco in order to get insurance money), effectively taking their side, speaking with them by speaking as they would have spoken. To describe how they spoke in Bergamasco, however, he switched back to Italian, taking up the outsiders' view once again, before giving voice to these póer bortulì by offering up four examples of typical Bergamasco interjections as illustrations of how they sounded: "**alura, cià, me, pòta**" (well then, right, me, who knows). These are all typical Bergamasco interjections or discourse markers[19] (if someone – Bergamasco or otherwise – knows just one word of Bergamasco, it will be **pòta**, which serves as an all-around exclamation and is hard to gloss precisely), and include vowel sounds that are common in Bergamasco and less so in Italian (the /u/ in **alura**). This is perhaps how these póer bortulì sound to outsiders – like they are just mouthing incomprehensible sounds, which have little or no meaning and no syntax. But the insurance men understood them – or at least their desire to make a justified claim – and asked them to repeat what they had said in Italian. Giorgio split this sentence between Bergamasco and Italian, stating in Bergamasco "those who understood" and switching to Italian to describe *how* they understood that the póer bortulì were in the right, and then back to Bergamasco to describe what the insurance men did: they asked the póer bortulì to repeat what he had said. He directly quoted the insurance men at this point, switching entirely into a rather formal Italian (with formal verb markings indicating politeness and social distance), and staying in Italian to describe what the insurance men made the póer bortulì do: speak in Italian. To describe the result of this effort, he switched once again to Bergamasco, telling us how everything came out contrary (to what they meant) and how they lost their case, switching to use the Italian phrase "*la causa*," which is used to describe court cases and adds a funny juxtaposition of legalese to the story.

This pattern of extensive switching continued after the audience laughed in response to what was essentially the punchline of the joke (that they spoke poorly and lost their case). Giorgio followed his anecdote by summing up what it showed: how important and how much security and pleasure Bergamasco affords. That the anecdote seemed to demonstrate exactly the opposite of this is what makes this transcript so interesting and apparently contradictory.

I believe that the fact that Giorgio described the importance of Bergamasco in Italian both before and after the anecdote points us in a productive direction for understanding what was going on here: the view that, these days, Bergamasco can and perhaps should be appreciated from the distance allowed by speaking Italian. Just like Maria observed that the architect and I could only see the positive aspects of Bergamasco because we already had our national languages, Giorgio supported the positive pleasurable aspects of Bergamasco from the safe distance of knowing and using Italian. Speaking Italian, here as elsewhere, indexed Giorgio's high level of education and his high socioeconomic status – or at least the probability of these.

But this anecdote also illustrated a particularly Bergamasco way of describing the world. Here is what Rina, with whom I transcribed it, had to say about the anecdote later in an e-mail when I asked her about it:

> *Mi sembra una cosa tipica nostra, puoi riassumerla con "dire pane al pane e vino al vino", ovvero parlare con grande franchezza, senza darsi arie, dire le cose esattamente come stanno al fine di esssere molto chiari e molto sinceri (questo è un valore dalle nostre parti, mentre in altre zone ci considerano rozzi/ruvidi/poco gentili).*

> It seems to me a typical thing of ours, you can understand it to be like "say bread to bread and wine to wine" [a Bergamasco saying],

or really to speak with great frankness, without putting on airs, to say things exactly how they are with the goal of being very clear and very sincere (this is a value of our parts, while in other areas they consider us rude/rough/not very nice or polite).

Rina explained that to tell a story like this, in which the problems of Bergamaschi are laid bare and discussed, is part of the common value system in Bergamo, where straightforwardness and honesty are highly valued. While this airing of dirty laundry might make outsiders cringe, for Bergamaschi this story tells it like it is – or was. Hence it has value as it fits within a local epistemology that values honesty over hiding problems.

Rina had other potential explanations for why Giorgio constructed his narrative in this way. Commenting on the words that Giorgio puts into the póer bortulì's mouths, Rina went on:

> *La frase in bergamasco spiega benissimo, con un'immagine viva e familiare all'uditorio, che tipo di persone erano quei clienti. Usando il bergamasco gli ascoltatori si saranno sicuramente immaginati davanti agli occhi quei "**póer bortulì**." Se avesse usato l'italiano sarebbe stato come fare una perifrasi per non voler usare il termine più diretto e più preciso, avrebbe implicato il vergognarsi di quel termine, vergognarsi di essere bergamasco.*

The phrase in Bergamasco ["**alura, cià, me, pòta**"] explains really well, with an image that is lively and familiar to the listener, what type of person the clients were. Using Bergamasco the listeners would have definitely imagined before their eyes these "**póer bortulì**." If he had used Italian it would have been like a paraphrase, because he didn't want to use the more direct and precise term, it would have implied an embarrassment of that term, embarrassment of being Bergamasco.

These words immediately evoke an image of a particular speaker – a póer bortulì. But Rina suggested that to do otherwise, to have had them speak in Italian, would have been for Giorgio to paraphrase their speech, effectively hiding their own modes of expression. This would have implied embarrassment of these men and more broadly of being Bergamasco. The value of accurate representation trumped even the value of having these men speak clearly. This story of the apparently ignorant póer bortulì was an instance of Bergamaschi looking themselves in the face, and seeing the truth, warts and all, and still laughing about it. The laughter and pleasure arose out of experiencing "who we are" (like, but not entirely like, the póer bortulì) against who outsiders are (potentially immoral and wily, like the insurance men). Giorgio's occasional alignment with these outsiders throughout the story emphasized as well how far Bergamaschi themselves have come, from manual laborers to bank presidents. At the same time, the story asks those present to reflect on who they have become. "Our kids don't speak it anymore" is a phrase that evokes both regret and relief.

Throughout this story, Giorgio played with the delicate tension between the two languages, explicitly framing the story as one which demonstrated Bergamasco's worth, even as the content of the story showed how risky and potentially dangerous it was to speak in the Bergamasco way, whether in Bergamasco or in a mix of Bergamasco and Italian. But as the audience's laughter, Giorgio's obvious satisfaction with his story, and Rina's comments demonstrate, this story did afford pleasure to its listeners. It afforded the pleasure of aligning oneself with a locally held and valued sense of self that prizes honesty and straightforwardness, while at the same time not being condemned to the life of being taken advantage of that the story describes (and perhaps was true of their predecessors). Speaking and understanding both languages well allowed for this balance to be achieved.

Conclusion

Considering these heteroglossic practices and language ideologies together allows for a nuanced understanding of the social aesthetics of language in Bergamo in the early 2000s. Transcripts show how speakers negotiated between the power and prestige that speaking Italian represented and the sentimental ties to local place and cultural authenticity that were signified through speaking Bergamasco. As we have seen, striking this balance was difficult, more so for some speakers, like Carla and Marco, than for others, such as the architect and Giorgio. Speaking with no Bergamasco at all was sometimes judged as being artificial or "embroidered," while to speak it in certain circumstances was to be funny, warm, connected to home, family, your ancestors. Yet speaking too much in a Bergamasco way could make you sound like the póer bortulì of old: inarticulate, easily taken advantage of, and certainly not fit to become the boss someday. Different age groups and classes had to strike this balance in their own ways. Older speakers were expected to speak more Bergamasco, as they grew up, for the most part, speaking it as their first language. People in higher class positions could afford to prize and play with the vernacular, bringing it out around the card table, or discussing its semantic richness with a foreign researcher. Those in lower, working-class positions might have spoken more in a Bergamasco way and paid the price for it, by sounding rough and uneducated, as Francesco and Ernaldo did when they joked about going up to the blackboard – peasants who found themselves in the classroom.

In the next chapter, I fill out this social aesthetics of language further by considering in depth the role that gender played. As suggested by stories that named mothers as those responsible for children's linguistic competence and socioeconomic futures, gender plays an important part in the social aesthetics of language in Bergamo. Many Bergamaschi's ideas about how the two languages sounded, as well as stereotypes about typical speakers of Bergamasco and Italian, lined up with data that suggested that Bergamasco was more the language of men while Italian was more closely associated with women. Women, through their roles as care-givers of young children, were expected to speak more and better Italian while men could sometimes revel in the roughness of speaking Bergamasco. This gendered divide had resonances in speakers' affective relations to their language use, as well as contributed to the linguistic hierarchies that placed certain languages, practices, and speakers above others.

3

Gendering Language

One cold, dark January evening, Maestro called the dialect writing course to an end early so that we could have a party. Beppe, an aspiring poet who had taken the course several times, was turning 64 and had brought a package of *dolci* (sweets) to share with the class. Maestro produced a cold bottle of sweet dessert wine from the Ducato's small refrigerator, and we all pushed our chairs back and gathered around the table in the front of the room to toast the birthday and socialize. At one point in the conversation, Dalia, the only young woman in the course beside me, observed that Bergamasco is a *"lingua maschilista"* – a male chauvinist language. This produced some laughter from the other class participants, but no one disagreed with her. Signora Zocco, the middle-aged woman who sat next to me, agreed, and they began to tease the Maestro that the Ducato itself is a maschilista organization, pointing out that there had never been a *Duchessa* (Duchess). The Maestro said that, indeed, there never would be one, either. It was impossible to imagine.

This was my first explicit indication that gender also played a part in the social aesthetics of language in Bergamo. I had had other intimations. A frequent critique of my own Bergamasco pronunciation was that I did not make my voice sound *basso* (low, bass) and *gutturale* (guttural) enough to sound right, which was attributed to my being female (see Cavanaugh 2005 for a discussion of accent). It seemed as if most of the poets I was meeting were men, and the character from the *Comedia dell'Arte* who Bergamaschi claimed as their emblem, **Giopì** (a close relative of *Arlecchino* or Harlequin), was male. I had heard more young men than young women both speak it and claim to speak it. Additionally, usually when I told people that I was researching Bergamasco, they would say I needed to go up in the mountains behind Bergamo in search of the last Bergamasco pastori, who spoke the most *stretto* and *duro* Bergamasco. I would not hear the real Bergamasco around here in town, they told me. And it did not seem like I would hear it from women, either.

Sounding Bergamasco

The social aesthetics of language in Bergamo in the early 2000s clearly involved gender. In the last chapter, we heard Marina, who grew up speaking Italian, worry about her barely discernible accent in a prestigious context outside of Bergamo, a concern that young men like Ernaldo and Francesco or Giana's two sons hardly seemed to share. Indeed, when Bergamaschi described to me who they expected to hear speaking the vernacular, there was a consistent tendency to associate Bergamasco with men, both explicitly and implicitly. This often occurred in conjunction with describing the language as rough ("*rozzo*") and unrefined ("*non fine*"), characteristics they associated with men.

For example, Roberta, the dialect theater director, demonstrated this when, while talking about soccer fans as likely speakers of Bergamasco, she said: "*Infatti quando vengono intervistati, lei prenda, quando escono dallo stadio i bergamaschi che vengono intervistati: 'Com'è andata la partita?'* **'Oh pòta nè!'**" ("In fact, when they are interviewed, let's say, when they come out of the stadium, Bergamaschi who are interviewed: 'How did the game go?' 'Oh, pòta, nè!'") Roberta deepened her voice for the second, Bergamasco utterance, but not the first, Italian utterance, using in addition the Bergamasco exclamation **pòta**, thereby conjuring the familiar aural representation of a rough, inarticulate – and implicitly male – speaker. Roberta's performance demonstrated that proper Bergamasco pronunciation involved an articulatory set characterized by low-pitched tones, more common for male voices, at least in terms of speakers' meta-linguistic judgments. Roberta herself often spoke fluent Bergamasco; as director of a dialect theater company, she was deeply invested in the value of the language and closely associated herself with it. This contradiction – between her voicing of a "typical Bergamasco" as male, and her own personal commitment to and use of the dialect – immediately suggests the complicated layering of meaning that surrounded the relationship between language and gender.

The cluster of associations of roughness, men's voices, and Bergamasco seemed most deeply felt by younger speakers. This was articulated during a group interview in a high school class when, having had several young men say that they spoke some Bergamasco, I asked the young women if they spoke it as well. One young woman said they spoke it only a little (*"poco"*). Two young men described the dialect as *"un po' rozzo"* ("a little rough") and *"un po' volgare"* ("a little vulgar"), but another young woman disagreed, saying that it is not rough, but is rather "hard in terms of pronunciation" (*"Proprio duro come pronuncia"*), more like a man's voice (*"con la voce da uomo viene più"*). Another young woman agreed, stating that the dialect is *"poco femminile"* ("not very feminine"). For these youth, sounding rough, vulgar or hard meant sounding unfeminine. The young women's disavowal of speaking Bergamasco was aligned with their experience of how the vernacular sounded to their own ears as well as how it sounded to their male peers.

A little later during the same interview, a young woman speculated about the association of Bergamasco with men, saying she had noticed that various boys who had gone to work directly after middle school tended to speak almost entirely in dialect.[1] A young man responded that this is because these boys tended to work in construction, surrounded by older workers who spoke the vernacular. For these students, as for many people, speaking Bergamasco indexed certain types of male-dominant work and workplaces, namely manual and unskilled labor, such as construction work. While Bergamaschi in the past who spoke the dialect were often referred to as *contadini*, those who speak Bergamasco in the present were often identified as *muratori* (construction workers, lit. "wallbuilders"). Besides speaking Bergamasco, both of these groups were presumed to have had the minimum amount of education (the end of middle school currently being the earliest time to leave school legally), to work with their hands – and to be men.

The image of the hardworking, uneducated, and unsophisticated *contadino* was central to Bergamasco cultural conceptualizations of self. Indeed, the peasant has played an important part in how Italians across the peninsula define themselves.[2] With over half of the population scarcely a generation away from being rural agriculturalists, usually involved in some form of share-cropping, the image of the peasant remained too close for comfort. As Krause argues, "well into the twentieth century, the peasant continued to stand for the most degraded, backward internal Other within the Italian peninsula" (2005:597) (see also Counihan 2004; Schneider and Schneider 1996). There were few actual contadini and pastori still alive while I was doing my research, and most of them were older and lived in rural areas. They were, however, powerfully emblematic of Bergamo.[3]

In this, they are similar to Giopì, who "*è rimasto la tipica espressione della gente di sua terra, fiera della proprie tradizioni, nemica di tutte le prepotenze, entusiasta per tutte le libertà*" ("has remained the typical expression of the people of his land, proud of their own traditions, enemy of all pretenses, enthusiast for all freedoms") (Milesi 1932:25). Indeed, for Giopì, "*e che cosa importa se non ha una laurea?*" (and what does it matter that he has no degree?) (Milesi 1932:31). Giopì manages to fill his empty stomach and (usually) win the girl – a servant like himself – through his mix of stubbornness and wile. Bergamaschi often embraced such images of Giopì and the peasant and shepherd precisely because of their roughness and lack of sophistication. As Rina posited in the last chapter, they liked to "say bread to bread and wine to wine."[4] Presumably, such frankness would be uttered in Bergamasco.

This embrace of roughness was an uneasy one, however, and for certain speakers more than others. Young Bergamasca women, especially if they were educated past middle school, were often subjected to a certain degree of social censure for speaking Bergamasco at all. We have already heard about Marina's self-criticism for having the accent in a formal context, where she feared its indexical links to lack of education and ignorance. There were other associations as well. As one male teenager told me during another group interview: "*Una ragazza che parla bergamasco non è che sia sexy. Perchè manca di eleganza*" ("A girl who speaks Bergamasco, it's not that it would be sexy. Because it lacks elegance"). In other words, to this young man, a young Bergamasca woman who spoke her dialect would have been less desirable that one who did not. Speaking Bergamasco, then, indexed not just working-class men, but also a potentially sexually undesirable female self, at least for some younger Bergamaschi. Indeed, among the many young couples that I knew in Bergamo, none of them spoke Bergamasco to one another, even when they could have and did speak Bergamasco to other people in their lives. Even for Dalia in the Ducato's dialect writing course and Ella, one of my transcription consultants, who were both explicitly interested in saving Bergamasco, speaking Italian was the norm in their romantic relationships, except perhaps during joking moments when they might lower the pitch of their voices to utter a joking "pòta!" When I asked why they did not speak Bergamasco with their *fidanzati* (boyfriends, plural of *fidanzato*), they said it just would not have felt right.

For these young people, linking maleness to Bergamasco cooccurred with other indexical associations, such as class and age differences, as well as romantic desirability. These associations recall the phenomenon of covert prestige (Trudgill 1972), in which working-class men value their own non-standard ways of speaking as markers of in-group working-class values and status, while women tend to be more oriented toward the standard. But whereas covert prestige appears to provide a social reproduction loop, explaining how working-class speakers reproduce working-class values through their practices (e.g. see Willis 1981), in Bergamo these clusters of associations contributed to Bergamasco being deemed to be unattractive – virtually unusable – to young, educated women.

Indeed, the ultimate example of this cluster of indexical associations with male lower-class work are the same pòer bortulì who were described as suffering at the hands of the insurance men in the last chapter. The following comments by Marco are illustrative of a portrait I heard many times of the imagined last speakers of Bergamasco.

Example 3.1

MARCO: *Difatti se tu **vai su** in certi paesi proprio più in su, parlano solo [ride] solo di quello. Se poi ti sposti ancora sulle vette delle montagne, che c'è su ancora magari qualche pastore, [ride] l'italiano non lo parla propio.*

MARCO: In fact, if you go up in certain little towns higher up, they speak only [laugh] only that [Bergamasco]. If then you go even more up on the tops of the mountains, there are still perhaps some shepherds, [laugh] they don't speak Italian at all.

JC: *Ci sono ancora persone che non parlano l'italiano?*

JC: There are still people who don't speak Italian?

MARCO: *Eh ma son difficile trovarle. Cioè abitano propio . . . bisogna camminare tre o quattro ore senza macchina . . . a piedi. Su per i monti, le Alpi.*

JC: *E' bello che esistono ancora.*

MARCO: *E' bello però* **pòta!** *Loro non hanno nessuno a cui tramandare la loro . . . eh . . . chi hanno? Non sono mica sposati . . . hanno solo quattro mucche e basta. Hanno solo quello di accudimento, eh. Non è che hanno moglie e figli che possono tramandare una . . . C'è nessuno. Son su solo loro. [ride] Loro e magari un a-altri mem[bri?] — altri soci come loro che dopo la sera fanno su la compagnia e dopo si metton dietro [ride] a fare qualche bevutina, a giocare a carte alla sera e basta. Non è che abbiano . . . son solo loro. E basta.*

MARCO: Eh, but they're difficult to find. That is, they live really . . . you have to walk three or four hours without a car . . . on foot. Up in the mountains, the Alps.

JC: It's nice that they still exist.

MARCO: It's nice, but damn! They don't have anyone to leave their . . . eh . . . who do they have? They are not even married . . . they have just four cows and that's it. They have only what they can take care of, eh. It's not that they have a wife or kids who they can leave a . . . There's no one. It's just them up there [laugh]. Them and maybe one o-other mem[bers?] — other buddies like them who in the evening keep each other company, and then they get to having a little drink, playing some cards at night, and that's it. It's not that they have . . . they're only them. And that's it.

Marco's portrayal of these male shepherds as the last monolingual speakers of Bergamasco, hidden up in the highest parts of the mountains above Bergamo, was in keeping with how they are generally depicted, although it offered more details about their lives than usual. In this portrait, they are isolated and apparently technologically backwards (you have to get to where they are on foot). They are not only men, but single men, with no wives or families, no one to leave their material (and linguistic) possessions to; it is just them, as Marco emphasized (and their four cows). Indeed, they are so isolated and impoverished that Marco could not quite articulate exactly what it is that they might leave to a wife or children. They speak to just a few male friends who are like them, with whom they may meet in the evenings to have a drink and play some cards, social activities that are deeply male-associated in Bergamo, connected to a long tradition of men socializing in neighborhood *osterie* (taverns), having a *bevutina* (little drink) of wine, and playing some cards.

There are literally no women in this portrayal of a world lived entirely in Bergamasco, neither young nor old, such that Bergamasco and its speakers seem to live in a world isolated not just from modernity and success, but also from the feminine influences of wives, mothers, and daughters. Since there are no women with whom these monolingual men apparently speak, at least on a day-to-day basis, the association of Bergamasco with men in this portrait is remarkably complete: women do not exist in this world or indexical order. And the men who populate these mountain-tops do not seem to be any more desirable as romantic partners than the Bergamasco-speaking young woman described above, due to their undesirable profession and lack of upwardly mobile aspirations. Indeed, as Krause has argued, the figure of the peasant in Italy "impinges in meaningful ways on social life, in general, and family making, in particular" (2005:610).

Women's personal attractiveness and men's work emerged as important elements in the value of language in Bergamo. Linguistic practices indirectly indexed both genders' desirability as romantic, reproductive, and productive partners, mediated through more immediate indexical associations with particular personal characteristics, such as roughness or elegance.[5] Women were assessed as potential partners at least in part due to their sexiness or lack thereof expressed in how they sounded when they spoke. Men were more commonly evaluated according to their work – old-fashioned and isolating, or modern and integrated into the larger society. Within the pictures these speakers sketched, speaking Bergamasco – for women, in addition to Italian; for men, monolingually – was linked to characteristics and attributes that were undesirable.

For Bergamaschi, especially those who are younger, speaking in a Bergamasco way indexed particular personal attributes, activities, and professions, which were in turn understood to be male and working class. These indexical associations were expressed explicitly, as in Marco's description of the lives of shepherds, but also implicitly, as in Roberta's voicing of a male Bergamasco-speaking soccer fan. Personal characteristics such as roughness came into play in the heterosexual marketplace (Eckert 1996), where the desirability of an imagined female may have been diminished through sounding Bergamasco in the ears of young Bergamasco men, and where the association of Bergamasco with certain types of work could make men who spoke too much Bergamasco sound like undesirable partners as well, especially for middle-class, educated women. These associations in turn had an impact on what men and women spoke, at least at the level of self-reported speech repertoires, and resulted in different attitudes towards Bergamasco and its speakers across men and women.

Women as Linguistic Care-givers

Associations of women with Italian and men with Bergamasco may indeed have resulted in different patterns of use across speakers of different generations and genders. Consider, for example, how Mario, a male high school student, described language use in his home and family:

Example 3.2

Io vedo i miei nonni parlavano il bergamasco sia in famiglia che fuori. Un po' perché si conoscevano tutti, erano poche persone. Mio papà lo parlava in casa e poi fuori parlava in italiano. Io lo parlo molto [meno] in casa. Cioè per esempio con mia mamma parlo molto l'italiano. Parlo di più con mio papà il bergamasco. Però capita spesso che mio papà dice una frase in bergamasco e poi magari usa una parola in italiano all'interno.	I see my grandparents who spoke Bergamasco within the family as well as outside of it. A little because they knew everyone, and there were only a few people [in their community]. My father spoke it [Bergamasco] at home and then outside he spoke in Italian. I speak it [less] at home. That is, for example, with my mother I speak Italian a lot. I speak more with my father in Bergamasco. However, it often happens that my father says a phrase in Bergamasco and then maybe he'll throw in a word in Italian in the middle.

3 generation model

This description essentially echoes how many young Bergamaschi depicted linguistic repertoires within their families: both grandparents have always spoken Bergamasco to everyone, and may or may not have spoken Italian as well. Parents generally could speak both, although their patterns of use differed: fathers used Bergamasco and bivalent language more often than mothers, who spoke more Italian, particularly in the home. Mario, in turn, reports speaking mostly Bergamasco with his father and Italian with his mother.

Women's roles as primary care-givers of Bergamasco children were central to this type of association of women and men with different languages and practices. Italian's role as the language of education meant that there was a premium on children knowing Italian, a common tendency in situations where a national standard is the language of education (Bourdieu 1991; Bourdieu and Passeron 1977; Eckert 1980; Heller 1994). However, although school was once widely regarded as the site where children learned Italian, more recently children of all class positions were expected to enter school already speaking it, so that they would not have to endure the linguistic difficulties and social humiliations their parents and grandparents suffered in school as they struggled to learn Italian (Cavanaugh 2004). In addition, Bergamasco was seen to interfere with children's acquisition of Italian, so that even women with limited competence in Italian attempted to raise their children as monolingual Italian speakers, with varying results.

The central role of women in the capacity of care-giver in linguistic shifts has been well-documented in different ethnographic contexts, although how this role is taken up varies widely. Women have been shown to be leaders in language shift (Gal 1978; Garrett and Baquedano-López 2002), speaking a more standard language variety than men in order to "marry up," for example (Gal 1979; Kuter 1989), or to increase their employment opportunities outside their communities (see Labov 1966b; Trudgill 1972). Conversely, in other situations, women in general and mothers more specifically have been regarded as bearers of tradition, carrying the burden of ensuring that younger generations grow up with knowledge of their culture and traditions (Clancy 1999; Hoffman 2006, 2008; Paugh 2001; Zentella 1987, 1997), while in yet others women may be responsible for speaking the language to their children, while men are charged with carrying on the group's traditions (Fader 2007).

In the following transcript, Paolo, Carla, and Daniele comment on the changes that have affected how Bergamaschi speak since the post-War period. This segment preceded their discussions of what comprised speaking alla bergamasca discussed in Chapter 2. They agreed that a decline in Bergamasco was due at least in part to societal expectations that mothers would teach their children Italian.

Example 3.3

1 DANIELE: *Le mame a case, dicevano* . . .

2 CARLA: **Mé tocàa fàga ü regàl, mia a l'època.**

3 DANIELE: "*Non farò mica io la figura che i miei figli non sanno parlare italiano?!*"

4 CARLA: *Eh, bé, certo.*

5 JC: *Ah, sì?*

6 PAOLO: **E ghe l' insegnàa sò màder.**

---

1 DANIELE: *The mothers at home said* . . .

2 CARLA: **It was my responsibility to give them a present, it wasn't so long ago.**

3 DANIELE: "*It won't be me who's embarrassed because my children don't speak Italian?!*"

4 CARLA: *Right, sure.*

5 JC: *Really?*

6 PAOLO: **And it was one's mother who had to teach it.**

This passage helps us understand a number of things about the choices that mothers like Carla made to speak Italian and not Bergamasco to their children. A mother of four children who spoke primarily Bergamasco herself, Carla described having to teach her children Italian as giving them a "present," something extra which they could treasure, but that was her responsibility to bestow. She noted that it was not so long ago; her children grew up in the 1960s and 1970s, a period which most Italian and Bergamasco scholars identify with great social, economic, and linguistic shifts. Having raised children during a time of transition, Carla marveled in line 2 at how much had changed so quickly, pointing out that this type of linguistic choice happened "**mia a l'època**" (lit. "not an epoch ago" or not a long time ago). She said this in Bergamasco, the language she spoke most of the time, suggesting that undertaking such a course would not have been her choice, if not for societal pressure. The prestige and ability "to relate oneself to a world more vast than that of the neighborhood" ("*di rapportarvi a un mondo piu` vasto di quello che è il rione*"), as Maria put it in the previous chapter, which was part of being able to speak Italian, influenced the language socialization choices that many mothers made as they strove to ensure their children had all the advantages they could give them.

Daniele then emphasized in line 3 that it was the mothers' responsibility to teach it, and that they were motivated by embarrassment, by a desire not to fail in the face of other mothers' successes for their children. He spoke in Italian, directly quoting one of these young mothers, as if positioning her on the side of Italian, rather than Bergamasco. In saying "*Non farò mica io la figura,*" he used the phrase "*fare una figura*" (meaning literally "to make a figure") – common in Bergamo as throughout Italy – which means to present oneself poorly, or in an embarrassing manner.[6] Young mothers, mindful that they were held responsible for "properly" raising their children, knew that this included raising them to speak Italian. For fathers, like the one described by Mario above, public use of Italian was enough, and they could safely speak Bergamasco or bivalent forms in the private sphere of the home. For mothers, however, public scrutiny potentially extended into their practices within the home – through the evidence of these practices in the form of their children's competence in Italian – making all their linguistic choices more open to censure.

This young mother's voice was given a double edge in the beginning of the phrase when he said "*Non farò mica io . . .*" ("It won't be me . . ."). *Mica* is a form of negation, closely associated with northern Regional Italian, which when paired in Italian with *non*, as it is here, means basically "not at all." But it closely resembles the most common form of negation in Bergamasco: **mia**, which occurs after the verb and is not paired with another negation marker before the verb, as in **l'só mia** (I don't know).[7] The similarity of the negation forms *mica* and **mia**, as well as the postverbal positioning of the form seemed to add up to "sounding Bergamasco" to many Bergamaschi. Indeed, my transcription consultants often pointed out mica as evidence of a speaker's Bergamasco origins, as Ella did in the clogs discussion in Chapter 2. So, while mica is used in other parts of Italy, such as, for example, in Rome in phrases such as *Mica è scemo* (he is not stupid),[8] using mica in this postverbal position when speaking Italian sounded particularly Bergamasco to Bergamaschi. In this instance, mica indexed the double positioning of the imagined young mother that Daniele quoted: she will speak Italian to her children, but she herself is Bergamasca. And one can imagine that the Italian that they learn will sound distinctly Bergamasco. The sentimental, local importance of Bergamasco was present in these mothers' efforts, even if it was severely limited and balanced by their desire to give their children Italian. It won't be them, Daniele asserts in their voice, to embarrass themselves and their families by having their children speak in the wrong way. Carla agreed with his assessment, and Paolo emphasized once again, in Bergamasco, that it was all up to the mother: **"E ghe l' insegnàa sò màder"** ("and it was taught by one's mother").

This conversation illustrates a placement of accountability that was widespread in Bergamo. It also suggested the range of linguistic difficulties facing the mothers entrusted with teaching young Bergamaschi how to speak. Young mothers, especially those who belonged to the working classes and aspired to join the middle class, recognized that it was their responsibility to give their children the "gift" of Italian, and may have resorted to using both languages together – as Carla did in the part of this conversation discussed in the last chapter and in many other conversations – to enhance their own often-limited abilities in Italian. "Speaking Italian" in practice became "speaking Italian in the Bergamasco way." Carla, Roberto, Paolo, and Daniele ultimately laughed about it, but this heteroglossic linguistic purgatory – and the social middle ground it indexes – was often criticized as being neither here nor there, neither Italian nor Bergamasco.[9] The concerns described by Daniele, Paolo, and Carla clearly centered on socioeconomic advancement, due to the important role of schools in socioeconomic advancement. As locally understood, this advancement could only happen when the acquisition of Italian began at home and was solidified in school (see also Zuanelli Sonino 1989).

Anecdotal evidence suggests that a number of children in the 1980s and 1990s continued to enter school with an incomplete knowledge of Italian, in spite of the best efforts of their mothers. Annabella, a recently retired elementary school teacher in her mid-fifties, complained to me about the number of children who had arrived in her school during the more than two decades that she taught speaking a mixture ("*miscuglio*") of Italian and Bergamasco. The mothers of these children would reassure her when their children started school that their children spoke only Italian, and indeed, Annabella believed that the mothers tried. She said they "*fanno una testa così*" while holding her hands out wide on either side of her head (literally, "they make a head like this" about it, essentially going to great lengths). However, instead of solving the problem, Annabella maintained that these young mothers' efforts complicated the issue. These children arrived at school mixed up about language in general, as they had been told that they should and did speak only Italian, but then were exposed to, and proceeded to learn, this "*miscuglio*" of Bergamasco and Italian.

Women were held responsible not only for the language socialization of their own children, as Carla was, but also for their linguistic failures with all children for whom they played a care-giving role. This was especially true for grandmothers, who often played an important part in care giving because most Bergamasco families had both parents in the workforce by the end of the 1990s. Grandmothers tended to speak Bergamasco to their grandchildren, although they were often charged by their daughters or daughters-in-law to address their children only in Italian. Like Carla and Mario's and Rina's grandmothers, these grandmothers were of a generation that tended to be more dominant in Bergamasco than Italian, and may have attempted to use as many Italian words as possible, but continued essentially to speak Bergamasco, so that children learned this bivalent miscuglio. These bivalent varieties could be used for humor, but also potentially limited a speaker's socioeconomic advancement, just as speaking only Bergamasco had for previous generations.

Language's connections to gender were caught up in complex indexical associations with class, socioeconomic aspirations, and generation. The image of a young, Italian-speaking woman as mother, who was also implicitly well-educated and of a higher social class, was held up as an ideal which did not fit the linguistic or social realities of many speakers. Access to education and the knowledge it brought – most importantly standard Italian, but also the linguistic competence to keep Bergamasco and Italian separate – were part of what divided members of the middle class from contadini and muratori. These indexical associations also help to flesh out the image of Italian-speaking women as attractive discussed above: such women embodied personal refinement and social mobility, which surely reflected on their potential "sexiness" or desirability.

Like the poor shepherds up in the mountains, keeping each other company, men were cut out of the images of social reproduction portrayed in stories about women as care-givers of various types. Young women were judged in terms of their sexiness or elegance, adjectives that described their romantic desirability and perceived suitability as reproductive partners, but also their presumed higher education levels and socioeconomic upward mobility. As they grew older, these women, like their mothers and grandmothers before them, were evaluated on how well they took care of Bergamasco children. Since the 1960s, such care included giving the gift of Italian, and avoiding as much as possible the taint of Bergamasco. Across these life-cycle stages, however, and although such sociolinguistic choices were intimately bound up with socioeconomic aspirations and realities, the indexical association of Italian with idealized women's traits and activities allows for a partial erasure of class (Irvine and Gal 2000). In these portraits, women are not producers, do not seem to exist in the realm of production at all, but merely take care of themselves and the children, all in Italian. Just as the unmarked nature of Italian meant that I heard much less elaboration about what it meant to speak it (much more discussed was what it meant not to speak it or to speak it badly), the activities associated with Italian indexed not just women but an unmarked background of normalcy. At the turn of the millennium, that unmarked norm was middle class, characterized by employment in non-manual labor jobs and new types of consumption patterns (Martinelli et al. 1999).

Revitalizing Activity

Women in Bergamo, through their role as care-givers and the linguistic responsibility associated with this role, had become increasingly associated with Italian; Bergamasco was clearly more associated
with men, in terms of perception, and perhaps also in terms of
practice. Between 15 and 25 percent more men reported speaking
Bergamasco than women in sociolinguistic dialectological data collected in the 1970s (Berruto 1978), as well as survey data collected
in the 1970s and 1980s (Mora 1975, 1982, 1983). My experience
in Bergamo since the late 1990s supports this, especially among
speakers under the age of 35. So while age and class played important roles in what people spoke in Bergamo, gender was an essential
contributing factor.

In this division of sociolinguistic labor, men were not responsible
for how children spoke – their linguistic responsibility was saving
Bergamasco, either as its imagined last speakers or in their leading
roles in linguistic revitalization activities, such as those run by the
Ducato di Piazza Pontida. The Ducato, whose support of Bergamasco poetry and play production will be discussed more at
length in the next chapter, began its existence as an all-male social
club. During the dinner at which the group was officially inaugu-
rated – a long meal with a great deal of Bergamasco poetry written
and recited for the occasion – the group crowned their chosen
leader as the first Duke. An interesting element in this origin story
concerns the crown itself, which was constructed on the spur of
the moment from materials on hand – paper and bread from the
table rolled into tight balls to sit on its cartoon-ish peaks. Two of
these balls, however, would not stay attached, and eventually were
tied together with string and left to hang, draped over one section
of the crown. These balls were pronounced to represent a part of
the anatomy shared by all the men in the group (the word has the
same double meaning in Italian and Bergamasco as it does in
English), a symbolic value they continued to carry.

In the 1920s and 1930s, the group's meetings were held in restaurants and osterie and consisted of long meals, copious amounts
of wine, and much joke-telling, poetry recitation, song singing,
and general merry making – all in Bergamasco, all by men. Looking

through their fittingly named newspaper, Giopì, from those years, all of the poets, playwrights, puppeteers, journalists, and other participants in the Ducato's activities in the early times were men. This appears to have continued until relatively recently. Since the mid-1980s, women have formed an increasing presence in the group, doing many of the day-to-day tasks of running the group and its many activities, such as answering the phone at the Ducato's headquarters, or taking money at public events. However, as of 2007, there was only one woman among the *Cavalieri* or *Senatori* (positions of power) and she, the wife of the Duke, was the only woman to have ever reached any position of power. There still has never been a *"Duchessa"* (female *Duca*); Maestro's belief that the idea itself was nearly unthinkable was echoed in an article in Giopì in 2003.

What was true for the Ducato di Piazza Pontida held true for revitalization activities more broadly. Although as of the late 1990s and early 2000s, there were a few women poets, and one woman dialect play director (Roberta), women for the most part could be found in supporting roles in these activities: as actors, audience members, and event organizers. Archival evidence indicates that this was even truer in the past. And just as there were ideologies about language and gender that made sense of and helped explain gendered differences in linguistic practice, so too were there ideas that circulated in Bergamo about women's and men's relative importance and roles in revitalization activities.

This became strikingly evident in one of my many conversations with a prominent expert on Bergamasco. During a discussion of dialect poetry, he informed me that "*le donnazelle non sono capaci ad essere poeti*" (women are not capable of being poets), using a diminutive form of women to emphasize his point (*donnazelle* rather than *donne*). "This is because they are not capable of expressing true, deep sentiments," he went on. "They may write little verses that rhyme prettily, but no woman has joined, nor will ever join, the ranks of the great Bergamasco poets." He dismissed the names of the few Bergamasca women poets I offered as counterexamples as dilettantes, not "*poeti propri*" ("real poets").

His assertions about women as poets had implications beyond the purely literate, since Bergamasco poets were seen as not simply poets, but producers of cultural and personal memory. As I elaborate in the next chapter, poets were often portrayed – by themselves and by others – as Bergamasco's best and most important champions. Women, then, in this view, were not fit to be defenders of their own language, just as they were not supposed to pass it on to their children. This condition is built into their emotional, and perhaps even physical, selves, as they were described as not being able to experience the right type of sentiments – deep and personally and culturally authentic. They were erased (Irvine and Gal 2000) from revitalization efforts – their participation in this culturally valued activity either unrecognized or unappreciated – just as women were erased from the image of the lives of the póer bortuli Marco sketched above. Men could produce (Bergamasco) poems; women could reproduce only (Italian) children.

Even when women poets were recognized and their work valued, as happened in 2000 when a woman won a prestigious local poetry award sponsored by the Ducato, it was clear that this was an exception rather than the norm. During the announcement of the winner, the emcee expressed considerable surprise at how many women had entered the contest. He called the presence of "*molta poesia al femminile, poesia di poetesse, poesia scritte da donne*" ("much poetry of the feminine, poetry of poetesses, poetry written by women") "*una particolarità*" ("a particularity") and "*una originalità della quale siamo contenti e della quale ci compiaciamo*" ("something original about which we are very happy and which pleases us"). Notice the repetition and rephrasing of the concept of female poets, which seemed to require a substantial amount of linguistic work to attempt to phrase correctly, as well as how their participation warranted special note, as being "original" and "particular." Although it was pleasing to this jury (so pleasing that they indeed awarded one of these female poets the grand prize), it was a novelty worth noting, discussing, and trying to phrase correctly. The short, nearly haiku-like nature of this author's poems, which contrasted sharply with the longer, more stanza-driven norm of Bergamasco poetry, was noted during the prize-giving and perhaps contributed to her selection. Her gender was far more discussed than the form of her poetry, however, in both the awards ceremony and in casual conversation following it, making it clear that women were the marked category in terms of this activity. I have never heard similar remarks about male poets, and find them hard to imagine.

Conclusion

Bergamaschi frequently described their language as "rozzo," and closely associated it with contadini, pastori, pòer bortulì, Giopì, and poets – all men. At the same time, speaking Italian, while unmarked in many circumstances, seemed to be the responsibility of women. I believe that this gendering of roles and languages is linked to the accessibility of gender for stereotyping. As Agha (1998) has argued, gender is an obvious and available category for typecasting, as it were, which may be more accessible and discussable than other types of social divisions within a community, such as class and generational differences. Women seemed to be "naturally" linked to the nurturing of children, while men seemed just as "naturally" characterized by their roles within the sphere of work. These associations were, however, anything but "natural." Rather, they were produced and reproduced as part of the broader social aesthetics of language in Bergamo, which linked ideas about particular types of speakers and selves to ideas about the two languages in use.[10]

In this chapter, we have explored the links between women and men and particular personal characteristics and activities. The roughness of Bergamasco pronunciation indexed male manual labor, especially for younger speakers, even those whose grandmothers may have addressed them in Bergamasco. This was reinforced by men's roles as the champions of Bergamasco, as well as the preponderance of male Bergamasco symbolic figures like Giopì and peasants. Women's roles as care-givers of children included the linguistic responsibility to give their children the gift of Italian, forging an indexical link between mothers and Italian that extended to all younger women. Class intertwined with gender as well, to make young educated women the least likely – in local understandings as well as practice – to speak Bergamasco. This association between class and language, in turn, made speaking Bergamasco – or simply in a Bergamasco way – an obstacle in the path of young women aspiring to move up in the socioeconomic hierarchy. This linguistic reproductive dead-end bodes ill for the vernacular, as fewer and fewer children were potentially growing up speaking Bergamasco in the home, although it may have been available to them through other avenues, such as friendship networks and fathers' linguistic practices.

In the next chapter, I turn to poetry and theater in order to look more closely at the activities that were explicitly undertaken as a means *per salvare il dialetto* (to save the dialect), as the Duke put it. In considering these activities, I ask what is entailed in regarding these particular activities as essential to the future of Bergamasco. Declaring that something is in need of saving is also to imply that it is being lost, so I explore what Bergamaschi themselves describe as being lost within their community and what can be gained by supporting certain types of cultural activities. In doing so, it is necessary to consider the meaning of the past and the future and how the two languages were associated with each, generally to the benefit of Italian and detriment of Bergamasco. While Bergamasco plays and poetry were enjoyable because they utilized and built on the sentimental associations of Bergamasco with local ways of living situated within the recent past, they simultaneously – and often indirectly – reinforced the hierarchical positioning of Italian as the language of power, prestige, and the future.

4

Bergamasco on Stage:
Poetry and Theater

When I was beginning my research in Bergamo, telling everyone I met that I was there to study the language and what it meant, people (after overcoming their shock that an outsider would want to study Bergamasco at all) consistently pointed me towards two important cultural activities in Bergamo: poetry and plays. Going to hear poets read their poetry and attending play performances would show me Bergamasco values and character, particularly since those who participated in these activities usually knew Bergamasco better than other people, especially old expressions and words that people did not tend to use anymore. Poets could teach me about the riches of the vernacular; in play performances, I would see real Bergamasco culture in action. Plus, these events were enjoyable, and would make me laugh or maybe even cry, people said.

If Bergamasco was valued as the language of *confidenza* and for its connections to home, family, and local ways of life, then performances in it were seen as examples of these values writ large. Because of this, Bergamasco poetry recitals and theater performances were activities undertaken for pleasure but also as a means of ostensibly "saving" or revitalizing Bergamasco. Through these types of performances, both audience members and performers could immerse themselves in the enjoyment of a world lived nearly exclusively in Bergamasco (although Italian may slip in at telling moments), reinforcing the associations between the language and life lived in Bergamasco ways. Saving Bergamasco – keeping it spoken and understood and reveled in – was the aim of many of these events, although the fact that they were set apart from the heteroglossic sphere of everyday interaction may have ultimately had a negative impact on the language.

It is no coincidence that these two activities in particular lie at the heart of the largely symbolic project to "save" Bergamasco. Poetry and theater have a long illustrious history in Italy (as elsewhere) of being highly prestigious genres, drawing on literary traditions that include Dante, Petrarch, and Goldoni, to name only a few. Poetry and theater in vernacular, further, can simultaneously draw on two different axes of value: they are at once "high" genres, written in "authentic" linguistic varieties (Brevini 1999; Pagliai 2000, 2003; Zanetti 1966, 1969, 1978). As fixed texts, with written forms that adhere to generic expectations and endure beyond performance, they may "entail more power than context-dependent texts because of the way in which they culturally and ideologically reproduce the same idea over and over again" (Philips 2000:195). Additionally, the recurrence of humor and nostalgia in both helps to negotiate between and resolve the contradictions that arise from trying to be both authentic and prestigious at the same time, with varying results.

In Chapters 2 and 3, I discussed everyday language use in Bergamo to explore the "tense intersection" of Italian and Bergamasco in practice and meaning. I looked at what people did with language when they spoke, and what they thought about how they used language. In this chapter, I turn to two types of practices that Bergamaschi undertook which very purposefully involved putting their ideas – and ideals – about language into action through performance. Play performances and poetry recitals were crystallizations of Bergamasco ideologies of language, in which Bergamasco was highly sentimentalized, keyed humor, and was located in the past, and Italian was either absent entirely or indicated a person, thing or idea from outside the tight circle of Bergamo. The indexical world that such performances created was one in which home and family were Bergamasco, and outsiders were Italian. At the same time, this Bergamasco world seemed to exist in the past, while Italian was the language of the present and future. Performances of these two genres helped to "routinize and unify the past" (Herzfeld 1991:45). Such efforts in effect help make the past into folklore, or traditions associated with a particular group's past, which Herzfeld and others have argued is a common occurrence in undertakings to valorize a culture (Folklorization, while often explicitly portrayed as an effort to "save" what was important from the past, helps to separate out the content of these practices as things of the past, set apart from the modern flow of everyday life (Giddens 1979).

Experiencing Bergamasco Poetry First-hand

It was a beautiful summer day to spend in the mountains. Roberto and his wife, Franca, picked us up early in the morning and we drove a couple hours to their friends' house high up in one of the valleys above Bergamo. We followed Roberto's parents, Paolo and Carla, in their car, and chatted about the landscape, the mountains, Bergamasco, and what the day ahead might be bring.

This was the first day-long outing I had made with this family and I was both excited and happy as well as nervous and anxious at its prospect. Although I had been getting to know Paolo rather well over the previous several months, talking with him at length in his workshop and cantina, and attending poetry readings around town with him, I had only met the rest of the family a few times, and had never spent a whole day in all of their company. There is something slightly exhilarating and terrifying about stepping into a near-stranger's car in the early morning light, knowing that you are headed for parts essentially unknown for what is likely to be a rather long day (indeed, we did not get home until midnight that night). I have heard ethnography described as the art of over-staying your welcome until you become part of the social landscape (Kulick, personal communication), and I was rather aware of that feeling this day, as I had only briefly met our host and never our hostess. I could not help but wonder how welcome we were or how intrusive we would feel, to them and to ourselves. Indeed, the whole day was something of a mystery before we set off, for although Paolo and his good friend who was our host had invited us a few weeks before as we stood around chatting in Paolo's butiga, it was unclear what the event would consist of and who would attend. It was like being invited to a new type of party by a new group of friends: what to wear? what to bring? Not wanting to miss a valu-able ethnographic opportunity, I brought all of my usual equipment (tape-recorder, microphone, tapes, extra batteries and tapes, a camera, extra film, a notebook), and so felt rather conspicuously laden with material evidence that I was a different type of guest than the others.

This feeling of conspicuous other-ness faded as the day progressed, of course, for the event was not about me and my research interests, but a house-warming. There was a party of a dozen of us invited to the newly renovated mountain vacation home of these old friends of Paolo's for a long day of eating, strolling, joking, and conversation. The party was in celebration of the completion of the house's renovations: once a roughly built stone **cassina**,[1] at least a century or two old, it had been extensively restored and expanded into a rustically luxurious mountain lodge. The hosts, Rico and Elena, and the rest of the group that day were all successful, prosperous professionals, nearly all of whom had originally come from working-class families. Most of them were between 40 and 60 years old (the architect, Stefano, and Paolo and Carla, in their early seventies, were the oldest), had grown up speaking Bergamasco as well as Italian, and still did so regularly, especially in a relaxed social setting like this among friends. Most of the guests that day had aided in the renovations in some way: in addition to Paolo and Roberto, who had helped with the ironwork, there was Stefano, the architect, and an engineer, Umberto. They were all old friends. My moroso and I had been invited to enjoy how a real Bergamasco Sunday afternoon should be spent: among friends and family, eating, drinking, talking, laughing, enjoying the mountains, and the poetic talents of a real Bergamasco poet, Paolo **Frér**.[2]

First, we were taken on a tour of the house, during which various high points were lingered over, such as the basement room designed for aging and storing cheese and salami, and the huge wood plank staircase that led from floor to floor. Then, we settled down to a long, sumptuous, Bergamasco pranzo. Our hosts prided themselves on offering authentic Bergamasco fare, made from local products as much as possible. The *salumi* (assorted cured meats, like salami and pancetta) that made up the first course had been made by a friend and aged in their basement; the *casonsei* (local ravioli) and *foiade* (triangles of pasta with mushrooms) of the pasta course were homemade; the salad greens and other produce had been picked from their garden; and the main course's roasted meats, accompanied by the obligatory polenta, had been purchased from neighboring small farmers who raised and butchered their own animals. Local

Valcalepio wines accompanied the whole meal, which was followed by various local cheeses, including Bagòss, a very rare cheese made only in that valley. We ate and ate, drank wine and talked and joked; the meal went on for at least two hours.

After our coffees, a cry went up around the table; people started to clink their forks against their glasses and yell, *"Paolo! Poesia, maestro! Dai!"* ("Paolo! Poetry, maestro! Come on!") After much laughter, scraping of chairs, searching for eyeglasses, and making sure that my recording equipment was all set up correctly, Paolo rose and began the afternoon's recitation. He performed a number of his poems, many by heart, a few with folded pieces of paper in hand to remind him if he lost his thread. His voice, sonorous and deep, filled the dining room. Each poem was met with laughter and applause, and in between people called out to request favorites, or comment on how clever a particular phrase had been. **I Mé Pé** (*I Miei Piedi*; My Feet), the following poem, was one of Paolo's most often-requested poems. It was called for several times before he consented, and was received especially enthusiastically.

Figure 4.1 Paolo at the head of the table, raising his glass to his audience after finishing a poem (photograph by Scott Collard).

Example 4.1 I Mé Pé[3] (My Feet)

Quando che sére ü zùen,
  i mé pé
A i éra bèi . . . ma bèi . . . de
  là de bèi . . .
Stèss di cane de l'òrghen
  de la césa
Facc sö a scala: perfècc,
  pròpe zömèi
De dovrà de modèi per ü
  scültùr
E per disègn 'n de stöde
  d'ü pitùr.

When I was a youth, my feet
Were beautiful . . . but beauti-
  ful . . . beyond beautiful . . .
Same as the organ pipes in the
  church
Made up to scale: perfect, real
  twins
As if they were models for a
  sculpture
And for sketches of a painter.

Gh'ére i dicc lóngh e
  drécc e füsolàcc,
E i se müìa compàgn ch'i
  fòss di mà:
Püdìe ciapà 'n di dicc fina
  la pèna
E scriv bèl tónd, sensa gna
  mai sbaglià,
E püdìe stà sö i ponte di
  mé pé
Pròpe stèss de la
  Fracci . . . o zó de lé.

There were toes long and
  straight and molded,
And when they moved they
  could be taken for hands:
I could even hold a pen in those
  toes
And write beautifully, with never
  an error
And I could stand on the bridge
  of my feet
Just like Fracci[4] . . . or even better
  than her.

Mé curìe a pé nüd sira e
  matina
De sima a fónd de töte ste
  contrade,
E sènsa mai proà gna ü
  dulurì
Anche a ciapà de bröte
  sigolade.
Püdie infilà i scarpe come
  ü guant
E, ai mé pé, ghe ülìe
  pròpe é tant.

I ran on my bare feet evening
  and morning
From the top to the bottom of
  all these streets,
And without ever suffering even
  the smallest of pains
Nor brutal stubbings to mar
  them.
I could slip on shoes like putting
  on a glove
And I loved my feet, I wished
  them well.

Adèss i ròbe i s'è tüte
  cambiade:
I dicc i è slargàcc fò,
  quase ön'entàia;

Now, things are changed
  completely:
The toes have widened out,
  almost a fan;

Fiache, cai e dürù 'mpó sura e sòta;	Slow, whining and hardened a bit above and below;
E 'nfina töte e ónge i me se scàia . . .	And down at the end of the nails they splinter on me . . .
I va decórde sèmper tra de lur	They never get along amongst themselves
Dóma per cassà fò . . . impó de udùr.	Except to toss my way . . . a bit of odor.
I me fa sènt dulùr "scapa diàol!";	They make me feel pain "devil begone!";
Ü l'völ indà de ché, l'óter de là;	One of them wants to go here, the other there;
Chèl mansì a l' me döl a la matina	That left one gives me pain in the morning
E l'óter a la sira l'fa cridà;	And the other makes me cry out in the evening;
E cae fò i scarpe con d'ü tal fastöde	And getting off my shoes is such a big pain
Che pròpe i pé i m'è vegnìcc in öde.	That I'm actually beginning to hate my feet.
A la sira me slónghe sura 'l lècc	At night I lay myself down to bed
E i mète còmocc sura ü gran cüssì,	And lay them comfortably on a big pillow
Pò ghe fó sö sta béla romanzina:	And then I start telling them a good night story:
"Ve recomande tant . . . lassìm durmì!";	"I mean it, really . . . let me sleep!";
E 'ntat con d'öna mà, èco, i carènse	Meanwhile with one hand, there, there, I caress them
E ai dé passàt e a töt ol rèst a pènse . . .	And I think of the days past and all the rest . . .
A pènse ch'i è nassìcc apröf,	To think that they were born so close together,
Cressìcc töcc du pròpe 'n de stèss ambiènt,	Grew up both of them in the same place,
E crède che a capì sto cambiamènt	But I believe that to understand this change
No l' sièss gnamò riàt che tal sapient . . .	Doesn't take a wise man . . .
Opör i fa pò a lur compàgn de mé:	After all, they're just like me:
Urmai i è dré . . . a ragiunà co i pé.	At any rate, it's left to me . . . to reason with my feet.

The audience, chairs pushed back from the table, listened intently to Paolo's performance, calling out occasionally to agree or comment or just to guffaw. Afterwards, we applauded and whistled and begged for more. Paolo continued, reciting three more poems before he said we'd had enough, and sat down. Conversation continued at the table, about the poems, Paolo as a poet (all praise), how lucky I was to know such an important Bergamasco poet and man, all of this loud and overlapping. I was teased about whether I understood it all (not every word, but I had the tape to review later), and quizzed as to my Bergamasco abilities in general. All this verbal activity contrasted with Paolo's poems in an important way: it involved the usual mix of Bergamasco and Italian that I'd grown used to, not the purified Bergamasco that Paolo employed in his poems. Here is an illustrative example of the heteroglossic nature of the conversation, taken from when Paolo had just explained that his next poem might be considered a little self-promoting, as it was about his own butiga:

Example 4.2

CARLA: *Pubblicità!*	CARLA: *Publicity!*
ELENA: *E' l'anima del commercio.*	ELENA: *It's the soul of commerce.*
UMBERTO: **Chesta l'è** autoreclam!	UMBERTO: **This is** self-promotion!
PAOLO: *Autoreclam,* **ó faìt mal!**	PAOLO: *Self-promotion,* **I've done badly!**
UMBERTO: **No, no, te et faìt benone!**	UMBERTO: **No, no, you've done well.**
RICO: **Scolta Paolo, a gh'è ne mia un'òter compàgn de te!**	RICO: **Listen, Paolo, there's no one else like you!**

Everyone at the table (except my moroso) used both languages, moving between them frequently according to topic, interlocutor, or other reasons not evident from the transcript/recording (such as a passed bottle of wine or dropped napkin). This fluidity characterized the whole day's verbal interactions, with the marked exception of when Paolo was reciting his poems.

No one commented on this contrast; nor did I especially notice it until I transcribed the tapes from that day with Ella. She commented that it seemed to be a particularly Bergamasco day, however. Even if every word was not in Bergamasco, the fact that so much of it was used – indeed the whole flavor of our interactions that day – seemed to her to be particularly Bergamasco, and she relished some of the Bergamasco turns of phrase, such as Umberto's use, at one point, of the phrase "**e compagnéa bèla**." Lexically, it would be the same in Italian ("*e compagnia bella*"), but the pronunciation and the sense (of things or people well-grouped together) were all Bergamasco to her.

Why I Mé Pé?

Through its humor and delicious turns of phrase, I Mé Pé helps resolve the contradiction at the heart of Bergamasco poetry: how can such a rough, peasant language be considered appropriate to the refined, sophisticated genre of poetry? It addresses important, universal themes (getting old, the difference between the past and the present) through the lowly, bodily metaphor of the feet; this juxtaposition of high and low is part of what makes it funny, but also makes it good and satisfying to its listeners. It rings true to them, not only in what it says, but also in how it says it.

I Mé Pé exemplifies Bergamasco poetry as a performative activity and a literary genre. As an activity, this poem took place in what Ella and others describe as an authentic – and increasingly rare and idealized – Bergamasco setting: it was recited out loud, by the poet himself, with friends around a table after a meal, amid laughter and much socializing. These social characteristics of the poem and its recital were essential to it being judged "authentic" and "good." According to the participants, I Mé Pé and all the other poems of Paolo's that he recited that day at the cassina "fit" the situation perfectly. For Bergamaschi, gathering with friends and family for a large meal on Sunday afternoon was a traditional and pleasurable activity, one which was most properly executed if there was polenta and red wine on the table, a large group around the table, and – most traditionally – at least one poet at the head of the table to stand up and perform for the group, give them something to talk about, and make them laugh together. Paolo's audience wanted to hear his voice as he performed, see the expression on his face as he did so, and be able to raise their glasses to him as he finished. The experience of this type of shared sociality through performance was an essential part of what made the day enjoyable. Indeed, in spite of a growth in the availability of the written form of Bergamasco poetry, few people I spoke to enjoyed it through individually and privately reading it. This was perhaps in large part because so few Bergamaschi were familiar with the orthographic conventions for writing Bergamasco. It was also because poetry's oral performance was so much preferred as a social activity.

The poem itself is also a prime exemplar of poetry as a literary and cultural genre in Bergamo. Bauman defines genre as a speech style that is "a constellation of systematically related, co-occurrent formal features and structures that serves as a conventionalized orienting framework for the production and reception of discourse" (2000:84). That is, genres are recognizable types of language/speech, which share certain thematic, formal or structural, and pragmatic features and functions. These shared features and functions orient both producers and audience to poetry being a particular type of speech activity, bringing with them expectations about what types of topics will be treated, what types of language will be used, and what types of things will be accomplished through this recitation. So, for instance, the genre of sermon will contain certain topics (morality, say, more likely than movie star gossip), patterns of language use (predominantly one person speaking, with perhaps some call and response from the audience, in a different register of language than might be used for gossip), and pragmatic effects (the participants will feel as if they have participated in a shared spiritual experience, so that some may feel comforted, others shamed, etc.). Genres work because they echo past speech events (you know a sermon, presumably, because you've heard one before), but also because they rely on future effects (like more of them happening, or applause following them, or that social recognition will be gained for the speaker).

The genre of Bergamasco poetry evoked a past in which similar performances have happened for generations, and presupposed that they will continue.[5] Herein lies part of its power, for each performance connects the past, present, and future. I Mé Pé, as a performance, evoked the countless times that Paolo and other Bergamasco poets have stood at similar heads of tables and recited their poetry for the pleasure of others. In its very normality, it also presupposed that such events will happen and be enjoyed again in the future, continuing this Bergamasco tradition. Being a part of this activity linked participants to this past and presumed future, for their current actions were modeled on those of the past and will – alongside all those past poetry recitals – act as models for future occurrences. Caton (1990) suggests in his analysis of Yemeni poetry that poetry is an instance of a speech act or genre in which culture emerges from communicative action, and we see this clearly with Bergamasco poetry recitals. Paolo and his friends and family were actively constructing and participating in what they defined as Bergamasco culture through their actions that day.

This type of poetic performative tradition, linked to intimate social settings of confidenza enjoyed around a table, dates back to at least the 1920s, when the *Ducato di Piazza Pontida* was founded.[6] As discussed briefly in the last chapter, the Ducato began its existence as a social club, electing the Duke, its leader, by popular vote. Its meetings were held in restaurants and taverns and were basically social gatherings – all in Bergamasco and generously documented in the newspaper that they continue to publish, Giopì. The group, although its members were mostly part of the elite, has always dedicated itself to the tutelage and patronage of popular Bergamasco culture.

The strength and vitality of the Ducato and the cultural activities they have supported have waxed and waned since its founding. While the 1920s and 1930s are widely considered to have been the Golden Age of Bergamasco dialect and culture as well as the Ducato (Mora 1984; Zanetti 1978), Fascist restrictions against local dialects and cultures during this period ultimately led to Giopì being shut down and the Ducato going underground until after World War II. After the war, the Ducato and Bergamasco poetry never quite regained the vitality of the 1920s and 1930s, and experienced a period of slow decline in the 1960s and 1970s. However, during the late 1980s and 1990s, Bergamasco dialect performances began to enjoy a renewal.[7]

Paolo's recitation that day in the mountains happened during a period in which Bergamasco poets and their poetry were flourishing as they had not since the 1920s and 1930s, most with the support of the Ducato di Piazza Pontida. Although Paolo considered himself a member of the Ducato and had published his poetry in Giopì (as do most of the poets the Ducato supports) during the 1960s and 1970s, his participation in the group by the time I knew him had been reduced to receiving Giopì and casual social interactions with other members. This type of day, casual and privately social, fell outside the realm of the types of activities that the Ducato sponsored during my research, which were generally larger and more public (i.e., held in small theaters and lecture halls for anyone who cared to attend).

The poem itself depicts a particularly Bergamasco past, evoking a version of the lived past as desirable, accessible, and shared, a poetic theme common in Bergamasco poetry. It compares the treasured past with a present that suffers in comparison. These comparisons are couched in humor, however, so that, like Giorgio's potentially painful story about the póer bortulì, participants can laugh at the difficulties they have faced. As was often the case, this comparison is grounded in personal experience, although the central conceit of Paolo's feet affords an unusually embodied view of past and present, for Paolo's feet and hands had both by that time become gnarled and painfully arthritic from his decades of hard work in his forge. Throughout the poem, Paolo reflects on the agility, speed, and beauty his feet possessed in his youth (i.e. the past) and compares this with the pain and deformities that afflict them now. His age and the wisdom that it provides him are contrasted with the physical pain that his body now gives him. His feet are portrayed as agents of their own, standing in as synecdoches of the poet himself: moving fleetly in his youth, and proving stubborn and difficult in his old age. In the final stanza, he reflects on the irony of how he and his feet were all born together, and yet it is now left to him – in fact, no wise man – to reason with his painful, unreasonable, and irrational feet, a difficult if not impossible task. Throughout, the poem deals humorously with the serious subject of getting old and the physical difficulties that accompany this process.

Like nearly all Bergamasco poetry, I Mé Pé is situated in a particular place and time(s): the Città Alta during Paolo's lifetime. The Città Alta, a potent sociogeographical symbol of Bergamasco identity that Bergamaschi commonly reported as the best and most beautiful thing about Bergamo, was a common topic in Bergamasco poetry. Paolo's poem stood out among poetic treatments of the Città Alta, however, in that it describes a lived relationship to and active movement within this place, which is more often described from a static, admiring distance. Although there are no place names, such as street names, in the poem, it is clear that Paolo is talking about specific places, places with which his audience – as Bergamaschi and as friends of his – will be familiar. Paolo's poem talks about how his childhood and adulthood both took place in the Città Alta, the "same place" in which he and his feet grew up together. He refers to "all these streets" ("**töte ste contrade**") that he ran down as a child, as if pointing them out to his listeners; they are the **contrade** of his Città Alta, the place where he has tread his path. The Città Alta of today and the Città Alta of yesterday are contrasted in the poem, as he remembers how he used to run and points out the streets down which he can no longer. The morning and night, the times of day when he used to run as a child, are contrasted with the pains that his feet give him now at those times. The outside arenas in which his feet used to carry him so effortlessly are compared with the private atmospheres in which he suffers the pain of his feet now: "**sura l' lècc**" ("on the bed"), as he tells them a bedtime story, as he would his own children or grandchildren.

In terms of imagery, I Mé Pé relies extensively on vivid descriptions of the physical world. Clear, down-to-earth physical descriptions were common in Bergamasco poetry, a tendency that supports the idea that Bergamasco itself was particularly suited to everyday, concrete types of activities. Comparing his feet first to organ pipes, long and straight, and then later as widening into "almost a fan" provides the listeners with tangible, physical descriptions. Paolo repeatedly refers to his feet in material terms: they are "**nüd**" ("nude," "bare"), they tend to "toss a little odor" at him ("**cassà fò ... impó de udùr**"), and he puts them on "**ü gran cüssì**" ("a large cushion"). His feet, when he and they were young, could have been confused for hands, "**mà**," and they could hold anything, even a pen. He contrasts this with how "slow, whining and hardened a bit above and below" ("**Fiache, cai e dürù 'mpó sura e sòta**") they have become, down to the toenails, which have begun to splinter. Instead of his shoes slipping on and off "like a glove" ("**come ü guant**") as they did in his youth, in old age the pain of putting on and taking off his shoes gives him such pain or annoyance ("**fastöde**"), that he has come to almost hate his feet.

This type of physical immediacy illuminates a lingering difference between Bergamasco and Italian poetry and between the two languages themselves: for centuries, Italian was used in formal and solemn circumstances, and was in essence a literary language, able to talk about Arcadia, but not fields; Woman, but not women; War, but not the realities of battle.[8] Nencioni calls the Italian spoken until roughly 30 years ago "*aristocratica, scritta dai ceti colti, e parlata da pochissimi*" ("aristocratic, written by the upper classes, and spoken by only a few") (1994:xxviii). At the same time, in most parts of Italy, vernaculars were spoken by all social classes in nearly all circumstances except the most formal, especially in the intimate spheres of home and family, a situation that changed only gradually after World War II (De Mauro 1972:26). Paolo's description of his body in Bergamasco is particularly apt, for it sounds like what most people thought the dialect was best fit for: everyday intimacy and the details of everyday life, rather than the loftier topics more common to most Italian poetry (and increasingly, much Bergamasco poetry as well). Through this imagery, Bergamasco once again indexes the pleasure of the intimate circle of Bergamasco experience. As a poem about feet, I Mé Pé is meant to be humorous, and only indirectly addresses these more universal themes (aging, social change through time) that poetry, as a high literary genre, is thought to more appropriately engage. As such, it bridges the distance between poetic prestige and local authenticity that much Bergamasco poetry attempts to address, perhaps more successfully than most.

I Mé Pé illustrates many other conventions of Bergamasco poetry. Most obviously, it is written entirely in Bergamasco, and contains a number of Bergamasco idioms and plays on words.[9] Turns of phrase, like referring to stubbing his toes as "**sigolade**," a play on the word for "onion," received much appreciation as an acute use of older terms that have fallen into disuse. The use of particularly Bergamasco phrases, such as his advice to his feet, "**Ve racomande tant . . .**" ("I mean it"/"I'm telling you") – something which a mother says to a child, or an elder may urge while giving advice – sounded cozy, homelike, and familiar to his listeners, who could hear their own voices and those of their loved ones saying the same phrases.

Another hallmark of Bergamasco poetry present in I Mé Pé is a relatively simple poetic form, with a consistent rhyme scheme and metrical structure. The rhyme scheme for each of the seven stanzas is ABCBDD, and many of the rhymes revolve around **pé** (feet), the central theme of the poem. The metric structure is *endecasillabo* (11 syllables), a classic form in both Bergamasco and Italian poetry. This form traditionally demands that line-internal stresses fall on the fourth, sixth, and tenth syllables; the fourth, seventh, and tenth syllables; or just the tenth syllable. Paolo adhered to this structure most of the time, but was not overly strict with it. In not adhering too closely to the strict rules about poetic structure, Paolo demonstrated the flexibility that should be part of a Bergamasco poet's repertoire, for in his oral delivery, all the structures and rhymes lined up and made sense. The spoken form clearly took precedence over the written form in this as in all of Paolo's poetry, as it was in his performance of it that his poetry truly shone.

Poetry Performed

For Paolo and his friends and others like them, poetry was enjoyable; it made them laugh, and called to mind people and activities in their immediate personal past as well as their common cultural past. They shared in this pleasure together and could later recall such events as positive group activities, remembering, for example, that time that Paolo recited his poetry at Rico and Elena's house, a remembrance that would probably then lead to recalling how delicious the food was that day, the scenic walk that was taken later, how many laughs (**grignade**) we all enjoyed together. Indeed, that very day, multiple similar occasions were recalled by various participants, linking the present day's activities to a chain of others, such as a gathering of the Città Alta's hiking club a few weeks before at which Paolo had also recited some poetry, and other mountain gatherings at which similar traditional and delicious foods had been prepared and consumed. In these ways, the very type of sociality with which this poetry recitation co-occurred was one of the reasons this activity was most valued. It drew the group together around shared experiences and values such as enjoying the Bergamasco mountains, appreciating Bergamasco food, being able to laugh at the shared memories of the past. These shared values provided the indexical ground against which Paolo's poetry recital can be understood; each subsequent recitation indexed this day, and others before it, as well as anticipated the occasions to come.

Paolo's poetry recitation was also valued for provoking a poignant contemplation of a past that these people treasured. This positive orientation towards the past was evident in other parts of their lives, such as through investing in renovating an ancient structure, as Elena and Rico did; or participating in a profession which contributes to such renovations, as was true of Umberto, the engineer, and/or was based in time-honored practices, such as Paolo and Roberto, the ironsmiths. Sharing in this type of activity often co-occurred with participation in other Bergamasco-oriented activities, such as belonging to a local alpine or hiking club. Those who participated in these types of activities demonstrated a local orientation, valuing the Bergamasco landscape and traditions from the past. These people belonged to a larger, looser group that valued being Bergamasco and doing Bergamasco things. They may or may not have considered themselves activists in this regard, but they explicitly recognized the value in certain activities, ways of socializing, types of food, and even places in which to combine these activities (in, for instance, the mountains, in an old cassina made new again). Having poetry in Bergamasco, and spending the day speaking alla bergamasca were important components of this orientation.

During the time I did my initial fieldwork in 1999–2000, there was, if not a boom, then a definite flowering of Bergamasco poetry occurring. This was evidenced in the number of practicing and aspiring poets I knew and was told about; the growing number of poets contributing to Giopì; the increasing number of volumes of poetry available in local bookstores; the relative frequency with which poetry readings were held around town and the province (one or two a week, usually organized by the Ducato or a community organization or social club in honor of some locally important event); and the growth in the number of annual poetry contests (in 2000, I counted 13 in the province of Bergamo). I knew of few younger poets, as it seemed that writing poetry was closely linked to reaching a particular stage in life, becoming, as they put it, *"di una certa età"* (of a certain age). Most poets described to me how they had begun to write verse as they approached or went into retirement, a time of leisure, and, perhaps, increased contemplation.

The one poetic practice that was becoming increasingly rare, however, was the type in which we participated that summer afternoon. From archival and anecdotal evidence, as well as personal observation, this type of social gathering, complete with poet, is no longer as common as it seems to have been in the 1920s and 1930s. While Sunday or special occasion pranzo remained an important social event in Bergamo, only groups of friends like this one (older, relatively well-off but with roots in the working class, and, most importantly, interested particularly in Bergamasco ways of living) still made it a point to have a poet around. I accompanied Paolo on several outings when he recited his poetry, some similar to this one, but most more formally organized, put on by alpine clubs, neighborhood associations, or social clubs. Even the Ducato's biannual banquets, which centrally featured poets and their poetry, had become more formally organized events, scheduled twice a year and requiring participants to reserve places and buy tickets in advance. And while there must have been poets I did not know − or know well enough to be included in these types of events − who participated in informal gatherings where they read their poems, I knew of no others who did so on a regular basis, like Paolo. Increasingly, this ideal type of Bergamasco socializing was becoming rare, even as the amount of poetry being produced seemed to be on the rise.

Poetry as Cultural Revitalization

While our day in the mountain's informal poetry reading was relatively uncommon at that point in Bergamo, the tendency to regard poetry as an essential element of modern Bergamasco culture was not. Poetry was praised for being "real" and expressive of the *"memoria sociale della nostra gente bergamasca"* (social memory of our Bergamasco people), as the Duke put it in a speech in 2000. The same Bergamasco being spoken less often in the streets, he continued, *"rinasca . . . nella poesia, come lingua dei valori individuali e collettivi, come musica del pensiero e del sentimento personale e corale, come strumento di ricerca della memoria e dell'identità alle quali ci si tente di apparte-nere . . .*" ("is reborn . . . in poetry, as [the] language of individual and collective values, as [the] music of the thought and of personal and choral (group) sentiment, as an instrument of research into the memory and the identity to which we try to belong").

In this description, Bergamasco poetry is not simply something to be enjoyed in and of itself, although many people surely experi-enced it that way. It is also an "instrument" that will help save the dialect. Poets and their supporters often thanked audiences at poetry readings for their participation in keeping Bergamasco from disap-pearing. Introductions to volumes of poetry often advised readers that the dialect serves as a direct link to the past and commented positively on its ability to represent Bergamasco realities accurately. Ducato member Gabrio Vitali, discussing the poems of Carmelo Francia, the Ducato's most well-known poet (and teacher of the writing course), in the preface to the collection **Menabò**[10] (2000:10), stated: "*le parole del dialetto liberano in noi l'immaginazione non solo nostra, ma anche di coloro che ci hanno preceduto e del cui racconto esisten-ziale serbiamo almeno qualche lacerto di memoria: i genitori, i nonni, gli amici di quando eravamo bambini*" ("The words of the dialect liberate not only our own imagination, but also that of those who preceded us and of whose stories of everyday life we save at least a trace in memory: parents, grandparents, friends from when we were chil-dren). Similarly, former Duke Francesco Barbieri, in his preface to Rita Rossi's volume of Bergamasco poetry **Tra sògn e realtà** (*Between dream and reality*), observed that Rossi's poetry "*dipinge, con il personaggio, tutta un'epoca, un ambiente, una vita*" ("paints, with its character, all of an epoch, an environment, a life"). He further observed about her use of the particularly Bergamasco word **ingogià** (to knit) that "*nessun altro verbo, in nessun'altra lingua può esprimere così tante cose e con altrettanta efficacia*" ("no other verb, in no other lan-guage, can express so many things and with so much efficacy") (1996:6). This specifically Bergamasco action can only be described in Bergamasco, in other words, as no other language so accurately and immediately captures its realties and the past that it references. This praise of ingogià is similar to Daniele's description of how immediately expressive the word **malfàt** is, and how **sigolade** was admired by Paolo's audience.

These types of characterizations of the value of Bergamasco poetry draw heavily on ideologies of purism. These ideologies often focused on lexical items that express particularly Bergamasco values and activities, linking them to a perhaps idealized past when such terms were more commonly used. Indeed, Bakhtin asserts that "poetry always behaves as if it lived in the heartland of its own language territory, and does not approach too closely the borders of this language, where it would inevitably be brought into dialogic contact with heteroglossia; poetry chooses not to look beyond the boundaries of its own language" (1981:399). Although bivalent items like **smistàa fò**, which in Bakhtin's terms "approach too closely the borders" between Bergamasco and Italian, certainly occurred in poems, they were never the terms singled out for praise.

Indeed, it was common, as I Mé Pé demonstrates, to use archaic Bergamasco words and phrases in Bergamasco poetry in an effort to present a "purified" version of the dialect, unmuddied by the interference of Italian. This type of effort towards purifying a minority language of elements of the national language that have become part of everyday usage is common in minority language revitalization efforts across Europe, as Kabatek notes in his work on standardization efforts in Galicia (1997), as well as in other parts of the world (Blommaert 1994; Hill and Hill 1986; Hoffman 2008). In Bergamo, older forms of words were often regarded as sounding more poetic, and were savored by audience members as recovered treasures. Archaic terms also tended to be more different from Italian words than the words used during my research, as with **pirù** and **forchéta** (respectively, the archaic and modern terms for fork discussed in Chapter 2) compared to the Italian term, *forchetta*. As we saw in Chapter 2, one way in which a Bergamasco word was judged to be "authentic" was by having – or seeming to have – no linguistic elements from Italian. As Hill and Hill observe, "linguistic purism, like many attitudes about language, can be turned to a variety of purposes" (1986:57).

Although contemporary consumers of poetry may have appreciated archaic lexical forms in theory, in practice many needed a little extra help in understanding them. In the majority of contemporary volumes of poetry, there was a glossary in the back, so that readers could look up words or phrases they did not know. Many others had Italian translations that accompanied the Bergamasco texts.

Similarly, at Bergamasco poetry performances, poets often explained what certain words or phrases meant before or after they recited their poems, frequently as a way of explaining the poem as a whole, since these archaic words and phrases were often at the heart of what a poem was addressing. Some Bergamasco poets even recited Italian versions of their poems before or after the "real" Bergamasco versions in order to afford audience members of potentially all linguistic abilities the opportunity to know what the poem was about. The extensive use of archaic terms and phrases, then, might have limited comprehension of poetry, rather than enhanced it, in many cases.

Contextualizing Poetry

At informal poetry readings, in which poets and audience were co-participants in a shared social event, poetry helped to pragmatically construct or reinforce a sentimental attachment to the dialect. The more formal poetry readings, which became more common in the 1990s, share this goal, but have another one as well: to give Bergamasco and Bergamasco poetry prestige. These two goals generally co-occurred, as demonstrated by the commentary that framed much Bergamasco poetry, whether in the form of written introductions or verbal speeches given at the opening and/or closing of poetry readings.

Such framing texts served to translate the culturally specific into the universally poetic, essentially telling the reader or listener why these poets or this poet were important. Such comments were made by experts of some sort, such as the Duke or other illustrious members of the Ducato, other poets, or well-known local or national literary figures or scholars, lending them the weight of their personal social prestige. For instance, in 2000 the Ducato invited an expert to speak about the nature of contemporary dialect poetry in Italy during an evening celebrating *poesia dialettale* (dialectal poetry). The emcee introduced him by establishing his value as an expert:

> *È uno studioso di metrica e insegnante, docente di storia della letteratura italiana all'università di Bologna. È un critico ma è anche un poeta. Scrive*

anche nel suo dialetto, che è il dialetto di Modena, e è stato più volte a trovarci a Bergamo, sia in veste di poeta, perchè è stato finalista fra i più votati al Premio di S. Pellegrino di due anni fa.

[He] is a scholar of metrics and teacher, lecturer of the history of Italian literature at the University of Bologna. He is a critic, but also a poet. He also writes in his own dialect, which is the dialect of Modena, and has been to visit us here in Bergamo several times, in the guise of poet, as he was one of the most popular finalists at the San Pellegrino Prize[11] two years ago.

Note that this scholar was presented as especially well-fitted to comment on dialect poetry due both to his prestigious position at a university, but also because he himself was a successful poet, who wrote in both Italian and dialect. Indeed, having such a person participate in a local event like this poetry contest sponsored by the Ducato lent the event itself prestige and cast it as not simply a local event, but a national one that drew national figures and was positioned as part of a wider national effort to promote local dialects. His ensuing comments about writing dialect poetry focused on the tension between how to value Italian and dialect, which he characterizes respectively as *"lingua e arte alta, colta, e lingua e arte popolare"* ("high, cultivated language and art, and popular language and art"). The best dialectal poetry, he argued, has always been able to transcend this divide, addressing and illuminating both the mundane world of dialect and the cultivated, elevated world of Italian. Valuing dialect poetry for its ability to appeal to all readers, not just those who can appreciate the piquant acuity of Bergamasco words or phrases representing Bergamasco ways of living or feeling, represented a departure from why Bergamasco poetry was more commonly valued, and what it usually indexed.

Undeniably, these types of comments signaled that Bergamasco poetry was being framed as not just authentic and sentimentally important, but also as a literary genre capable of prestigious commentary on the human condition beyond the small circle of Bergamasco concerns, and worthy of literary criticism, not just judgments of cultural authenticity. The current Duke and others at the Ducato indeed explicitly expressed their desire to "raise the cultural level" of the group and the events it sponsored. In an informal interview, the Duke stated that instead of looking always to the past and how things have always been done:

> *E io invece siccome credo appunto, sono affermamente convinto che, che, che tutto sommato se non faremo qualcosa di un po' piu altamente culturale, è tutto, eee, è facile che tantissime delle cose vadano perse, sto puntando un po' di iniziative più, più mirate.*

> And I, instead, seeing how I believe really, I'm firmly convinced that, that, that when all is said and done if we don't do something a little more culturally elevated, it's all, ahhhh, it's almost certain that lots of things will be lost, I'm aiming to offer more, more pointed initiatives.

The Duke, then, sought to improve the "quality" of what the Ducato did, raising the tone or cultural level of the group, to move up and out of the small local world most often evoked in Bergamasco poetry. In the same interview, he told me that the aim of his new initiatives (like a newly established poetry series that brings in dialect poets from all over Italy) was "*avere dei contatti al di fuori della nostra stretta, ristretta cerchio*" ("to have contacts outside of our narrow, restricted circle"). In this, the Duke also aimed to expand the Ducato's domain to include upper-class and even non-local poetry lovers in search of universal truths about the shared human condition in verse.

In making these changes, the Duke hoped to attract members and supporters who might otherwise have hesitated to associate themselves with such a locally oriented and populist organization. Although membership in the Ducato was initially nearly exclusively a province of the elite (for who else had the leisure time and education to engage in such activities in the pre-World War II years?), its focus had long been the popular culture of the Bergamasco contadino.[12] Since the 1980s, however, it was beginning to expand to include members from the middle as well as working classes. By the end of the 1990s and beginning of the 2000s, the Duke increasingly aimed to move away from the group's traditional populist orientation, and reconstruct itself as more appealing to an educated, upper-class audience, not usually interested in strictly local issues or topics. This corresponded with the group's efforts to expand its largely aging (age 60 and up) membership by adding younger members. Although they have had some success, due at least in part to younger supporters of the Northern League joining their ranks, it remains to be seen if these efforts to raise the cultural level of their endeavors will succeed, or if they will draw in this desired audience.

Bakhtin maintained that literary genres are ideologically connected to "social groups and 'spheres of human activity'" (Briggs and Bauman 1995:581). In other words, genres like Bergamasco poetry are firmly anchored to the social contexts in which they occur, the social actors who participate in these contexts, and the social ends to which these actors aspire. As fixed texts, they can also circulate across social contexts, creating connections between various moments of recitation. Whether explicitly undertaken as instances of "revitalization" or "saving" Bergamasco or not, poetry performances link those who participate in them to a valued past through myriad indexical associations.

The past – treasured or not – is not the only baggage that Bergamasco poetry carries. As Bauman observes, insistence on generic regimentation and efforts to transform genres are closely connected to "hierarchies of value and taste (which genres are evaluated as relatively higher, better, more beautiful, more moral) and to the social regimentations of access to particular generic forms (who can learn them, master them, own them, perform them, and to what effect)" (2000:86). At the time of my research, the "best" poetry was written in Italian and addressed universal human values and experience. Ranked below it was any *poesia dialettale*, which was judged according to different criteria. "Good" Bergamasco poetry generally treasured the past over the present, esteemed the intimately local over what could be found outside of that, and celebrated peculiarly Bergamasco values, characters, and situations. One person's intimately local, however, was another's "narrow, restricted circle." I view efforts like the Duke's to alter the focus of the activities it supported as attempts to socially regiment what types of poetry would receive their official – and relatively important – sanction as both "real" and "good." Whether these efforts result in more than just superficial changes remains to be seen.

"La Zét D'Öna Ólta":
The People of Long Ago

The third Saturday night in October 2000, the auditorium at the Oratory of the church of *Borgo Santa Caterina*,[13] was packed, as it had been for the previous four Saturdays. Around 250 people were in attendance to see the last in an annual series of Bergamasco theater performances, which the oratory and parish had sponsored every fall for the previous five years. The play that evening, **"La Zét D'Öna Ólta (De Dét in del Ritràcc)"** ("The People of Long Ago (As Seen in a Picture)"), was put on by the *Tradizione e Novità* (Tradition and Innovation) theater company of Borgo Santa Caterina. The troupe was composed of roughly 20 members, with a core group who regularly attended rehearsals numbering about 15. The largest number of troupe members were older people over 60, with a few people between the ages of 40 and 60 (including Roberta, the director of the company). There were also a few members between 20 and 40, playing the important young lead roles; and an adolescent boy and girl. Although a relatively new company, founded in 1997, Tradizione e Novità was already gaining a loyal following, with many fans drawn from the neighborhood who enjoyed having a representative theater company, and others who just enjoyed Bergamasco dialect theater.

In 1999–2000, there were at least 20 amateur dialect theater companies performing in Bergamo and its province, and at least eight extended series of performances sponsored by local town administrations, neighborhood social centers, and the Ducato di Piazza Pontida. Dialect theater performances regularly drew audiences of anywhere from 20 to 250 people. Although these audiences were heavily weighted toward older members of the working class, they also consistently drew numbers of younger people from a range of class backgrounds. Participation in dialect theater performance was evenly distributed across genders, both in terms of performers and audience members. Local newspapers covered series and individual performances, advising readers of their occurrence on future dates, and reviewing them – always favorably – after they had taken place. Bergamasco plays were always referred to generically as *comedie* (comedies), and reviews often described them as *brillante* (scintillating) or *vivace* (lively), attending to particularly humorous characters or situations. It has been observed about Bergamo that "*Quando si parla del teatro dialettale, si pensa ad una platea di gente che ha già gli occhi e la bocca aperti pronti alla risata*" ("when one speaks of dialect theater, one thinks of an audience of people who have their eyes and mouths open, ready to laugh") (Mora 1984:11).

The play that evening was a love story, set in the town and province of Bergamo. The hero and heroine, a boy and girl from similar working-class backgrounds, fall in love despite the wishes of the young woman's mother, who aspires to marry her daughter to someone more *benestante* (well-off). Many characters and chances of fate conspire to keep the young lovers apart as well as draw them together throughout the play, but in the end they are united, and even her mother gives her blessing to their union. It is a familiar plot, but a pleasurable one for the audience. Most of the humor revolves around a love letter from the hero to the heroine that goes astray. First the heroine's mother finds the note and thinks it is from a neighbor, then the neighbor's wife finds the note and thinks it is from the heroine's father, and finally a housemaid finds it and thinks it is from a close friend of the family. The confusions that surround the letter's circumambulation through the characters were received with – and indeed, played for – much laughter, as untoward declarations of love, gossipy moments of sharing, the wrong person walking in at the right moment, and dreamy monologues about "what if?" were interspersed with numerous "*battute*" (humorous lines; lit. "beats").

This comedy, like the majority of Bergamasco plays, takes place **"d'öna ólta"** (literally, "at one time"). This phrase, a common one in Bergamasco as it is in Italian (*di una volta*), refers to a time in the past that occupies no particular moment, although it is more recent than its English equivalent, "once upon a time." Bergamasco comedies tended to be set in this past that exists outside of history, lacking political or historical particularities, but somewhere around the turn of the century. The description in the playbill – entirely in Italian except for the title of the play and the names of the characters – stated that the action takes place sometime "in the first decades of our century," and the characters are dressed in clothes that evoke the early 20th century, down to the wooden clogs on their feet (discussed by cast members in Chapter 2). The scenes are set in rooms lit by candles, and the characters haul water inside in buckets. Items from the Bergamasco past, like the **mònega**, a bed-warming device that was once common, and wooden polenta platters and paddles populated the stage. The characters are members of the industrial working class or contadini, having just what they need, but working hard in order to get ahead. This was the case in most Bergamasco plays, where even bourgeois characters, who appeared much less often, were generally depicted as hard-working and earnest.

This play contains an element that threw this "past on display" tendency of Bergamasco plays into higher relief than usual, a fact hinted at by the second half of the title, "(As Seen in a Picture)." At numerous moments throughout the play, the actors suddenly freeze and the stage goes dark, lit only on its very front lip. A grandfather and granddaughter dressed in modern clothes appear, looking at a photo album, and referring to the frozen scene before them as if it were one of the photographs they were examining. The granddaughter asks questions about what the people were doing or wearing, criticizing them for their repeatedly mended socks and saying that she is glad she lives in a time when there is central heating. Her grandfather tries to teach her about the past, telling her that they did not mind their worn clothes because they worked hard for them, or that they enjoyed the warmth of the fireplace.

At one point, the grandfather teaches the little girl a nursery rhyme in Bergamasco – the only Bergamasco during these scenes, which take place otherwise entirely in Italian – and her mother (his daughter) catches them reciting it together. She severely criticizes her father for teaching her child Bergamasco, for she does not want the girl to come out with a phrase in Bergamasco in front of their friends and make her look bad ("*fare una brutta figura*"). In other words, the daughter is embarrassed by her Bergamasco past and wants to forget it and make sure that her daughter is not saddled with its embarrassingly old-fashioned and lower-class practices. The grandfather is upset by his daughter's lack of interest and pride in her heritage, and in later scenes continues to try to interest his granddaughter in the things and the people of the past. The final scene of the play, immediately following the moment when the separated lovers are finally united, features the daughter realizing that she has been wrong in her rejection of Bergamasco, and the past and culture to which it is connected. She forgives her father, and they recite the nursery rhyme in Bergamasco together with her daughter, as the three of them look on at the photograph of the scene before them. The lovers, we find in the end, are the grandfather's parents, and his daughter has finally allowed herself and her daughter to be proud of and connect themselves with their heritage and traditions.[14]

This play does explicitly what the majority of Bergamasco plays do implicitly: it displays the people and customs of the past as something to be proud of, not embarrassed by. In fact, Roberta, the director (who also played the daughter) added these scenes of modern life in Italian as "improvements" to the old script (written in the 1930s) in order to make exactly this point. What she made explicit in this play, however, was implicit in most Bergamasco comedies. The characters in the past portrayed on stage are rarely sophisticated, well-off, or worldly, but are generally honest, hard-working, and sincere. This contrasts with the self-consciousness, consumerism, and lack of respect for traditions that many older Bergamaschi felt characterized modern Bergamasco society. One recurrent theme of this genre is that Bergamaschi may have gotten ahead financially, but have left too much behind culturally in the process if Bergamasco children and grandchildren do not understand and appreciate their past, if these children are not told about how Bergamaschi used to live, work, play, and love. This play went further than just portraying this dynamic, for it proposed a possible solution: Bergamasco parents – mothers, perhaps, in particular – should embrace the dialect and encourage their children to speak it and learn about their past, instead of orienting them only towards Italian and the future. Implicitly, it also presented a way to incorporate Bergamasco and the past into everyday life safely: within nursery rhymes, and through looking at photographs – representations of the past. Roberta was explicit that these scenes provided both a critique of what she saw as the overly common tendency for Bergamasco mothers to speak only Italian to their children, as well as a model for how to rectify that problem.

Characterizing Bergamasco Dialect Theater

Bergamasco dialect theater productions were, by definition, almost completely in Bergamasco. The occasional characters who were exceptions to this "Bergamasco only" rule and spoke Italian tended to be set apart in time or space from the Bergamasco characters. Such "outsider" characters come from somewhere outside of Bergamo, and may serve as conniving foils for the simple and honest Bergamasco characters. Alternatively, this "outsider" type of character might be like the modern family in "La Zét D'Öna Ólta (De Dét in del Ritràcc)," who are set apart from the main Bergamasco characters in time and comment on the more Bergamasco characters of this past time period.

The overall image depicted on the Bergamasco stage, however, was everyone speaking only Bergamasco at all times with everyone in his or her lives. As such, these plays presented models for living entirely in Bergamasco, models situated in times gone by, reinforcing links between speaking (only) Bergamasco as an everyday practice and the past. Moreover, as comedies, in which even the most apparently dire circumstances are ultimately resolved with a few good battute and shared goodwill (if not always sophistication and grace), plays presented an idealized past in which overbearing mothers, scheming outsiders, and strokes of misfortune are overcome through traditional Bergamasco cultural values: steadfastness and the application of will, hard work, and humor.[15] Even plays set in the present (in the 1970s, 1980s, and 1990s), of which there were noticeably few, treated "modern" issues with a decidedly "old-fashioned" bent. These plays often pitted wise, older characters against young, willful rebels who eventually come to appreciate the time-seasoned perspectives of their elders, and valorize "traditional" ways of living (such as extended families living together) over the rush of modern life. The fact that, like for poetry, all the language framing these plays, such as spoken introductions and concluding remarks as well as written materials such as play bills or reviews in Giopì or other newspapers, was nearly always in Italian only served to underline this contrast between Bergamasco in the dramatized, "on-stage" past and Italian in the everyday, "off-stage" present.

This point was underlined the evening of that performance of "La Zét D'Öna Ólta (De Dét in del Ritràcc)," which was also the night I made my debut on the Bergamasco stage. I played the small part of Maria, loyal friend to the heroine Rosina, who serves as a liaison between Rosina and her forbidden beloved, Rico. Before the curtain went up that evening, Roberta introduced me and, by extension, my research to the audience in Italian. She described how, as a researcher interested in the Bergamasco people, dialect, and culture, it was natural that my interests should include the Bergamasco theater, due to its importance in Bergamasco culture; she said she was honored that I had chosen their company to get to know. But although I had tape-recorded and observed numerous rehearsals and performances, my experience with the Bergamasco theater would have been incomplete, said Roberta, if I had not become a part of it myself. Hence, my participation that evening was a final step to understanding and appreciating what Bergamasco culture is all about. Immersing myself in the "real" Bergamasco culture, in other words, meant joining the cast on stage in the Bergamasco past.[16]

Theater as a Revitalization Activity

Like poetry, there is evidence to challenge the efficacy of theater as an activity of revitalization. These performances helped those who participated in them – whether as performers or as audience members – enact being Bergamasco, through the shared knowledge they presumed and the shared laughter they produced. The same indexical associations, however, between the dialect and the past were being reinforced in theater as in poetry. In theater, it was even clearer than it was in poetry that this is a past of poverty and hardship. The characters are honest, humorous, work hard and value one another, but the majority of them are also unmistakably working-class laborers and rural agriculturalists. The quaint artifacts and rustic surroundings in which they are set may appeal nostalgically to the audience, but no one really wants to return to a time when food was often scarce, long winters were warmed by stoves and fireplaces, adults and often children worked hard, and few were educated beyond a few years. In these scenarios, Bergamasco is not only the language of the past; it is the language of a time before comfort and prosperity.

This was another arena that the Ducato had designs to change. In the same interview excerpted above, the Duke observed to me that "*Vedi anche lì, per esempio compagnie teatrali. Compagnie teatrali in questi ultimi, dieci, o vent'anni ne sono sorte tantissimi. Però . . . però sono povere di, di, di cultura, insomma, no?*" ("You see, also there, for example theater companies. Theater companies, in these last ten or twenty years, there are lots of them. However . . . however they are poor in culture, basically, no?"). Like the Duke, there were a number of Bergamaschi who despaired of the populist, lower class ("poor") culture depicted in the Bergamasco plays, dismissing them as well as for being exclusively comedies. Indeed, a number of Bergamaschi I knew did not attend plays for exactly these reasons. The Duke expanded this view by saying, "*Non, no, no – è impensabile che uno vada a vedere una commedia in dialetto che tratti un argomento serio. Cioè, un argomento non serio, un argomento impegnato. Perché uno dice, 'Madonna mia, devo andare a vedere, va penso vado, se vado,* '**ndò per fà quàter grignà**'" ("No, no, no – it's unthinkable that one would go to see a comedy in dialect that treats a serious subject. That is, not a serious subject, but a demanding subject. Because one says, 'My gosh, I've got to go to see, to go see, if I go, I go to have a few laughs'"). The Duke's switch from Italian to Bergamasco to give voice to a presumed audience member (after several mis-starts in Italian), as well as his idiomatic use of the Bergamasco phrase "**fà quàter grignà**" ("have a few laughs," but literally "make/do four laughs"), perfectly evoked the audience he is railing against: in search of peculiarly Bergamasco laughs. This switch also underlines the close association of Bergamasco and humor in general.

This concern for the "poor" cultural level of plays, as evidenced in their failure to engage serious topics, was part and parcel of the Ducato's desire to raise the cultural level of the events it sponsors, and – by extension – perhaps change what Bergamasco culture itself consisted of. These concerns culminated in the Ducato calling a formal meeting in 2004 to inform the several theater troupes associated with it (*Tradizione e Novità* was one) that they were going to offer a course on theater, play production, acting, and the history of dialect theater in Bergamo, and urged the directors of these troupes to make sure their members participated. The company directors, many of whom had a lifetime of experience on stage in both Bergamasco and Italian, reminded them that theirs were amateur companies, always scrambling after funds and struggling to slot rehearsals into troupe members' busy lives. Besides, they felt that the comedies they produced were doing what they wanted them to do: entertain their audiences in the ways that the audience desired. Why try to alter something that was obviously going well? (And indeed, between 1999 and 2005, there were more theater companies and play productions around the city and province of Bergamo than there had been since the 1920s and 1930s.) Perhaps not surprisingly, in spite of their strong urging, the course had so few participants that the Ducato did not offer it again. Not everyone, then, sees the need to elevate Bergamasco culture above its rough, peasant roots in order to save it.

Notwithstanding this tension, attending these poetic and theatrical performances and performing in one showed me that a sizable number of Bergamaschi enjoyed them and participated in them on a regular basis, either as producers (poets, actors, and directors) or audience members. Participants made their own judgments about who and what were "good" and "bad" and what they liked and disliked. Just as certain poets were more popular than others, and particular poems were felt to strike stronger sentiments than others, some dialect theater companies were judged to be more talented than others, and certain plays were regarded as more entertaining than others. Criteria other than the "high" and "low" generic judgments, which dominated mass media and scholarly discussions of these events, were thus available and deployed by participants to distinguish better and worse instances of dialectal events. These assessments, however, did not escape the dimensions of the debate in the larger context entirely, for the basis of these criteria often revolved around degrees of "authenticity," related to the local character of these events.

Theater and Poetry as Pragmatic Genres

Bergamasco theater and poetry are pragmatic genres: they affect the world through their consumption and production. As Briggs and

Bauman observe, "by virtue of the profound social and ideological associations of genres, hierarchies of genres are tied to social hierarchies" (1995:597). Italian, though rarely present in the text of poems or in the lines of plays, was always present nonetheless "beyond their boundaries," as Bakhtin would have it, as was the linguistic hierarchy that positioned Italian above Bergamasco. It was the language that surrounded these genres, the language in which so much of everyday life occurred. It was the language in which prestigious, "high" poetry was written, and the language in which Bergamasco poems were analyzed and praised. It was the language that introduced plays (as well as the occasional visiting researchers who participated in them), and the language in which they were reviewed. It was the language in which younger Bergamaschi asked older audience members to explain a particularly Bergamasco turn of phrase or joke, and the language in which poetry contests were adjudicated. It was, of course, a local heteroglossic language, an Italian with Bergamasco cadences, phrasings, and words mixed in. But even this mixed language contrasted with the pure Bergamasco that characterized these two genres, aiding to reinforce the local linguistic hierarchy.

Bakhtin and Medvedev observe that genre "takes a position between people organized in some way" (1985:131). The genres of poetry and theater positioned Bergamaschi vis-à-vis their two languages, and thus helped to create and reinforce the indexical order in which these languages were deployed. The purified Bergamasco of plays and poetry indexed a Bergamasco audience and context, reinforcing links between the dialect and this community of speakers, and between those outside of this circle and Italian. Further, the archaic Bergamasco words and phrases that peppered these genres indexed the older age of the audience, and anticipated the pleasure with which these forms would be met. This pleasure presupposed a positive affective stance towards the Bergamasco past but also a safe distance from it, as it stood in contrast to the present, when these forms were not commonly used. The thematic content of Bergamasco poetry and plays furthered this orientation towards the past, through consistently depicting the past itself. The past depicted was one in which the material complications of poverty, socioeconomic and political struggles, and personal hardship were indexed by the material culture present on the stage (the clogs, buckets, and mònega), or presented as obstacles which the characters overcome simply by hard work, honesty, and will. In other words, they overcome adversity by being themselves: Bergamaschi. But as is clear from Giorgio's story about the difficulties faced by the póer bortulì in Chapter 2, and the multiple examples of the difficulties mothers confronted if their children grew up speaking Bergamasco and not Italian discussed in Chapters 2 and 3, this model was hard to reconcile with the social realities that most Bergamaschi have faced.

Many of the tensions between a sentimentally valued Bergamasco and a powerfully prestigious Italian were exemplified in the love note that figures prominently in "La Zét D'Öna Ólta (De Dét in del Ritràcc)." My character sneakily delivers this note to the heroine from the hero, when he is forced to emigrate to France in order to find work. All of the talk surrounding the note is in Bergamasco. The note itself, however, which the heroine reads out to the audience – and will be read repeatedly by multiple characters as they find it and think it is for them – states "My love for you will never end" in Italian (*"Il mio amore per te non finirà mai"*). Except for the conversations set in modern times between the grandfather and his daughter and granddaughter, this is the only Italian in the play. It is also the only written material in the play.

How can a love letter, a most intimate genre, be written in Italian? Doesn't this contradict the very position of Bergamasco as the language of deeply felt sentiments and social proximity – of confidenza? On the face of it, an easy answer is that writing itself is strongly associated with Italian due to it being the language of education, bureaucracy, and nearly all written genres in Bergamo, in spite of the growth of poetry volumes printed in Bergamasco available in local bookstores and the Ducato's annual class to teach writing it. Bergamasco remained, in this representation as in so many other areas of life in Bergamo, a language for speaking. All of the discussion about the note and its possible meaning, author, and addressee takes place in Bergamasco.

A few further features of the performance of this letter, however, help to clarify the push and pull of various sociolinguistic currents. First, the note is read aloud a total of four times; every time the various characters stumble and stutter over it, pronouncing the words with strong Bergamasco accents. Reading at all, even in Italian, is something with which they are not entirely at ease.

Second, the Italian itself is markedly formal: "*Il mio amore per te non finirà mai*" is very poetic, but not a common or everyday way to say "I love you" in either Italian or Bergamasco, which would more commonly be "*Ti voglio bene*/**Mé te üle bé**" ("I care for you"; lit. "I wish you well") or "*Ti amo*/**Mé te ame**" ("I love you"). This more formal Italian phrase is not what a Bergamasco would whisper into a lover's ear. Third, it is also several times removed from its animator and author, the hero, passing from him to a messenger to the object of his affections, all via the written word. That these words are as alienable from their intended recipient as from their author is demonstrated repeatedly as the note is passed from character to character. Indeed, the note has no meaning until it is read aloud and then discussed in Bergamasco, and then the meaning shifts through each debate until finally the hero and heroine are reunited and come clean to everyone that the note is "really" about their love. At that point, the two lovers declare their love for one another in Bergamasco, and her parents finally relent and let them marry. The spoken Bergamasco declaration of love makes it real, not the indexically slippery Italian written note.

Contrast this with the ways in which Bergamasco and Italian are used and discussed during the framing scenes. In these, the grandfather teaches his granddaughter nursery rhymes, the names of household objects, and simple idioms in Bergamasco, although their talk about these things is in Italian. The conversations between the grandfather and his daughter are also in Italian, until the end when she relents and they recite together the nursery rhyme that the grandfather has been teaching the granddaughter. Bergamasco, in the form of these words, phrases, and little songs, is objectified in a way that parallels the Italian love letter, for their significance as artifacts and symbols of something else are open to reinterpretation by different speakers. The grandfather treasures them, the daughter scorns them, and the granddaughter finds them strange but appealing. Not until the daughter decides that her Bergamasco past can be safely embraced does the true meaning of these Bergamasco bits of language solidify: they are a bridge to the past that has made up the rest of the play, just as the Italian love letter is a bridge between the lovers that must be claimed in Bergamasco to assume its true meaning. Like the letter, the value of the Bergamasco words and phrases such as the nursery rhyme lies not in their being written down; rather, they must be remembered and spoken out loud.[17]

Conclusion

Enthusiasm for artistic forms and performances may or may not have been accompanied by support for other types of Bergamasco. Fans of Bergamasco poetry, or even poets, for example, may have portrayed themselves as a supporter of the dialect through their interest in poetry, but also claimed not to speak Bergamasco to their children or grandchildren. If they did speak it, they may not have expected these children to address them in Bergamasco in response. Also, they may or may not have been interested in other types of support for the dialect, such as changing education policy to allow the vernacular to be taught in schools, for instance. It seemed self-evident to most Bergamaschi, even those who support the vernacular, that Italian was the only language appropriate for education and its associated activities. Poetry and plays were one thing; education and successfully participating in the Italian public sphere in order to get a good job, for instance, were another. In this, the Bergamasco situation differs greatly from other minority language situations, such as those of Corsica (Jaffe 1999), Catalonia (Woolard 1989, 1994), and Morocco (Hoffman 2008), for instance, where having the minority language spoken in government institutions like schools is a priority for activists. As I will discuss in Chapter 6, most language activists in Bergamo have long resisted such explicit politicization of language for various reasons.

Bergamasco poetry recitations and play performances co-existed with dominant or "high" cultural norms, as language activists – until recently, exclusively members of the upper classes – shaped these activities to stand as symbols of Bergamasco culture in general. Bergamasco poetic and dramatic undertakings were most commonly classified as "local" and "popular" cultural performances, and valued as such. As local or "situational" events, linked to a particular place and culture, they were essentially precluded from being judged according to "universal" criteria of aesthetics or intellectual value that are applied to artistic performances of "high" art. Similar to colonial subjects who are often imagined by their colonizers as culturally situated rather than universal or abstracting speakers (Lemon 2002),[18] interests and events considered local in Bergamo, as across Italy, were consistently judged according to the criteria of "authenticity," and were not seen to be of wider, more universal

interest. Rather, dialectal events were considered enactments of the
culture of the masses – instances of folk art – and were usually
evaluated according to how accurately they reflected the norms,
values, and lifestyles of these groups, rather than for their abstract
aesthetic value. So, for example, most Bergamaschi I spoke to would
positively evaluate a poet's description of a childhood game he or
she played for accurately describing a local pastime that had fallen
into disuse, rather than in terms of how the poem itself was constructed. As there were formal expectations around poetry, however,
such features were probably also a factor in audience evaluations,
even if they were less often explicitly voiced.

In France, Bourdieu describes what he calls the "popular aesthetic" of working-class tastes for cultural production, as:

> based on the affirmation of the continuity between art and life,
> which implies the subordination of form to function. This is seen
> clearly in the case of the novel and *especially the theatre*, where the
> working-class audience refuses any sort of formal experimentation
> and all the effects which, by introducing a distance from the accepted
> conventions (as regards scenery, plots, etc.), tend to distance the
> spectator, preventing him from getting involved and fully identifying
> with the characters (1984:4, my emphasis).

The performance of Bergamasco plays and poetry worked to
create such links between producers and audiences. Laughter, sentimental longing, and nostalgia for the past helped to create a direct
connection between what was being depicted and the audience's
experience. Bergamasco poetry and plays have come to stand for
the dialect itself, which in turn indexed Bergamasco culture as a
whole. As one city administrator publicly observed at a poetry
contest sponsored by the Ducato: "*Il dialetto è la nostra parte più viva,
più intensa di noi stessi e dobbiamo difenderlo a tutti i costi, perché sono
le nostre radici*" ("The dialect is the most alive, most intense part of
us, of ourselves, and we must defend it at all costs, because it is our
roots"). Attempts to create distance between these productions and
those who participated in them were met with resistance for reasons
such as adhering to literary genres, following social traditions, and
utilizing scarce resources like actors' time.

At the same time, as the Bergamasco past was most often one of
peasants and poverty and the Italian present was filled with progress

and prosperity, Bergamasco poetry and plays brought into sharp focus a central conundrum for people interested in saving Bergamasco language and ways of living: is authenticity enough? For some activists, it was not, and they sought ways to boost the prestige of the Bergamasco dialect through its poetry. Attempts to give it prestige, however, were often resisted for creating the distance that Bourdieu describes between audience and performance. For most of those who participated in these genres, it was enough to feel close to the scenes depicted, perhaps have a laugh or two, experience a nostalgia for a time of closeness within the Bergamasco circle. Such affective attachments were what made these genres so pleasurable; efforts to substitute these pleasures for other, more rarefied, experiences are sometimes reviewed suspiciously and resisted, as was the case with the theater companies refusing to attend the Ducato's course on dialect theater.

In his poem about his feet, Paolo, who lived his whole life in the Città Alta, spoke not of restoration or preservation, but of continuity in place and movement within that place, while life itself is what changes as one grows old. Paolo's poetry shared his lived experiences with his audience through the assumption of shared knowledge – of Bergamasco phrases and words, of particular **contrade**, of the joys of fleet-footed youth and predictable but honorable pains that a life of hard work causes in old age. Paolo's poetry and his own experiences, in other words, provided a view of experiencing both the dialect and the streets of the Città Alta, which did not remove either to a safe, diminishing distance, but which used them as the material of everyday life. Connections between place, language, and time were thus made intimate and lived – not employed to "save" practices deemed in danger.

The next chapter considers Paolo's topic, the Città Alta, as another symbol of Bergamasco-ness. Bergamaschi looked to the Upper City as the symbolic heart of their city and province. Although there are a number of similarities between what made the vernacular and the Città Alta powerful symbols of Bergamaschità, ultimately their material forms created distinct possibilities for how Bergamaschi experienced them.

5

Modern *Campanilismo*:
The Value of Place

Traveling northeast to Bergamo by train or *autostrada* across the Po river valley from Milan, one is aware of a simultaneous inter-mixing of urban beauty and industrial ugliness, the ancient and the contemporary, material wealth and a poverty of *belle viste* (beautiful views). As the city draws closer, the traveler sees the seemingly unending procession of industrial and residential deve-lopment through which the train or the car is passing. What was once countryside between Milan and Bergamo has become an endless *peripheria* (periphery): Milan's suburbs run into the small towns slowly spreading across the plains of the province of Ber-gamo and melting imperceptibly into the periphery of the city of Bergamo and then the *Città Bassa* (Lower City). Slowly the *Città Alta*, or Upper City, appears in the distance, perched on a hill and ringed by its Venetian *Mura* (walls), the Orobian Alps mountain range rising in the background. The silhouette of its towers and domes brings to mind the Middle Ages and Renaissance, when cities needed walls in order to protect themselves and their riches from invasion.

Unlike hill towns in other parts of Italy, such as Tuscany or Umbria, which popular imagery tends to depict as perched atop picturesque hills ringed with vineyards or olive groves, the city of Bergamo is hemmed in by its own development. The myriad small firms and large industries which line the autostrada from Milan to Bergamo attest to a greater material wealth than can be found in

Figure 5.1   The Città Alta as seen from behind (photograph by author).

those more rural hill towns, although the view is certainly less charming. Likewise, in those more scenic spots, one seems invited to look at them and imagine only the past. In Bergamo, from the first glance onwards, one is forced to reconcile the admixture of past and present, old and new, antique and modern.

This impression strengthens when you enter the town and approach the Città Alta from the lower city. Advancing up the main thoroughfare, the Città Alta hangs like a jewel above you: chestnut trees and majestic marble *palazzi* (palaces)[1] rise above the light-colored Mura, and the grand marble *Porte* (gates) display the impressive lion that indicates this was once part of the *Serenissima*'s – Venice's – reign. The Città Alta appears timeless and preserved, a pristine icon of a glorious past. Walking through its cobblestoned streets (where traffic is extremely regulated), history seems to adorn every façade, as colorful frescoes, age-stained wooden beams, wrought-iron balconies, and empty blackened torch-holders suggest centuries of lived-in use. In the early 2000s, walking up the main thoroughfare, which contained a number of churches, fountains, small piazzas and a medieval tower or two, one passed numerous cafés, restaurants, bakeries selling pizza by the slice, ice cream shops, clothing boutiques, and other tourist-oriented shops, with a few stores dedicated to everyday conveniences (a grocery store, a butcher, a dairy store and bakery, greengrocers). The grand central piazza, the *Piazza Vecchia* (Old Square), dominates the center of the Città Alta, ringed by cafés, expensive restaurants, the *Biblioteca Civica* (the main public library), an entrance to several departments of the University of Bergamo, and the *Palazzo della Ragione* (literally, the Palace of Reason, an 11th-century building built over a portico, which was long the seat of government for the province and town), beyond which lay the *duomo* (main town cathedral). Numerous small streets radiate out from the Piazza Vecchia. Following one of them, you ducked under a portico, tripped down a small back alley and came upon a *lavatoio*, a large marble public laundry facility, situated in a small but picturesque piazza. The lavatoio's multiple slots for different users brought to the imagination women up to their elbows in suds, gossiping with their neighbors and sharing everyday tasks. The collective history of this specific place seems inscribed in the marble, the wrought iron, the cobblestones.

On weekends at the beginning of the millennium, the Piazza Vecchia and main street were packed with people strolling and socializing. There were groups of teenagers calling to one another, family groups from grandparents down to freshly scrubbed infants, and groups of friends of all ages, stopping when they ran into someone they knew, lingering in front of shop windows. A few of these groups were tourists, obvious with their guidebooks in hands, but most were Bergamaschi, come up from other parts of town or the province to enjoy their Città Alta for the afternoon or evening.

Public spaces were filled with various ways of speaking. Indeed, riding up in the *funicolare* (funicular tram) from the Città Bassa at midday on a weekday, you might have been surrounded by a group of older men, pensioners on their way to socialize at the *Circolino*, a social club and casual restaurant. There, they may have met friends, played cards or *bocce*, had a small glass of wine or two (a **calesì**, in Bergamasco), as well as a number of **grignade** (laughs). They were probably speaking in Bergamasco, while the college students who filled the Circolino's garden on a nice day, taking advantage of its cheap, good food, would have been chatting and discussing their classes in Italian. The groups of high school and middle school kids riding in the same funicular, busy texting on their cellphones and laughing and joking in Italian with one another, were heading home after school, or perhaps going with friends to grab a piece of pizza. Shopping along the main street, one would have heard a mix of Bergamasco and Italian at the greengrocer, butcher, and bakery, where certain customers spoke Italian, others Bergamasco, and those who waited on them answered accordingly. Customers and employees at the numerous clothing boutiques, fancy restaurants, and other businesses catering to non-residents were more likely to speak Italian than Bergamasco.

Dodging off the main street into the *Piazza del Mercato del Fieno* (Hay Market Square), chances were good that you would find a small group outside Paolo and Roberto's **butiga** (workshop, forge). While the clang of hammers working iron rang out, this group – neighbors passing by, customers, friends stopping in for a visit – would be exchanging stories, catching up on their lives, perhaps reminiscing about when they were young, usually in Bergamasco, though they may have occasionally switched to Italian to accommodate newcomers, like an American anthropologist.

Around the corner from the butiga was a neighborhood center that on Monday afternoons was occupied by a large group of women between the ages of 30 and 85 who got together to knit, embroider, cross-stitch, and crochet. They shared tips about yarn, needles, sewing patterns, and who had the best prices; one of the older women tutored novices. Their conversations wove together Bergamasco and Italian, depending on speaker (e.g. most of the younger women spoke predominantly Italian, while the older women spoke Bergamasco), and topic (e.g. talking about technical matters like thread size or pattern layouts was always done in Italian, while catching up on neighborhood news was more often in Bergamasco). Some speakers, like Sara and her mother who attended sporadically, did not speak Bergamasco at all; others, like Antonia, a retired schoolteacher and long-time resident who lived nearby, spoke more Bergamasco than Italian.

Across the Città Alta, then, patterns of language use varied. Down another small cobblestoned street near the butiga, one found twice-weekly sessions of free hairdressing and pedicures for the elderly at the *Centro Sociale* (Social Center), where conversation was almost always in Bergamasco. In several locations across the Città Alta, university classes were taught in Italian, as well as those in the elementary, middle, and high school. The small children who often surrounded the fountain in the center of the Piazza Vecchia nearly always spoke Italian, though their care-takers (parents, grandparents, or some combination thereof) may have spoken either or both Italian and Bergamasco. The Grand Civic Library that formed one end of the Piazza Vecchia would have been filled with whispers in Italian as patrons asked about collections and consulted amongst themselves; those who worked there, however, might have spoken either language when they passed each other in the halls or took a break together for lunch. A newspaper could be bought in Italian, while the latest defeat of Atalanta, the beleaguered local soccer team, would have been dissected and lamented in Bergamasco. Church services were in Italian; the language of the confessional, however, was often Bergamasco.

Within private spaces, there were similarly numerous patterns of language use across the Città Alta. The language spoken in private homes could have been Italian, Bergamasco or both, depending on where the residents were from, how long they and their families had lived there, and how educated they were – in other words, all the factors that shaped the heteroglossic use of language across the city and province. Families who had lived in the Città Alta the longest (generally, over several generations) were the most likely to speak more Bergamasco than Italian in the home; newcomers tended to speak more Italian.

Linguistically, the Città Alta was as mixed as the rest of Bergamo. Symbolically, however, it stood as the heart of *Bergamaschità* (Bergamasco-ness), whether as a distant silhouette glimpsed during a daily commute from below, as a destination for socializing on Saturday nights, or through its invocation in multiple poems. The vernacular, as we have seen, could index a range of meanings, both positive and negative. The Città Alta, however, primarily evoked a sense of what was best about Bergamo. Like the vernacular, there have been a number of efforts, past and present, to "save" the Città Alta in various ways and to various effects. And as with the dialect, attempts to save the Città Alta have been fraught with unintended consequences.

Campanilismo: Place-Making and Meaning-Making

In Italy, there is a widespread idea that where you live or are from equals who you are. This is the well-known Italian concept, *campanilismo*, which holds that everyone who lives within sight and sound of the same bell-tower (*campanile*) shares the same everyday characteristics and practices: they eat the same things, attend the same church (to which the campanile is attached), laugh at the same types of jokes, speak the same dialect, and generally share similar lifestyles. Campanilismo – which may in practice center on various symbolically potent localities, such as entire municipalities (it is sometimes called *municipalismo*), common lands, neighborhoods, or small rural settlements – equates spatial proximity with cultural community, indexed through language. While championed by some people as a form of local civic pride, campanilismo in its various forms has also been denounced as contributing to close-minded judgments about people from other places that prevent Italians from uniting as a truly "modern" nation-state (Duggan 2007; Galli della Loggia 1998; Galt 1991; Sciolla 1997; Tullio-Altan 1995). It is not just about shared characteristics and practices. It is also and essentially about shared attitudes, toward your own place and the place of others – in terms of social status (i.e. place in the social order) as well as in terms of geography. Whether positively or negatively viewed, attachments to localities – what Tak calls "local patriotism" (1990) – contribute to how Italians think about and categorize themselves ("we here are like this") and others ("those people from X are all alike").[2] For example, Heatherington argues that in Orgosolo, Sardinia, the common lands are the sociogeographic root: "The local social memory of interdependence with the Orgosolo commons is evoked, shared, reshaped and made real by everyday work and hospitality and by a superabundance of historical narratives contained in murals, old photographs, festival celebrations, Sardinian poetry, and even certain key works of anthropology and literature. The landscape itself is widely perceived by residents to be the ultimate visual text legitimizing local interpretations of history" (2005:149). For the people of Orgosolo, their commons stand as the very symbol of who they are, were, and want to be. This is due to symbolic practices such as storytelling and mural painting, but also the everyday practices through which people related to it, such as grazing animals or gathering firewood.

In the town and province of Bergamo, people attended to what Blu calls their "home places," where they lived and worked (1996). Whatever part of Bergamo they were from, Bergamaschi felt attached to the particularities of that place – its piazzas and pizza parlors, its streets and idioms (Grasseni 2000). At the same time, a lot of this sentiment was aimed at the Città Alta no matter where people grew up, as Bergamaschi across the town and province viewed the Città Alta as theirs in some way. This was expressed through poets' verses, in everyday conversation, in political debate about the community, in newspaper articles. It was reinforced by the common tendency to view the Città Alta as a desirable destination for a *passeggiata*, or social stroll. The Città Alta's distinctive silhouette, as seen on the opening page of this chapter, was ubiquitous, appearing on newspaper headings, local product labels, the *comune*'s (city administration) website, restaurant menus, and bus tickets, iconically extended to signify Bergamo as a whole.

As Basso has noted, "what people make of their places is closely connected to what they make of themselves as members of society and inhabitants of earth" (1996:7). By examining several illustrative examples of what the Città Alta meant to different people, we can profitably trace particular individuals' experiences and narratives to explore the use of the Città Alta as a material and symbolic resource in Bergamo at the beginning of the millennium. As Miriam Kahn argues, "places are complex constructions of social histories, personal and interpersonal experiences, and selective memory" (1996:167). Bergamaschi related to their places and their history in ways specific to them, rather than just as static dimensions of space and time.

It is essential not to consider these relationships as simply holdovers from some pre-modern, pre-national, pre-global past, in which people lived only locally. While many of Bergamaschi's sentiments draw on a particular past, they are not reducible to that past. Giddens has argued that with the advent of modernity, "time and space became 'empty' categories, specifically separated from one another as distinct dimensions of existence" (1994:xii).[3] I argue that Bergamaschi's relationship to their place is thoroughly modern, as the multifaceted, dense social, economic, and political networks that supported campanilismo in the past have given way to different ways of inhabiting and relating to places, affectively, symbolically, and practically. I maintain that it is precisely through understanding specific inscriptions of space and time that analysts can better understand how people, as Giddens puts it, live "in the world" today (1994:xiii). These connections between people, their places, and the histories that join them cannot be easily predicted, but rather require in-depth analysis of local ways of meaning-making and social practices that form the affective dimensions of this relationship. To say that Bergamaschi are connected to their place is to say little; to explain the nature of this bond and how it varies across individuals and has changed over time is to shed light on the complex ways in which places all over the world matter to those who live there.

In Bergamo, as in many places, language is one of the primary social practices involved in making places meaningful. However, language's role in the complex construction of the Città Alta as important was not necessarily obvious at first glance; the Città Alta is not the site where Bergamasco was most often spoken or where Bergamaschi said the best or most stretto version of the dialect was spoken (this is always to be found among the mountain peaks to the north of Bergamo). However, both the place and the language were potent, multiplex symbols of Bergamaschità – being Bergamasco. As such, both are caught up in the same crosscurrents of authenticity and prestige, tradition and modernity, the past and future. In practice, these apparent binaries may be recruited to support certain actions or positionings, or they may simply dissolve into what Kathleen Stewart has called "ordinary affects," the bustle of everyday life in both its public and intimate forms (2007).

Continuity of Place

Angela, who was in her early fifties and worked as a tailor out of her home, had lived in the Città Alta all her life, as did her parents, grandparents, and their predecessors as far back as she knew. Her two sisters lived in spacious apartments in the same palazzo they grew up in, although it was now a little different. When the three of them were growing up, there were about 20 families who lived in that building, each family packed into one or two rooms that faced the courtyard. Everyone's doors were always unlocked, because they trusted each other, but also because there was nothing to steal as they were all so poor. There were six outhouse stalls in the central courtyard, which everyone in the building shared. All the children – and there were a lot of them, as families were bigger and had lots of children back then[4] – played together. They played Bergamasco games, like **la sgaréla** (a local version of stickball), as well as tag, hide and seek, and games of their own devising. Nearly every palazzo in her *vicinie* (neighborhood) was like that, full to overflowing with families and kids, all poor. A few of the palazzi were actual palaces, owned by nobles or other rich people, who only occasionally lived there and whose courtyards were playgrounds for only their own children. There were numerous shops on Via Porta Dipinta, the main street near her home, like a *fruttivendolo* (produce stand), a *latteria* and *forno* (dairy and bakery, respectively), a barber, a hardware store, and of course the *osterie* or taverns where men gathered to play cards, drink a calesì, and socialize – all in Bergamasco, of course.

By the late 1990s and early 2000s when I lived there, Via Porta Dipinta was thoroughly changed. The shops that sold daily, mundane necessities had disappeared entirely. The latteria had become a shop selling pizza by the slice; after being shuttered for many years, the barber's shop had become first a jeweler's, and then an artist's ceramics shop. Indeed, these were the few commercial shops open at all in that area, and residents had to go either up – to the main shopping street in the Città Alta – or down – to one of the many supermarkets in the Città Bassa – to fulfill their shopping needs. There were a couple restaurants, but they were no longer the local watering holes that used to dot the Città Alta's landscape and provide socializing centers for its men. One was a *birreria* (beer hall) that loudly overflowed with youth from all over the city and province on weekend nights, eliciting numerous complaints from neighbors about the noise.

The street had changed in terms of inhabitants as well. As of the beginning of 2006, official statistics showed that the number of youth under the age of 19 who lived on Angela's street was 43, about as many as she described for just her building during her childhood in the 1950s (see also Angelini 1989 on this trend). The street was lined with exquisitely restored buildings, some with recently uncovered frescoes on their external and internal walls, inhabited by those who could afford the high costs of renting or owning there. In public, at least, Italian was the most common language used, although there were quite a few nights when I lay awake listening to the high-volume Bergamasco being shouted by drunken youth (mostly male) as they exited the birreria,[5] and it was relatively common to hear greetings and private conversations in Bergamasco between friends and acquaintances.

Along with a number of paintings, nearly all of which depict the Città Alta, Angela had a large black and white photograph hanging in her dining room from roughly 50 years ago. It showed her grandfather, standing in the Piazza del Mercato del Fieno and tending to a little stand. He is selling roasted chestnuts, a quintessential Bergamasco food (and a major staple in the Bergamasco diet in the past), and has a hand-lettered sign that announces "*bibite fresche!*" (cold drinks). A few years before, Angela's family had seen the photo in the newspaper, and her father recognized his father in it. None of them had ever seen it before and now regarded it as a family treasure, showing previously unknown details of a normal day in their grandfather's life. It also showed many of the changes that have affected the Piazza del Mercato del Fieno since the photo was taken: where the small post office was in the early 2000s there was an osteria, and while the piazza itself had become one of the few parking lots in the Città Alta, there is not a car in sight in the photo, just lots of pedestrians. This photograph, though initially unfamiliar, showed the Città Alta in which Angela and her sisters grew up, the Città Alta in which multiple generations of her family have grown up and lived, finding livelihoods as they could, part of the crowded masses who claimed it as their home.

Most of the people Angela grew up with in the Città Alta had moved away by the time I knew her, although occasionally she ran into someone on the main street – the **corsaröla**, as the locals called it in Bergamasco – and then they caught up. The old friends often said how much they missed living in the Città Alta, where shops, friends, family, and your whole social life could be right outside your door, within a short walk. Things were too expensive there for many people at that point, however, and according to Angela (and most statistics), the Città Alta was primarily populated by the wealthy, some Bergamasco, but also many Italians from elsewhere and foreigners. For instance, there was a German man who lived in Angela's building, in a beautifully restored apartment. He kept it for when he was in town on business, but stayed there rarely. Angela thought this was a bad thing, and that that apartment should have had a family in it, with children, who could be neighbors and part of the social life of the Città Alta. Angela remembered that when her kids were in elementary school in the 1970s, there were lots of children and they all played together; the mothers were friends, too. According to her youngest sister, whose children were much younger than hers and had been in elementary school more recently, it was not like that anymore – the mothers were aloof and snobbish and not part of the tight-knit social network that characterized Angela's experience in the Città Alta. She thought it was because these newcomers tended to be wealthy, and base their social lives elsewhere. Like the children of the elite when she was growing up, these children played in their own courtyards or spacious homes, socializing with other children from similar backgrounds. One can imagine that Italian was the only language allowed in these rarefied play-spaces.

Indeed, it was expensive for most people to live in the Città Alta. When I lived there in 1999–2000 (and several times afterwards) on the same street that Angela grew up on, locals were always shocked to hear how much I paid in rent (although it seemed inexpensive to me after having lived in Manhattan during graduate school). Some older families could still afford it, like Angela's, who bought their places before it got expensive, or those whose rent was based more on their social ties than the market price, or who qualified for the few *case popolare* (public housing) scattered around the Città Alta. But for most Bergamaschi, living in the Città Alta was a luxury they could not afford.

It was also not an easy place to live. There were not many shops for daily necessities, and it was much more convenient to go to one of the large "*ipermercati*" ("super-" or, literally, "hyper-markets") that dotted the edges of town to stock up on groceries once a week rather than shop everyday for what you needed immediately, as people used to do. Also, for Angela and most people I knew who lived in the Città Alta, driving was difficult, due to heavily restricted parking and narrow, often heavily trafficked roads in and out of the

Città Alta. Add to this the crowds that took over the Città Alta on the weekends and holidays, and living there was a luxury that many chose not to indulge in even if they could have afforded it. For instance, in 2000, a woman I knew from a dance group I participated in was trying to sell the apartment on the corsaröla that her mother had recently left to her. Livia, who had grown up in that apartment, had lived for years in the Città Bassa with her husband and son. "I have beautiful views of the Città Alta from here," she told me, "and that old apartment is dark and loud and needs a lot of work. Why live there when I can sell it for a good price and live more comfortably here in the Città Bassa?"

For Angela and her family, however, living in the Città Alta tied them to one another and to their shared past in ways they chose not to live without. Reflecting on the crowds in particular, Angela said that they were just one of the tradeoffs. For her, Sundays were a day to stay off the streets of the Città Alta, which were crowded with strollers and groups eating ice cream. "*La lasciamo a loro la domenica*" ("We leave it to them on Sundays"), she explained to me, about her decision to stay at home.

Like Paolo's poem from the last chapter, Angela's experience and recollections presented the Città Alta in terms of continuous lived experience. They recalled, either explicitly as Angela did or implicitly as Paolo's poem did, the poor past and compared it with the rich present, and found the latter problematic in various ways. They valued the strong social connections and communal way of life that characterized their past there, and recognized the poverty that underlay it. Only rarely did recollections like these include reflections on the ills of poverty, however: the high rates of infectious diseases from the poor hygiene conditions that accompanied so many people living so close together; the high infant mortality rates that resulted from these same conditions, as well as the lack of access to medical care experienced by most people (Ravanelli 1996) (see also Della Valentina 1984; Rumi et al. 1997); the widespread alcoholism that went along with men's socializing in the osterie; and the physical degradation of the place itself and its buildings and streets, making life lived there often squalid and difficult (Angelini 1989). Yesterday's ills could be recast as amusing, such as Angela's recollections of all the neighborhood children playing together; reduced to representations such as black and white photographs that allowed access to forgotten mundane details of everyday existence; or erased from memory altogether.

Some of the Città Alta's residents, however, made sure that I knew that it had not always been as beautiful and livable as I found it. Paolo, Roberto, Carla, Stefano, and others informed me that for decades starting at the end of the 19th century, the Città Alta was known by a less than flattering Bergamasco nickname: **La Sità di Tri P**: **Poarècc, Précc, e Pöta vècc** (which felicitously translates as "The City of the Three Ps: Poor people, Priests, and old Prostitutes"). Indeed, although the Città Alta had once been home to all sorts of people, since the end of the 19th century it had increasingly become filled with primarily poor people, living eight or ten to a room, with few or no public conveniences. Each of the 13 *vicinie* (neighborhoods) had their own church, run by several priests who held regularly attended daily masses and ran thriving *oratori* (oratories, which are youth and social centers) for their parishioners. And certain back streets were well-known for housing multiple bordellos, which were often attacked in newspaper editorials (Ravanelli 1996).[6]

Angela's image of her past in the Città Alta attested to the strong attachment of those who grew up there to this place and its particularities, and essentially claimed it as her own, through her life spent there, her family's ongoing multiple connections to it through living there, the density of her social networks that were anchored there, as well as the connections to that place imbued by past generations of relatives having lived there. As she explained to me, Angela and her sisters did everything together and always had; their children played together, they gathered often along with their father, a widower, who lived alone near her, and their families even vacationed together. The whole family spent a good deal of time together, and for much of it, they spoke Bergamasco. With the youngest sister and the children, they tended to speak Italian, as well, but a heteroglossic mix tended to characterize most of their interactions. Across the generations of her family, we can see the shift from all Bergamasco to Bergamasco and Italian that has characterized speaking practices all over Bergamo since the 1960s. It was easy to align Angela and her family's continuing commitment to the Città Alta with her claim that they still spoke predominantly Bergamasco as expressions of campanilismo, however; both display a positive orientation toward Bergamo and its symbolic heart, the Città Alta.

The contrast between past and present that emerged in Angela's recollections made the past seem – at least in certain ways – attractive, in ways that are similar to how Bergamasco was portrayed in the play discussed in Chapter 4; difficult but worth remembering and being proud of. Angela's recollections emphasized just how much and in which ways things have changed in the Città Alta, but did not linger on the process of this transition; things simply used to be one way, and now they are different. As Friedland and Boden note, the modern world is often "characterized by profound personal and collective historicity, where the present marks frequent breaks with the past" (1994:10). Angela may have explicitly portrayed her connections to the Città Alta as growing out of a continuity (her family has "always" lived there), but the contrast she depicts between a past of tradition and a present where only some people live as she does makes her thoroughly modern (Giddens 1979).

To get a sense of how this transformation occurred, let's turn to the experiences of people who were part of the transition, moving into the Città Alta in between Angela's childhood and the present. These newcomers were part of the mechanism of change, but they were also acute observers of it.

Experiencing and Embracing the Transition

When Stefano the architect decided to buy a building in the Città Alta in the early 1960s, he was going against the tide. Everyone who could was selling their property – often for very little money – and moving to the Città Bassa, opting for modern conveniences over disintegrating buildings in need of gutting. Many people who did not own property were leaving, too, some forced out when their landlords sold their building to someone like Stefano, others searching for similarly priced housing in the Lower City or, if they qualified, seeking to get into the many *case popolare* that were springing up all over the periphery of the Lower City. The people leaving sought new buildings with roomy apartments with electricity, running water, and modern appliances, close to public transportation and nearby parking. The Città Alta, City of the Three Ps, offered none of these conveniences. Statistics show that between 1951 and 1986 – by which time the Città Alta had become "*il quartiere più chic di Bergamo*" ("the most chic neighborhood of Bergamo") (Ravanelli 1996:356) – its population more than halved, dropping from 7,950 to 3,170 people (Angelini 1989), where it roughly remained in the late 1990s.

Stefano's friends and relatives were shocked when they heard he had decided to move his architectural studio into his newly purchased building in the Città Alta once it had been restored. No one will come to see you, they said, you will lose clients. But they were even more scandalized when he announced that he was going to move his family into the rest of the building. Why would you do that to your children, everyone, including his close relatives, wanted to know. What types of lives will they lead in that old, dark and dirty place, with its narrow streets and poverty all around? To these critics, Stefano seemed to be moving his family to live within the strictest, narrowest circle of Bergamasco society.

But Stefano's children were almost grown, and he saw the beauty of the place, or at least its potential for beauty. He appreciated the narrow, cobblestoned streets, the ancient façades of the buildings, the uncovered frescoes hidden beneath layers of whitewash in many of the old palazzi that had been split into one- or two-room apartments, crammed with numerous family members. As an architect, from a family long committed to the well-being of the Città Alta, Stefano saw what it might become and he wanted to be part of the transition, no matter how difficult living there was at first. Being from an elite family, Stefano spoke both Bergamasco and Italian, easing his interactions with various types of Città Alta's residents. And although Stefano described to me how beautiful and refined the Bergamasco his mother spoke had been, his children grew up speaking little of it. They were in little danger of becoming trapped in this *rione* (neighborhood).

The situation was not much changed by the time Tullia and Davide had moved there a decade later. Newlyweds, Davide worked in his father's business and Tullia taught school; living in the Città Alta was cheap for them, and Tullia, who grew up in Perugia in central Italy and studied history and literature, was captivated by the aesthetics of the place, as well as the idea of it. She loved the old buildings, the sense of history that came from simply walking across a piazza and looking at the medieval, Renaissance and Baroque *palazzi*, as well as the close-knit community of their neighborhood that slowly warmed to them. After their daughter, Marina, was born a few years later, she became more a part of that community, going to school with neighborhood kids.

But, like Stefano, they were never totally integrated into the Città Alta's social worlds in the same way that Angela and her family were, because of their multiple ties elsewhere, as well as their high social class position relative to many of the Città Alta's residents. Davide and Tullia worked outside of the Città Alta, and although Tullia later brought her mother from Perugia to live nearby in the Città Alta when her health started to fail, the rest of their families lived elsewhere, Tullia's in Umbria and abroad, Davide's in the Città Bassa and the small town in the mountains from which his family originated. Their friends were young professionals like themselves, and lived all over, some in the Città Alta, but many in other neighborhoods. Tullia described to me how their daughter did not really socialize with her schoolmates. For instance, although one of her old classmates from elementary and middle school lived next door, the two families were different in terms of professions and educational levels. How could they have spent time together socially when they came from such different class backgrounds? "*Se le famiglie non si frequentano, non possono frequentare i figli*" ("If the families don't socialize, it's not possible for the kids either"), as Tullia put it. She hoped that things would change when Marina went to high school at the *liceo classico* (classical high school, the highest ranked type of Italian high school), which is in the Città Alta just a few minutes' walk away. But she was literally the only resident of the Città Alta in her class; all the other students came from elsewhere, so once again Marina was socially isolated. The irony, according to Tullia, was that just a few years behind her, things started to change. More well-off families moved to the neighborhood and started sending their kids to school there, forming a peer group.

Over the years since they moved in, Davide's business had prospered and they renovated the apartment they owned in Via Porta Dipinta near Angela's childhood residence into a luxurious living space with modern conveniences. In the process, they uncovered and reclaimed many of the grand features of their space, such as frescoes on the walls and ceilings in many rooms. They also slowly expanded it and added enough outdoor space to build a large garden, terrace, and courtyard. Their living space was far from the cramped and challenging conditions that characterized Angela's childhood home and most of the Città Alta's habitations until recently. Like Stefano, they enjoyed the social aspects of the Città Alta, like knowing their neighbors and having a history in this neighborhood. But although they developed social ties and friendships through daily interactions with other residents, and solidified their connections to the place itself by buying a place there as soon as they could afford it, they remained slightly apart from it. Stefano, too, when I met him in 2000, was both a part of the Città Alta, but connected to other worlds beyond it. An old friend of Paolo's, he was present at the mountain house the day that Paolo recited **I Mé Pé**. One of the stories he told that day was about a project he had completed in the United Arab Emirates, far from where Paolo and Carla, or other long-time Città Alta residents like Angela, had ever ventured.

Davide, Tullia and Marina's language patterns are an illustrative parallel to their position in the Città Alta. The card game described at the beginning of Chapter 2 outlines how Italian was the most common language used in their home, although Davide used Bergamasco as well. In contrast, all members of the family of Marina's classmate, whose terrace adjoined Davide and Tullia's, could often be heard speaking Bergamasco. Differences in class positions as well as family histories (including contrasts in parents' and children's educational paths) shaped these linguistic differences, and the social networks enabled by them. Similarly, Stefano could and did speak Bergamasco when he chose; his children, in their forties and fifties when I met them, claimed to understand though not speak it. He said that his grandchildren (like Marina) spoke exclusively Italian.

Like many of their neighbors, they all dreaded the noisy weekend crowds, who clogged their streets. Stefano in particular worried that the Città Alta was being turned into a museum, a place for people to visit and admire, but not to live in, as it lost its services and daily-use shops to expensive clothing boutiques and pizza take-out places (the only laundry had closed by 2005, and there were only two greengrocers in 2007). Stefano, Tullia, and Davide were part of a change, arriving at its very beginning. They chose to live in the Città Alta, unlike most of their neighbors when they arrived, and their presence, educational choices and possibilities, money, and linguistic habits were part of what led to the change from the Città Alta being a place of poverty to be escaped from for most people to being an expensive, exclusive enclave. There were, however, other forces at work as well.

From Rich to Poor to Rich Again: The Changing Faces of the Città Alta

Starting in the middle of the 19th century, Bergamo's citizens began to realize that the Città Alta needed help.[7] By the 1920s, the Città Alta had become *"tagliata fuori della vivacità delle nuove dinamiche urbane"* ("cut out of the vivacity of the new urban dynamics") of the times, while the lower city was growing at a huge rate (Irace 1997:181). Once the bustling, vital heart of commerce, government, cultural production, and residence of the city, the Upper City had slid into physical decline and economic neglect. The seats of provincial and city government moved to the Lower City at the end of the 19th century, followed quickly by banks and other essential businesses (Capellini 1989). A new grand theater, the *Teatro Donizetti*, opened around the same time in the Lower City, leaving the Città Alta's historic *Teatro Sociale* as a second-class venue for the city's performing arts. The rich and burgeoning middle classes followed suit, building new, modern houses in the *sobborghi* (surrounding neighborhoods) of the Lower City.

This was when the Città Alta became known as La Sità di Tri P. The city's leaders saw the physical degradation and poor public hygiene of the Città Alta as central to its problems. The Città Alta's narrow, sewer-clogged streets, poor ventilation, and over-crowding had led to several cholera outbreaks in the late 19th century, and although one project to *risanare* (renovate, but literally "resanitize") the Città Alta had been undertaken in the same period with funding from the federal government, conditions remained largely unchanged (Angelini 1989; Belotti 1989). More drastic measures were needed if the oldest, most historic, and scenic area of the city was not to be lost altogether to neglect and degradation.

In the mid-1920s, the *comune* of Bergamo sponsored a competition for plans to rehabilitate the Città Alta. The plan submitted by a Roman architect named Chitò was favored by the administration's Fascist leaders, but met with widespread public protest. An example of this protest is shown in Figure 5.2, which appeared on the front page of Giopì in March 1924.

Figure 5.2   The Old Lady Città Alta and her poem. Front page of Giopì, March 1924.

It is a striking image of the Città Alta as a decrepit, naked, old woman, ensconced within her walls among the distinctive palazzi that compose her silhouette. She is kicking away the Roman architect Chitò, scattering his plans for the *"Risanimento Città Alta."* He is clutching a butcher's knife, the instrument of the central feature of his plan: to cut a wide swath through the middle of the Città Alta for a grand boulevard and a tram, knocking down a number of historic buildings and totally reconfiguring the Città Alta in the process. Another of the pages being scattered says *"Sventramento,"* which means both "demolition" and "disembowelment," referring to this aspect of the plan. **Ol Bechèr** (the butcher), as the architect was popularly referred to, is nattily dressed, from his top hat to his fashionable ankle-boots, contrasting sharply with the Città Alta's gap-toothed grimace and naked belly, breasts, and legs. She may be in need of a makeover and new vestments, but this outsider with such little respect for her own vitality is not the one to supply them.

Above this ink drawing is a poem, entitled *Parla la Città del Silentium* (The City of Silence Speaks). Written by the first Duke of the Ducato di Piazza Pontida and signed with his poetic nickname **Alégher** (Happy), this poem – written in Bergamasco, with a few Italian phrases – ventriloquizes the Città Alta and her disdain for Chitò and his risanimento plan. Referring to him as **ol Bechèr**, she calls herself "**ü vere reliquare**" ("a true reliquary," or container of sacred and ancient objects) and "**la grand Sità/d'arte e di coltüre**" ("the grand City/of art and culture"), which she says is evidenced in "**ogne finestra e porta**" ("every window and door"). She also recounts her resources for booting this butcher down from her walls: the many talented people she can call on the defend herself, the "**fiöi** *degli antenati*" ("children of the ancestors"), who are "**miga di salam**" ("not salamis" – i.e. not dumb or easily taken advantage of). She may appear old and decrepit, but she is powerful and knows where her strengths lie: in her grand past as shown in her neglected but still culturally valuable material appearance and in many Bergamaschi's desire to defend her against the disrespectful and potentially ruinous plans of outsiders.

This image and poem are a multifaceted depiction of campanilismo, in which a place literally speaks about what makes it distinctive and special in its native language. Many of the features that this

Old Lady Città Alta asserts make her unique are those which have long shaped debate about her worth: the value of her material composition as aesthetically valuable as well as essentially linked to Bergamo's history. Of course she speaks Bergamasco; then, as now, the symbolic links between place, local language, and local culture were immediately available for mobilization in support of local interests. At the same time, the use of Bergamasco here helps to forge the indexical link between Bergamasco and poverty, physical decrepitude, and decay. The Old Woman speaking Bergamasco is pinned within her own walls and needs saving, by her residents, by her speakers. Her eloquence speaks not of worldly sophistication and beauty, but of historical value and cultural authenticity. It is easy to imagine those who populate her speak similarly and are in need of similar types of (linguistic and material) aid and intervention. It is also telling that the form of this speech is a poem, as I have argued that poetry is regarded as a primary means for saving Bergamasco.[8]

This and other, perhaps less pointed, protests proved effective, and Luigi Angelini, popular local architect, public figure, and member of the Ducato (as well as father of Stefano), who most locals regarded as the best suited to undertake the project, was eventually put in charge. Unlike Chitò's controversial plan, which sought to change the face of the Città Alta radically, Angelini's was premised on improving upon what was already there. His plan for the *"conservazione al massimo grado del carattere ambientale di Città Alta"* ("conservation to the greatest degree the ambient character of the Città Alta") (Ravanelli 1996:291), called for destroying a few of the most decrepit buildings in order to open up some especially small, crowded streets, allowing for better light and ventilation for the surrounding buildings. He proposed improving hygienic conditions through building better sewers and public laundry facilities for residents, and adding electricity and indoor plumbing to many residences that had none. Clearing a piazza to build the lavatoio described at the beginning of this chapter was among the first parts of this project undertaken in the 1930s; later stages took several more decades to complete. Stefano later joined his father's efforts to renovate the Città Alta while preserving what they saw as its essential character (Forlani 1998). These efforts continued, in various forms, through the 1970s.

Much of this work required moving working-class families into new housing in the periphery of Bergamo while their buildings were either demolished or restructured. Generally, they were promised the chance to move back to the Città Alta once the renovations were complete. Renovations often took years, however, and members of extended families and social networks were often split apart in the initial moves and put down roots in new neighborhoods. Not all were ultimately given the opportunity to move back; many who were declined, seeing little point in uprooting themselves once again to go back to neighborhoods that would lack the same social milieu that had characterized them previously. The difficulties of accessing the Città Alta also influenced such decisions, as people weighed the conveniences of living below, on wide, modern streets, near public transportation and ample parking, with the difficulties of navigating the still-close spaces and always scarce parking up above, and opted to stay where they were. Those who did return were often relocated to different *vicinie* than they had lived in previously, making re-establishing social networks more of a challenge than it might have been otherwise.

Other changes occurred in the Città Alta, all with the aim of improving it. Under the auspices of Pope John XXIII (Bergamasco by origin), a large new seminary complex was built in the Città Alta in the 1960s. Traffic, which until the mid-1970s was virtually unregulated in Bergamo, became increasingly officially limited. The University of Bergamo was founded in 1968, and its main headquarters and most of its *facoltà* (departments) were located in the Città Alta. In the early 1970s, the jail that had been located in the Città Alta since the time of Napoleon was closed, after a mass prisoner revolt rendered most of the jail uninhabitable; a new jail was opened on the periphery on the Lower City, and the building became the Circolino social club.

Stefano, Davide and Tullia were the vanguard of the change that set in more vigorously by the early 1980s. As decades of renovation of individual buildings and the infrastructure of the Città Alta as a whole drew to a close, the Città Alta began to be seen as desirable and attract upscale residents. This corresponded with a generally high level of prosperity that had been achieved in Bergamo, which was described as the richest city in Italy in 1990.[9] People from the growing upper and upper middle classes from Bergamo and beyond began to buy up buildings and apartments, drawn by the picturesque streets, the unmatchable views of the Lombardian plains stretching out below the Città Alta, and the feeling of exclusivity offered by the limited traffic and quiet, otherworldly, other-timely air of the Città Alta. Bergamo is a relatively short commute to the industrial center of Milan and its suburbs (under an hour, if traffic permits), and it became a place for the privileged to live in peace and quiet, and still commute to work on a daily basis.[10]

By the 1990s, the Città Alta had also become a tourist destination. By then, many of public monuments in the Città Alta had been restored, like the *Rocca*, a Medieval fort at the Città Alta's highest point, and the *Campanone*, its tallest bell-tower, as well as various fountains and churches. The number of visitors to the city's museums and monuments rose dramatically during the 1990s. At the same time, university students became a strong presence in the Città Alta.[11] Most commuted to school during the day from the Città Bassa or other parts of the province, and their cars filled public parking lots and overflowed into zones set aside for residents. Restaurants and cafés catered to their demands.

The very restorations that saved the Città Alta physically appeared to have contributed to the downfall of the social fabric that once bound its residents together. Even as their quality of life improved in terms of public hygiene and living conditions, rising rent and real estate prices, strict parking and traffic regulations, coupled with the increasing loss of shops that provided daily necessities made it difficult for many families who had lived in the Città Alta for generations. Local newspapers featured numerous stories about parking in particular, reporting how often non-residents violated parking restrictions, or the ongoing political discussions about the need for a public parking garage. Frequent letters to the editors from Città Alta residents complained about these same problems, as well as what they depicted as a general tendency for the city's administration to ignore the particular needs of the Upper City.[12] In 2000, the *Associazione per Città Alta e i Colli* (Association for Città Alta and the Hills [the area immediately behind the Città Alta, long considered part of it]) along with the Bergamo chapter of *ItaliaNostra* (Our Italy), an environmental group, sponsored a photography and video exhibit entitled "*Orrori ed Errori di Città Alta*" ("Horrors and Errors of Città Alta"). This exhibit, according to a flyer, sought to show images of *"l'attuale situazione della realtà urbanistica e ambientale di Città Alta e dei Colli"* ("the current situation of the urban and environmental conditions of Città Alta and the Hills"). The show included photos of trash-strewn corners, graffitied walls, and illegally parked cars, and was supposed to help viewers "learn" about the Città Alta's problems so that Bergamo as a community could address them.

Concerns about the quality of life of the Città Alta's residents have been constant over the past century in Bergamo, though their substance has shifted as the Città Alta has gone from being a place where all kinds of people lived to being a place where only poor people lived to, most recently, being a place where predominantly only the wealthy could afford to live. Social networks like Angela's and Paolo's, grounded in families who have been in the Città Alta for generations, persevered, although they were a lot scarcer than they once were. Newcomers – whether or not they sought to integrate themselves socially to some degree, as Stefano, Davide, and Tullia have done – were the more public face of the Città Alta these days. Their concerns about parking and trash seemed relatively trivial compared with the public hygiene issues that used to characterize the Città Alta.

Symbolic *Campanilismo* and the Modern 3 Ps: *Pizze, Passegiate, Panorame*

Sara, Federico, and, later, their infant son lived in an apartment in the Lower City with a spectacular view of the Città Alta from their terrace. Although Sara and Federico both worked in the Lower City – he as an engineer, she as a teacher – and their everyday lives did not take them to the Città Alta, they spent time there regularly. Federico had an uncle who lived there and had a woodworking shop near Davide and Tullia's apartment, and they also had a few friends living there, but mostly they went up to the Città Alta to walk around and enjoy the view and the atmosphere. Much of their leisure time involved driving the short distance to park just below the Città Alta and then ascending to walk up the corsaröla or around the wall or sometimes both. Sara and Federico's use of the

Città Alta was typical of most Bergamaschi. They could not afford to live there, nor did they express a desire to, using it instead as a site of recreation and enjoyment.

Dalia, a classmate in the Ducato's Bergamasco writing course, lived just outside of the city in the Val Brembana, but spent most of her time in town where she worked. In her mid-thirties, and engaged to a fellow Bergamasco, she could not imagine ever living anywhere but Bergamo. She observed in a conversation with me that Bergamaschi, like most Italians, were "*mammoni*" (adults extremely connected to their mothers). She used this term to illustrate Bergamaschi's attachment to place: proud of it beyond reason and unceasingly loyal to it. She said that when she came home from being away, she had only to see the Città Alta to feel at home, content, calmed: "*Quando torno da un viaggio, non so, anche da Milano, quando vedo Città Alta lì su, mela sento fiera, e lo so che sono a casa*" ("When I return home from a trip, I don't know, even from Milan, when I look up and see Città Alta up there, I feel proud of it and know that I am home").

On a recent trip to Bergamo in 2007, I ran into Ella, one of my transcription consultants, and her fidanzato, Alessandro (also Bergamasco), while walking in the Città Alta in the evening. Scott and I had just arrived in Bergamo with our new baby, and were staying in the apartment in Via Porta Dipinta where we had lived previously. We immediately set out on a passeggiata – a stroll up the familiar streets to see what had changed, with the hope of running into friends. We met Ella and Alessandro in the middle of an intersection crowded with pedestrians, and after exchanging greetings continued with them up the thoroughfare. Ella said that they had just returned from a weekend away, and realized that they missed the Città Alta, as they had not been up in weeks. Since she finished her university degree in *Lingue* (Languages) the year before, she had fewer occasions to go to the Città Alta. From their home in a small town nearby on the plains outside of Bergamo, they had jumped on his motorcycle and sped up, knowing that parking would be easier than if they drove. We ate gelato as we strolled and caught up.

In June 2000, Bergamo was the cover story in the travel magazine, *TuttoTurismo*. The article was written by Franco Brevini, professor of the sociology of literature at the University of Bergamo, and struck a personal tone. In it, Brevini mentioned that he is half

Bergamasco, and wove together his daily experiences in the Città
Alta (seeing the Città Alta emerge from the seasonal fog as he drives
in from Milan, parking his car, getting his morning coffee, doing
some research in the library) and numerous conversations he had
with locals, such as the mayor, the heads of the university and Civic
Library, a singer-songwriter who writes in Bergamasco, and a local
art expert and amateur historian. His theme is that Bergamo is a
good place to live (and, for his readers, a good place to visit), but
as the article talked exclusively about the Città Alta, the effect is
one of bolstering the divide between the beauties and richness of
the old Upper City and the brisk modernity and focus on work
that characterizes the rest of Bergamo. The only modern aspects of
the Città Alta seemed to be its high rents (which he compares to
those in central Milan) and the university, which at the time was
quickly expanding. Alberto Castoldi, the director of the university
is quoted saying, "*Ma oggi una parte del futuro la stiamo prepariando
prioprio quassù*" ("But today, we are preparing a part of the future
up here") while discussing the university's expansion in the Città
Alta to seven thousand students by 2000.

Brevini sprinkled the article with Bergamasco words and phrases,
some of which were simply descriptive, such as when he described
the "*doppio sogno*" ("double dream") of Bergamo in the following
terms: "*Quello* **de sura**, *cristalizzato nel suo splendore da secoli. Quello*
de sóta, *animato dall'opera religione del* **laurà**" ("That **of above**,
crystallized in its centuries-old splendor. That **of below**, animated
by the religion of **work**"). If outsiders knew any words of Bergamasco beside **pòta**, it was often these two descriptors, **de sura**
(upper) and **de sóta** (lower), as they applied to the Upper and
Lower Cities, respectively. These instances added local color to his
descriptions, and indexed the particularities of Bergamo through
using terms in Bergamasco that would probably have been under-
standable to the outsider. In addition, having the word for "work"
in Bergamasco indexed and thus reminded the reader of the well-
known Bergamasco stereotype of the rough, hard-worker. The form
of these words, which were set apart from the rest of the Italian
text by being in italics, indicated to the reader that something
particularly local was being referred to, even if they could not
understand the meaning of the words indexing campanilistic associations between language, place, and a distinctive social group.

Brevini also used Bergamasco (with Italian translations) when quoting overheard conversations in the Città Alta. The authorities he spoke to all used Italian, but locals of all ages and genders on the streets of the Città Alta, at the Circolino social club, and at the parking garage all spoke in Bergamasco, again set apart from the rest of his text in italics. This portrayal of the use of Bergamasco by its residents helped to create an image of the Città Alta as a place apart – apart from the rest of Italy and Bergamo, where they spoke Italian; perhaps apart from modern times, as he stressed the splendors of the past that characterize the Città Alta (*"Su il passato, giù il presente e il futuro"*/"Up top, the past; down below, the present and future" (Brevini 2000:93)). These Bergamasco excerpts, many of which were instances of overheard local gossip (such as three young women recounting what they said to a young man who had been rude to them), reinforce the image of the Città Alta as an insular place, whose residents have their own local concerns. This contrasts notably with the sophisticated Italian used, for instance, by the director of the library and the editor of *L'Eco di Bergamo*, the most widely read local daily newspaper.

Brevini's portrayal of the Città Alta as crystallized in its centuries-old splendor and simply waiting for tourists seeking cultural adventures was not unique. Numerous guides to the city describe it in similar terms, and, in addition to the frequent letters to the editors in local newspapers complaining about the state of the Città Alta, letters and op-ed pieces dwelling on how precious it was were also common. These generally focused on its visual appeal, like the letter addressed to readers of *L'Eco di Bergamo* under a large photograph of the Città Alta lit up at night. The caption under the photo, a quote taken from the letter, exalted the readers to "*Fermatevi un istante davanti a Città Alta illuminata*" ("Stop for a moment before the illuminated Città Alta") (February 2, 2000). It urged its readers to forget about everything else (such as work, politics, their rush home from work, friends, and other everyday concerns) and "*sentiti preso dalla magia dei colori*" ("feel taken by the magic of the colors") of "*lo spettacolo*" ("the spectacle") of the Città Alta. Similarly, a feature that appeared in the other daily newspaper, the *Giornale di Bergamo*, was entitled "*Città Alta visione di sogno*" ("Città Alta vision of a dream"), and traced the various ways that the Città Alta had appeared in the author's dreams, sometimes hidden by the seasonal mists that often cover the town, sometimes bathed in bright sunlight, but always like *"un quadro"* ("a picture") that *"si ripresenta nello splendore risaputo della sua bellezza"* ("represents itself in the once more realized splendor of its beauty") (June 13, 2000). These newspaper pieces, like the magazine article by Brevini, presented the Città Alta as beautiful and otherworldly, to be appreciated for its visual appeal. The Città Alta was set apart from the viewers' everyday lives, to be enjoyed and consumed like art; it was not a site of everyday life, but something to be gazed upon from afar and experienced as a place apart from the quotidian.

The newspaper pieces quoted above extolled the view of the Città Alta from below, implicitly placing their readers in a position to enjoy the view but not interact with the place. They shared this tendency with much of the poetry in Bergamasco about the Città Alta, by, as we have seen, playing a central role in connecting Bergamaschi with their shared histories and values. Indeed, many poems also stressed the importance of place.[13] Most volumes of poetry had at least one poem that meditated on the poet's hometown, familial home, or other biographically important locale. The Città Alta also appeared repeatedly in poetry, where it was praised for its physical beauty and its rich past. For instance, Rita Rossi described it as **"ü quàder/süspìs in cél"** ("a painting/ suspended in the sky"), and Abele Ruggeri referred to all **"che 'l tò passàt a l'dìs e l'val!"** ("that your [Città Alta's] past says and is worth!"). Ruggeri's poem, entitled simply **Bèrghem de Sura** (Città Alta), also referred to the Città Alta as being **"sura ü pedestàl"** ("on a pedestal"), imagery that sets the Città Alta apart as an admired jewel or piece of art.[14] This type of praise for the Città Alta helped to construct a particular indexical ground, where the Città Alta, the most treasured of Bergamasco locales, was a beautiful sight, to be admired from afar. The use of Bergamasco as the language of these poems almost redundantly emphasized the local values being lauded. Campanilismo's links between place, sociocultural identity, and language, so intimately conceived and lived, are thus transformed into attachments to a place that needed only to be viewed and visited, not inhabited. That poems about the Città Alta were in Bergamasco while op-ed and letters to the editor in newspapers were in Italian is telling, delineating once again the symbolic distribution of these two languages across spheres of use.

This was markedly different than how the Città Alta was depicted in Paolo's **I Mé Pé**, where the Città Alta was a lived-in place, with **contrade** that were remembered for what one did in them, such that names themselves were uncalled for. Similarly, Paolo's **Cansù a Sità Ólta** (Song to Città Alta), while it did celebrate the Città Alta's art and physical beauty, also stressed its value as a lived place:

Example 5.1

**M' gh'à piassér de laurà
Mangià, bìv, e pò cantà
Che 'n del mónd, amò öna ólta,
L'è grand bèla, Sità Ólta.**

We have the pleasure to work
To eat, to drink, and then to sing
That in this world, one more time,
It is so beautiful, Città Alta.

Stressing quotidian experiences like work and eating and drinking, the poem also praised the "**Cà de prède, bune e 'ndace**" ("Houses of stone, good and straight") and other material aspects of the place as features of a lived-in landscape. Like Ruggeri's poem that stressed the value of the Città Alta's history, Paolo's poem asserted that it was kept together for centuries by "**nòss vècc/ Per lassàgala ai nòscc is-cècc**" ("our elders/To leave it to our children"). However, this Città Alta was not just a pretty "picture": it was "**bèla e nòsta**" ("beautiful *and* ours," my emphasis).

Experiencing Place

Campanilismo was multifaceted in Bergamo in the early 2000s, for it was not just a straightforward type of "local patriotism" but rather involved different people drawing on a range of symbolic and material resources to make sense of themselves in a here-and-now. As Thomas Gieryn asserts, places are doubly constructed: physically built as well as symbolically and narratively assembled, felt, and perceived. He observes: "place is, at once, the buildings, streets, monuments, and open spaces assembled at a certain geographic spot and actors' interpretations, representations, and identifications" (2000:466–467). Basso's work with the Western Apache demonstrates how the moral and social values embroidered across the sparse Southwestern landscape that the Apache call home interact with people's everyday lives and stories. He states, "as places animate the ideas and feelings of persons who attend to them, these same ideas and feelings animate the places on which attention has been bestowed" (1996: 55) (see also Basso 1999). By setting up this dialectic between place and the people's experiences – both within it and related to it – as the meaning of places, Basso's work pushes us to think of place as more than the setting, backdrop, or "given" environment within which social action is played out. Nor does he locate places' meanings as reductively connected to something simple called "history." Rather, social practices, especially practices such as storytelling and other types of "rememberings," link people and their places. Place is both symbolic and dynamic, as storytelling, for instance, may use places to illustrate a moral or narrative point, and the emplacement of events in certain locales informs how they are interpreted. Basso's work, then, illustrates the central role that can be played by language in the dynamic relationships between people and places.

In Bergamo, the myriad relationships between language and place were mediated by the complex concept of campanilismo, the modern form of which was not a simplified equation of residence, history, and identity, such that a clear boundary demarcates one small community from the next. The "narrow, restricted circle" that some Bergamaschi described involved geography, class, shared sociality, and language.[15] Likewise, modern campanilismo involved the complicated relationships Bergamaschi had with particular localities, relationships that helped define the community and its values. There are few factors that were seen to unite Bergamaschi in the early 2000s; they were no longer understood as eating the same things, laughing at the same jokes, or speaking the same way, although certain foods, types of jokes, and ways of speaking were held up as locally important. A positive orientation towards the Città Alta, however, was one thing that was shared.

The Città Alta and Bergamasco intersected in being symbols of an ideal, as elements in what made Bergamaschi distinct from even their closest neighbors. Campanilismo brings together versions of history, place, and language as components of this ideal: history as individually and locally narrated accounts of "what happened here," place as the context for these happenings, language as the indexical shorthand for these happenings, as well as the means for their expression. And just as the ways in which Bergamasco and Italian were used in Bergamo were different from – though connected to – idealized notions of language, so too were there differences between how the Città Alta was understood and how it was lived, joined by the belief that the Città Alta was a precious place, to be treasured.

Mock has observed that "some urban spaces can serve to symbolize a populace's identity and goals," even if no one resides there, as with the Japanese castle he discusses (1993:63). The fact that only a fraction of Bergamaschi lived in the Città Alta did not alter its standing as the symbolic heart of Bergamo. Nonetheless, there were a number of different ways to experience the meaning of the Città Alta. Some people felt acutely attached to the Città Alta because of its beauty and enjoyed weekend strolls through its streets or around its walls, although they did not live there. For them, it acted as a touchstone to Bergamasco culture, as well as a site of leisure time activities. Others, who grew up and continued to live there, felt deeply the social connections that characterized their everyday lives there, and, though they may have prized its beauty as well, the Città Alta signified a continuity of life, community, and shared values. Recognizing what had changed there was an essential part of their orientations towards their place, but did not lessen their attachments to it.

Conclusions: Worrying About the Città Alta

The fate and meaning of the Città Alta have been changing over the past century as its physical state has been transformed from one where everyone lived, to a space of poverty and degradation, to – most recently – an expensive, exclusive enclave and rarified sight from afar. Bergamaschi have played diverse roles in these shifts, transforming not just material, but also symbolic spaces in the process. Indeed, as Tilley notes, "spaces, as social productions, are always centered in relation to human agency and are amenable to reproduction or change because their constitution takes place as part of the day-to-day praxis or practical activity of individuals and groups in the world" (1993:10). The Città Alta demonstrates how malleable spaces and their meanings are to the efforts of those who lived there as well as those who did not. And while many processes that have affected the Città Alta have been explicitly undertaken in order to change it (like the Angelini plan and more recent letters to the editor), others – like staying there and socializing with family and friends who live in the same streets on which they grew up – were less explicitly engaged in the struggle over what the Città Alta was and meant.

In conversation with me, Stefano noted that when he was involved in planning for the risanimento of the Città Alta, there were dangers to be foreseen and avoided. He was afraid *"che diventi una città museo imbalsamata. Che diventi una città del sabato. E che diventi una città . . . delle pizze, una città del divertimento come San Marino. Dove vendono la torta, le cose. Ed è un po' quello che è successo"* ("that it would become an embalmed, museum city. That it would become a city of Saturday. And that it would become a city . . . of pizzas, a city of fun like San Marino. Where they sell cakes, things. And it is a little this that has happened"). Likewise, a local historian notes that since the 1980s, the Città Alta has become *"una 'città' però senza più i suoi personaggi, i suoi artigiani, le sue botteghe"* ("a 'city,' however, without its special characters, its artisans, its workshops anymore") (Ravanelli 1996:356).[16] As its population has more than halved over the past several decades, so, too, have the everyday conveniences that once characterized life there decreased. Most of the Città Alta used to live, work, and play there; older residents even recounted to me that people rarely used to leave their own neighborhoods. Indeed, one couple in their sixties who owned and ran a specialty *salumeria* (deli) in the Città Alta and lived above it, told me how unusual and a little scandalous it was when they became fidanzati years ago, since they were from vicinie on opposite sides of the Città Alta. Those days seemed amusingly distant as they recounted the story, both to them and to me.

Worrying about the Città Alta becoming too pristine and touristy is a far cry from earlier concerns. One had to look hard around the margins of the Città Alta to find any trace of the poverty that until relatively recently characterized so much of it, and most of the remaining decrepit buildings were surrounded by scaffolding, in the midst of being renovated. In spite of complaints about trash and overcrowded parking, the Città Alta of the early 21st century was for the most part well-preserved and inviting.

Gieryn argues that "in spite of its relatively enduring and impos-ing materiality, the meaning or value of the same place is labile – flexible in the hands of different people or cultures, malleable over time, inevitably contested" (2000:465). Such lability has proven to be the case in Bergamo, especially regarding the Città Alta. For most Bergamaschi when I lived there, it was a treasured place, seemingly beyond alteration or extreme change; its cobblestones, frescoed façades, and marble palazzi seemed to be effortless representations of a time **d'öna ólta**. Like the past represented in Bergamasco poems and on stage, however, this "once upon a time" was, on closer inspection, an idealized, timeless construction, as buildings and mon-uments from various time periods stood side by side in renovated splendor. Change has always characterized the Città Alta, as is true for most inhabited spaces. For example, at the end of the 19th century Ciro Caversazzi, a *"uomo di cultura"* ("man of culture," i.e. wealthy man), believing that the Medieval was a more attractive and worthy period of architecture than the Baroque, had the formerly important *Palazzo della Marchesa* and everything in it torn down because it was Baroque. *"Certo il visitatore di oggi, non avendo memoria di quel che c'era, non può lamentarne la perdita"* ("Certainly the visitor of today, not having any memory of what was there, cannot lament the loss") (Forlani 1998:52).

Many Bergamaschi when I did my research did not know that the Città Alta was once the City of the Three Ps, nor did they remember the degradation and overcrowding that used to character-ize so much of it. Those who did tended to value that past, looking at it as a time of community, when the Città Alta was a thriving site of work, play, and family. Some, like Angela, kept old photos of that time on their walls in order to remind them, while their everyday lives there kept them traversing the same familiar contrade and **piasse** (piazzas). Others, like the ironsmiths, whose butiga has occupied the same 12th-century tower since the early 19th century, made participation in their community an explicit priority.

Later, on the same evening in 2007, after Ella and Alessandro had headed home, Scott, the baby, and I walked home in the still crowded streets and literally ran into Roberto and Franca, almost making him drop the empty tray he was carrying. After our initial surprised greetings, they explained they were coming home from a community dinner in the oratory nearby, for which Franca had made a cake. Now they were returning to their apartment across the piazza from the butiga, having sent Roberto's mother, Carla, home to her apartment next to them earlier with friends. It had been Saint Erasmus' saint's day (a locally important celebration we had joined them for in other years), they reminded us, and they recounted who had been there and how the day's festivities had gone. This year's celebration was not as elaborate as a few years ago, when Roberto had built a new iron gate for the small chapel of St. Erasmus in the Città Alta, and the celebrations had included the wealthy benefactors who had funded the gate. "This year it was just us," they said, "just the usual group." Remembering years past, it was easy for me to imagine the quick, overlapping Bergamasco conversation that would have characterized their evening. We walked home together and I promised to stop by the butiga the next day.

Herzfeld has argued that in cases like Italy where the nation-state is weak, "localist versions of cultural intimacy prove more compelling than the national renditions" (2005:65). Anchoring their shared sense of self in the Città Alta, then, provided a more immediate cohesiveness for Bergamaschi than is offered by the state, just as Bergamasco offered a more intimate image of self than Italian. This was true despite the series of transformations that have affected the Città Alta over the course of the past century, both physically and symbolically. Bergamaschi's affective relationships with the Città Alta have been multiple, but always connected to its material form (finding pleasure in its beauty, lamenting its degradation) and its history as the oldest and most important part of Bergamo until the 20th century.

The power relations that have shaped the physical and social makeup of the Città Alta have also shifted. Once, everyone lived there, wealthy and poor, powerful and powerless. As the rich and powerful began to leave, the Città Alta fell into disrepair. It was only when the economic and political elite began to take interest in the Città Alta, starting at the end of the 19th century but gaining impetus only in the 1920s, that Città Alta became prized as something in particular, a treasure and not just a location. Once the money came back as part of publicly and privately funded restoration projects, real estate prices climbed, and the Città Alta changed face again, becoming a retreat for recreation or residence for those who can afford it. However, families and individuals like Franca, Roberto, and Angela continued to live their everyday existences there. For them, and many others, the Città Alta was the heart of their lives, similar to how residents of Orgosolo in Sardinia feel about their town commons, which is "an object of ongoing 'love,' nostalgia, passion, worry, grief and jealousy precisely because it is considered essential to the experience and agency associated with being both Sardinian and Orgolese" (Heatherington 2005:153).

Both Bergamasco and the Città Alta had been *risanati* – scrubbed clean, their old forms recaptured or remade in modern, purified, and hygienic forms (Cameron 1995). Both were also on display, whether on stage, in written form, or as a scenic silhouette glimpsed from below. This restructuring was saving the material forms of the Città Alta and Bergamasco, although their everyday use had been transformed. Once, every kind of person lived in the Città Alta, and Bergamasco was the language of virtually every sphere of their lives, except for the very elite, whose children played alone and learned to read, write, and speak Italian as they grew up. By the time I lived there, both the place and the vernacular were at once essential to and separate from the modern everyday life of most Bergamaschi. The differences between their material forms, however, have important resonances for their possible futures: the Città Alta will persist in its glory, its walls, palazzi, scenic streets attesting to an imagined, desirable past, while only a few will call it home. Bergamasco language also has a bifurcated path ahead; its heteroglossic form in contemporary use will continue to be used, even as its speakers see it as "inauthentic" and impure, while its purified, archaic forms will increasingly be found in the pages of books and on stage, set apart from everyday life. The texture of language use that formed the social aesthetics of language points toward continuing shifts in this direction.

This social aesthetics of language in Bergamo was clearly shaped by Bergamo's place within the larger political, economic, and social contexts of Italy and Europe. Bergamo was one of many small towns facing the issue of how to preserve material forms from their past, such as city centers, artwork, and the like. Likewise, Bergamasco is one of nearly countless local "dialects" in Italy, as well as one of hundreds of regional or minority languages in Europe and around the world whose speakers are seeking ways to make using them compatible with modern life. Speaking in Bergamo, then, was necessarily linked to larger debates about the role and values of minority languages across Italy and Europe, and the choices that Bergamasco speakers made about their language were shaped by decisions made by Italian politicians in Rome, and European politicians and bureaucrats in Brussels, as well as local circumstances. In the next chapter, I turn to this larger context, situating Bergamo and its language within the nation, the European Union, and global debates about the value of locality and its expressions.

6

Bergamo, Italy, Europe:
Speaking Contextualized

In Bergamo, as across Italy, the politicization of language – when language has emerged as a political issue – has occurred at distinctive historical moments when language has become a symbol of various sociopolitical and economic issues. During these moments, the values and patterns of use of Italian and vernaculars are compared and contrasted, and these differences are recursively aligned with particular social divisions (Irvine and Gal 2000). As Gramsci observed, "Every time the 'language question,' in one form or another, surfaces anew, it signifies that a series of other problems are becoming dire, concerning the necessity to stabilize an intimate and secure rapport between the governing groups and the popular masses of the nation" (quoted in De Mauro 1972: 324). At the beginning of the new millennium, the language question in Bergamo and Italy involved debate provoked by the Northern League about the role and value of local (northern) languages vis-à-vis Italian, as well as discussion that aligned newly arrived immigrants' linguistic competencies with their perceived desire and ability to integrate into Italian society.

These contemporary language issues resonated with past debates. Fascist language policies of the 1920s and 1930s shaped modern reactions to the Northern League's linguistic stances; the experience of past waves of southern immigration into Bergamo set the stage for understanding more recent immigration from further afield. In the midst of it all, local institutions such as the Ducato di Piazza Pontida interacted with and responded to national and international forces, helping create a particularly Bergamasco language politics. The emergence in the early 1990s of the Northern League, a political party that cast itself as the champion of all northern local cultures, languages, and traditions, complicated the Ducato's long-held stance as the strongest supporter of Bergamasco, as well as many speakers' affective – and potentially political – alignment with Bergamasco. This dynamic recurred across Europe, where a number of what Holmes (2000) refers to as "integralist" parties like the Northern League have sprung up over the past two decades, complicating the role of minority language activists in national politics. Integralist groups, which valorize ethnic nationalism in support of isolationist policies, played a vocal role in the European debate about integration into the European Union (EU) and the value of nations, regions, and smaller places in this process.

Contemporaneously, Europe as a whole was experiencing a previously unimaginable level of immigration from northern Africa, Latin America, Eastern Europe, and parts of Asia. The news in Italy in the late 1990s and early 2000s was often full of stories about boat-loads of immigrants who had attempted to land on Italy's long coastlines, or were intercepted trying. Those who arrived successfully – both legally and illegally – headed for where there was work, and Bergamo's consistently strong economy drew them in large numbers. What these new residents with their foreign languages meant to the linguistic situation in Bergamo was being negotiated, both in terms of policy and on the ground in everyday interactions. However, it seemed clear that the arrival of these immigrants from beyond Europe's borders, coupled with the simultaneous expansion of those borders, challenged national and local efforts towards self-definition. Further, reactions to and interactions with immigrants from Senegal, Albania, the Czech Republic, and beyond were informed by past generations of Italian southerners arriving in Bergamo similarly pursuing gainful employment and a new life.

Susan Gal has recently reminded us that the analytical divide between the micro-interactional realm of everyday practices and the macro-level forces of institutions and governments, while a useful heuristic, limits the types of interconnections and continuities we may be able to recognize and track across institutions and interactions (2007) (see also Keane 2007). Further, such a focus on different scales may produce an analysis that misses the lived connections that join them. Indeed, Bergamaschi generally did not delineate between their everyday lives and the larger institutions where social analysts generally locate power. Instead, large-scale forces were experienced and made real through everyday practices. The power of politics – whether Fascist, integralist, or other – while easy to describe as originating elsewhere for the outside observer, found form and meaning in everyday life through people's ongoing interactions. For example, the porousness of Italy's or Europe's borders and the perceived inaction of the state to control effectively the arrival of newcomers was experienced through interactions with individual immigrants, as well as through the ideological filters of the media. So images of North Africans being incarcerated following their boat's interception by the coastguard were made meaningful by interactions with Senegalese street vendors who sold knock-off Gucci sunglasses on the *Sentierone* (central pedestrian area) of the Lower City, occasionally having to leave their wares and flee in the face of patrolling local police. Similarly, while institutions of power such as the state or the EU may have at times been conceptualized as residing elsewhere – "down there" (in Rome) and "up there" (in Brussels), respectively – most Bergamaschi experienced them in the mundane routines of everyday life, such as when they heard their Albanian housekeeper's stories about the war in the former Yugoslavia, or interacted with government bureaucracies to get a wedding license or change their official address.

As studies of language ideologies have repeatedly shown,[1] the links between speakers' notions of how to speak and why are informed by cultural processes such as morals and aesthetics, ideas of modernity versus tradition, and other conceptualizations that define an "us" as different than a "them." For speakers, such links need not be explicitly acknowledged or constructed, and most Bergamaschi did not give political and economic institutions and processes much thought in the course of their daily lives. Paolo did not write poetry as a political act; Federico did not tell us Bergamasco sayings as a way to combat the homogenizing power of the Italian state; and most Bergamasco mothers felt that choosing to speak to their children in Italian just made sense. Language was always available for politicization, however, for the social aesthetics of language was cross-cut with issues of power that could be handily taken up by interested parties, eager to tap into language's pivotal role as a symbolic resource.

Language Politics: Fascism and Integralism

One of the unique dimensions of the sociolinguistic and cultural landscape of Bergamo was the existence of the Ducato di Piazza Pontida. Since its inception in the 1920s, the Ducato's ranks have been filled with local political and economic leaders, as well as poets and artists, making it a potential powerhouse on the local political and linguistic scene. And yet the Ducato's might has always been curiously circumscribed. Rather than cast itself into the role of political advocate, the Ducato's voice has stayed unswervingly apolitical and its activities squarely cultural. Indeed, the very organization that might have stood as a bulwark against the shift away from Bergamasco and towards Italian seems to have contributed to this shift through consistently lamenting the loss of local ways of speaking and traditions, beginning when this loss was still a couple generations away (see Cavanaugh 2006 for a discussion). To understand these contradictions, it is essential to look at how the Ducato began during Fascism.

Previous to the Fascist period that followed World War I, the Italian government had implemented numerous educational policies and legislative measures to try to promote the use of Italian over the so-called "dialects."[2] These efforts culminated during Fascism, which viewed dialects as holdovers from less modern times, indicators of lingering and widespread illiteracy, and potent symbols of the many sociogeographical divisions that separated Italians from one another due to the peninsula's long history of being divided into numerous political entities (such as city-states, papal states, and the Bourbon controlled south). Languages other than Italian divided Italians from one another, and needed to be eliminated. As such, dialects were subject to legislative "eradication and suppression" (Foresti 1978:119) and the so-called "minority languages" (such as Franco-Provençal in Val D'Aosta and Ladin and German in Trento-Alto Adige) and "foreignisms" (words such as "café" and "cocktail") were heavily legislated against (De Mauro 1972; Klein 1986; Leso et al. 1978).[3] Beyond explicit legislation, the Regime's other strategies to limit and control the use of the dialects involved designating local cultural traditions – closely linked to their dialects – as "folklore," juxtaposed with the modernity and unity of the nation-state. Since the late 19th century, scholars had studied the lifestyles and customs of the masses as "folklore," identifying traditional ways of dressing, story telling, and music from different parts of the peninsula (Leydi 1996; Saunders 1984). Fascist authorities embellished this scholarly inquiry, organizing folklore festivals across the peninsula along nearly identical lines: peasants dressed up in their "traditional" costumes for parades, in which they played "traditional" songs and danced "traditional" dances. These parades reduced local cultures to the same set of constituent parts, and separated them from everyday life by putting them on display. Reducing local cultures to cookie-cutter similarity and equivalence was one way for the Fascist state to contain and control them, forging unity out of diversity, as Fascism overwhelmingly promoted national unity over local particularisms (De Grazia 1981; Krause 2005; Mack Smith 1988; Puccini and Squillacciotti 1980; Saunders 1984).

As briefly described in previous chapters, the Ducato di Piazza Pontida was born in a moment of protest against local Fascist authorities. After stepping up to dedicate a locally important monument that the authorities had been slow to do, the Ducato coalesced into a volunteer organization in support of Bergamasco culture, tradition, folklore, and art. Many of the Ducato's early leaders and members, including Rodolfo Paris, the first Duke, were editors of and contributors to Giopì, a local satirical weekly newspaper founded in the late 19th century. As discussed in Chapter 3, the character of Giopì is considered by many to be the emblem or mascot of Bergamo. He is an honest but uneducated servant, always depicted with three goiters (from lack of iodine, a supplement lacking in chestnuts, longtime staple of poor Bergamaschi), a stocking cap, a **bastù** (baton or club), and a sly smile. He is clever but simple, and often plots about how to get ahead, motivated by constant hunger pangs. The Ducato quickly adopted the newspaper as their official organ to report on the group's activities. Giopì himself appears on the front page of every issue (see the upper left–hand corner of the image of the Old Lady Città Alta in Figure 5.2), nowadays alongside the common adage about the Bergamasco character, "**Caràter de la rassa bergamasca: fiama de rar; sóta la sender, brasca**" ("Character of the Bergamasco race: flames are rare, under the cinders, it smolders"), deftly encompassing the localist, populist orientation of the group. Giopì symbolizes the independence, honesty, ethic of hard work, and personal reserve so commonly described as Bergamasco characteristics. By adopting him, the Ducato sought to attribute these same values to itself. The newspaper's focus had always been explicitly local, with overt political critique and satire as the bulk of its material. Indeed on the front page of the first issue published under the auspices of the Ducato, they printed a poem that asserted that **"chè 'l gà miga de padrù/ lè de tocc e de nissü"** ("here, there is no boss, he [Giopì] is everyone's and no one's").[4] In the 1920s, it began to downplay this aspect, although it never entirely gave up its capacity and tendency to protest against forces that ran counter to the local interests of Bergamo, as demonstrated by the poem and caricature of the Old Lady Città Alta discussed in the previous chapter.

The first Duke's poetic nickname, **Alégher** (Happy), aptly indexes the group's upbeat, humorous attitude. Under him and his successor (after his death in 1927), the Ducato expanded its social role to begin sponsoring and frequenting dialectal events such as poetry readings, the first radio broadcast in Bergamasco, and numerous local dialect theater productions. Due to the Ducato's activities, the 1920s and 1930s were widely considered to have been the Golden Age of Bergamasco dialect and culture, in spite of – and in part in response to – growing Fascist restrictions of local dialects and culture. Many of Bergamo's most well-known and beloved poets were writing at that time (mostly in Bergamasco, though some wrote in Italian as well). Play-writing in vernacular also thrived, as did the performance of these plays. There was a flourishing of traditional puppetry (**böratì**) performances in Bergamasco, many of which, of course, prominently featured Giopì. Sonnets and songs in Bergamasco, scholarly pieces on the differences between Bergamasco and other dialects, stories and poems written in other dialects, descriptions of Bergamasco traditions which were described as being lost, satirical cartoons caricaturing local politicians and other public figures – all this and more was to be found in Giopì during that period.

For the elite members of the Ducato – which included bankers, architects, lawyers, and doctors – the objects and practices they extolled were often not their own, but those of the contadini and working classes who made up the majority of Bergamaschi at that time.[5] Indeed, in many ways, the Ducato's folkloristic orientation dove-tailed with Fascist efforts to consolidate, appropriate, and control local cultures. Peasants and members of the working classes had little time or resources to dedicate to leisure activities such as membership in the Ducato, even as their everyday lives consisted of many of the very "traditions" which members of the Ducato lamented as being in decline. Gross observed a similar process in Belgium in the 19th century, when the bourgeoisie portrayed the working classes as their regional cultural "roots," and appropriated peasant and working class practices – most notably puppetry – as symbols of "their" culture (1987). By refusing to recognize the working classes as their coevals, these elites removed them from modernity, naturalizing class differences into different stages in the same progression towards modernity. In so doing, they also cast themselves as modern in comparison. In Bergamo, the Ducato's interest in local "traditions" (that is, things in the past) probably initially shielded the Ducato from Fascist censure. At the same time, as Giddens (1979) has argued, once a way of life is separated from the everyday flow of social interaction to be deemed tradition, it becomes open to question and needs to be defended. By lamenting their loss and symbolically locating them in the past, the Ducato cast these practices as non-threatening to the unity of the Fascist state.

As supporters of Bergamasco "traditions" which they claimed were being lost, the Ducato potentially contributed to this loss. In particular, in depicting the vernacular as needing to be saved at a time when evidence suggests that nearly all Bergamaschi spoke their language across most interactional spheres, the Ducato perhaps unintentionally aided Fascist efforts to make dialects a thing of the past. This occurred through the re-construction of the indexical ground against which Bergamasco was understood. Previously, the vernacular had just been what everyone spoke, a fact that was as unremarkable in everyday practice as it was problematic to national leaders. Its use indexed the quotidian, and the myriad things that went along with it being the language of everyday life for most speakers. When the Ducato proclaimed that the dialect and culture associated with it were in need of saving – something that probably seemed unquestionable to them in those times of political, economic, and social flux – they added this valence of loss to what Bergamasco stood for. In addition, the Ducato provided contexts in which using Bergamasco was explicitly lauded as a worthwhile activity, made valuable *because* it was being lost. Within these contexts, using Bergamasco came to index a positive affective stance towards local practices, as well as active participation in the group itself. Through depicting these practices as in need of saving – as located, in other words, in the past – members of the Ducato also distinguished themselves as modern, further along a cultural progression towards becoming Italian.

Eventually, however, even the shared orientation towards culture as folklore could not shield the Ducato from Fascist control. Throughout the Fascist period, participation in national institutions such as governmental agencies and bureaucracies grew as centralization policies led to increased monitoring of the everyday lives of Italian citizens (De Bernardi 1998; De Grazia 1981, 1992; Thompson 1991). As the 1930s progressed, Fascism's hold on more and more aspects of life outside of the strictly political grew. Giopì frequently published articles and even poems in praise of *il Duce* (always in Italian), claiming their place proudly as Italians in the modern nation-state.[6] This was not enough, however, and on October 16, 1938, Giopì came under the direction of the *Comitato Provinciale per le Arti Popolari* (Provincial Committee for the Popular Arts), a branch of the *Dopolavoro Provinciale* (part of the national organization which occupied itself with the leisure-time activities of Italian citizens) under the P.N.F. (*Partita Nazionale Fascista*, or National Fascist Party). This act was referred to as a prestigious honor on the first page of the last independently published issue. After only three more issues, however, Giopì was shut down entirely and the Ducato went underground, meeting in the tavern of one of the members whenever possible until the end of the war.

Cultural Champions

During the 1920s and 1930s, the Ducato established itself as a strictly apolitical organization, a "cultural champion" of all things Bergamasco. Although it would occasionally raise its voice in the form of satire on the pages of Giopì, it positioned itself *for* Bergamasco rather than *against* anything. Especially as Fascism's political hold on the nation became solidified over the course of the 1920s and its efforts to control the everyday practices of the populace increased over the 1930s, Giopì and the Ducato's willingness to criticize openly – as with the commentary on the "Butcher," Fascist Architect Chitò, in 1924 – diminished. The Ducato portrayed itself as ready to promote the dialect and local traditions as valuable, but limited this support to praising it in the pages of Giopì and sponsoring cultural events. Positioning itself in this way may have ensured the Ducato's survival as a group, at least for a while, but it also shaped the Ducato's place within Bergamasco society and politics in the decades that followed.

The Ducato, in other words, refused to take on power directly, but rather promoted – and helped to define – the affective connections Bergamaschi could and perhaps *should* have to their dialect and culture. Looking over the pages of Giopì since the 1920s (it started publishing again in 1947), one can trace how consistently the Ducato has presented itself and the activities it has supported as squarely "cultural" or folkloristic. Giopì, which has called itself a *"quincidinale bergamasco di cultura, arte, folclore e tradizioni"* ("a Bergamasco bimonthly of culture, art, folklore, and tradition") for the past several decades, published pieces on special cultural events around the province, books on local interest topics (everything from encyclopedias of local flora and fauna to studies of frescoes in local churches), and occasionally local current events, still from a slightly satirical point of view. Aside from a single regular feature, in which Maestro, Giopì's long-time editor, foremost poet as well as the teacher of the writing course, commented – often critically – on local current events, Giopì rarely touched on controversial subjects. This capacity for political critique through satire had so faded into the background that it raised considerable attention when it occurred. For instance, when Maestro wrote a piece in protest of a national transportation initiative in the vernacular in stinging terms in 2000, it was written about in the two daily newspapers with a degree of amazement and admiration for its audacity as well as for having been written in Bergamasco.

The one activity the Ducato has sponsored since its inception that was explicitly and vocally political was the **Rasgament de la ègia** (burning of the old one (fem.)), a full day event in which a figure of an old woman is burnt in effigy for one of the city's problems, preceded by a grand parade of floats and people in costume competing for prizes. During the time I did my research, the Ducato was best-known for this event, although its political aspect – a pointed critique of some dimension of the city or government, such as plans for renovating certain neighborhoods or how the city's sanitation services were run – was far lesser known. In local media coverage of the event, the variety of floats and costumes was far more emphasized than the issue that was being burnt in effigy. Throughout the day itself, the issue was generally only mentioned a few times, effectively back-grounded against a focus on the parade competition and spectacle of the bonfire. Once a year, the Ducato enjoyed extensive media coverage; the rest of the time, its presence was felt only occasionally, and nearly exclusively on the pages covering local cultural happenings, not current events.

The Ducato Today

Fascism created the sociopolitical context in which the Ducato had its beginnings; the Northern League has recently helped set the stage for its renewal. Through its explicit support for all northern dialects and local cultures, the Northern League provoked nationwide discussion about the role and relative value of local interests when it emerged on the national political scene in the early 1990s. Indeed, although campanilismo in various forms has long characterized how Italians think about themselves and others, it was not until the Northern League that such sentiments came to the fore in Italian politics and public debate (Levy 1996; Stacul 2001, 2005).[7]

After it re-formed following World War II, the Ducato failed to regain the vitality that characterized it and its members during the 1920s and 1930s. Even as the shift in everyday speaking practices began to occur in Bergamo in the 1950s and 1960s, the Ducato's role as champion of Bergamasco seemed more circumscribed than ever. Aside from initiating the first Bergamasco poetry contest in 1957, the *Penna D'Oro* (Pen of Gold), supporting the return of dialect theater in the late 1960s, continuing its biannual banquets, and sponsoring various events and studies of Bergamasco folklore, the Ducato seemed intent on returning to being a jocular context for socializing. The 50th anniversary of the Ducato in 1974 was celebrated by a series of events and publication of a volume that glorified its past, but recognized few new accomplishments.

Since the late 1980s, however, the Ducato has found new life. It began several new initiatives, including the yearly dialect language course; a choir, which sings primarily in Bergamasco; two six-week-long dialect theater series, one of which brings dialect theater companies from across Lombardy to perform; the poetry contest for poetry in dialect discussed briefly in Chapter 3; and two yearly folklore festivals, one local, one international. Even as it profited from the wave in localist sentiment that underwrote much of the Northern League's success in this period, the Ducato struggled to distinguish itself from the League. One ongoing point of confusion came from the organization's very name. Early important Northern League rallies were held in the town of Pontida, located on the western border of the province of Bergamo.[8] The Piazza Pontida (once called the *Piazza del Legno*, Square of Wood, for its market), where the Ducato has been symbolically and physically located since its inception, is named for being the starting point of a road that leads eventually to Pontida. This purely coincidental overlapping of names put the Ducato on the defensive early on, so that, for instance, its members often cited the Ducato's long history (which, of course, predates the League by several decades) in order to differentiate itself from the League.

In 2000, the Duke described the Ducato's contemporary mission as "*costruire una documentazione storica, una memoria*" ("to construct a historical documentation, a memory") for Bergamasco culture. From its initiatives, however, it was clear that constructing a future for Bergamasco was also at stake. A large part of this project was distinguishing the Ducato from the League. The Duke at that time was explicitly bent on modernizing and expanding the group. In addition to trying to "raise the cultural tone" of the group and its activities as discussed in Chapter 4, the Duke and his allies wanted to refashion the Ducato as *one* champion among many of *all* Italian local cultures and dialects, allied with other individuals and groups with similar goals. They were attempting to do this through supporting events that promoted "cultural" endeavors more broadly, such as events that prominently featured the literary prowess of Bergamasco instead of focusing exclusively on strictly traditional concerns that emphasized Bergamasco's links to everyday life experiences specific to Bergamo. The Duke maintained that Bergamasco would be strengthened only if Bergamo aligned itself with communities in similar circumstances throughout Italy. This shift in tone, as well as the inclusion of individuals and groups from the south in these endeavors helped to underline differences between the Ducato and the League.

In accordance with this aim, in 2000 the Ducato began to sponsor initiatives in support of dialects from all over Italy. Most prominent among these was a dialect poetry contest in which poets from all over the peninsula could compete, and the dialect theater series that included theater companies from all over Lombardy. The very title of the poetry contest, the *Premio Nazionale di poesia italiana in lingua dialettale* (National Prize of Italian poetry in dialectal language), is evidence of this outward-facing orientation. Scheduling it in a small performance space at the prestigious *Teatro Donizetti*, the grandest venue in Bergamo, underlined that this was being presented as an event of high culture. The first year of the competition, a poet from the southern city of Bari won. His poetry was remarkably different in terms of tone and style than Bergamasco poetry, a fact discussed at length during the three evening events in which the competition culminated. The similarities and dissimilarities between his dialect, Barese, and Bergamasco discussed, however, were never framed in terms of north–south divisions, which were scrupulously absent. The discussion stressed instead that all Italian communities with a local dialect share the same concerns and efforts. What is particular about Bergamo is found in Bergamasco, just as what is particular about a place as far away as Bari is located in Barese, making them in some ways equivalent to one another. As the languages of sentiment, Bergamasco, Barese, and all Italian dialects provide Italians with an immediate connection to themselves lacking in Italian. Bergamasco, then, should not be delimited by linking it to events that are strictly local or connected to its past. Instead, Bergamaschi must look beyond their own boundaries and join forces with other groups in similar sociolinguistic positions, shedding the language's associations with poverty and the so-called restricted circle of those who spoke it in that past in the process.

For these reasons, the Ducato must be involved in efforts to promote dialects in general, not only Bergamasco dialect in particular. As the Duke put it in an informal interview:

Example 6.1

Cioè, alcuna volta, per esempio, scherzosamente – ancora anche adesso forse qualche volta – dice,

That is, sometimes, for example, jokingly – still today even perhaps sometimes – people say,

"Ah te seèt de Bèrghem?"

"Ah, you're from Bergamo?"

"Sì."

"Yes."

"Alura bisògna ìga 'l passapórt, per végn a Bèrghem."

"Then you must need a passport, to come to Bergamo."

Perché sembrava proprio che i bergamaschi fossero un po' un mondo a se. Ecco, tanto per far capire. E, e la mia, la, queste mie iniziative – in particolar modo questo qui dei dialetti di Italia, è proprio perché per aprire il nostro agli altri e anche perché gli altri vengono di insegnarci, a farci capire cose, cose nuove, insomma.

Because it seemed really that Bergamascos were a little a world of their own. There, to show you. And my, this, these initiatives of mine – in particular this one of the dialects of Italy, it's really to open ourselves up to others and also so that others come to teach us, to make us understand things, new things, basically.

Here, the Duke explicitly describes his "initiatives" as part of an effort "to open ourselves up to others, and also so that others come to teach us, to make us understand things, new things." In describing how Bergamaschi are sometimes seen as occupying "a world of their own," the Duke goes so far as to cite a joke that one needs a passport to come to Bergamo. All of this is in keeping with the Duke's efforts to transform the Ducato's activities and goals. But a closer look at the transcript forces a tricky question: why does the apparent outsider who jokes about needing a passport to come to Bergamo speak in Bergamasco, especially as the rest of the Duke's utterance (and much of the interview) was in Italian? There is no simple answer. I believe, however, that this switch points up the obstacles that the Duke's efforts face. As the language of humor, confidenza, and "speaking bread to bread and wine to wine," Bergamasco has value, value that can be immediately felt and recruited in sometimes unconscious ways. Severing Bergamasco from these associations is not only a difficult – perhaps impossible – task, it also begs a question: if Bergamasco is no longer valued for these associations, but for other, "new things," then what *will* it be valued for?

These attempts to shift the Ducato's focus away from its traditional populist and localist orientation and toward a higher level of cultural sophistication and broader audience for its initiatives challenged the indexical potential of Bergamasco. This indexical interruption often required considerable effort. For instance, the Duke often stressed his own lack of sophistication and low level of education in public speeches in contrast to the sophisticated intellectuals he brought to the Ducato to achieve his goals. In doing so, he offered himself as a symbolic bridge between what he called the "narrow, restricted circle" of Bergamo and Bergamasco and his desired future, as when, at the end of the first Bergamasco poetry contest, the Duke said: *"Beh, forse vi siete resi conto, perchè sono emozionato. In mezzo a tutti questi intellettuali. A tutta questa gente così colta, io che ho fatto solo la terza avviamento, potete capirmi. Comunque sono abbastanza intelligente di trovarmi tanti amici intelligenti"* ("Well, maybe you are all aware that I have gotten pretty emotional. In the midst of all these intellectuals, all these cultivated people, I who did only the third form [finished middle school], you all can understand me. However, I'm smart enough to have found myself lots of intelligent friends"). The Duke presented himself here as similar to his audience in order to align himself with them and their interests. He assumed they, like him, were not highly educated, and perhaps felt out of place among so many university professors and other intellectuals. These intellectuals were, however, "friends" whom he had been smart enough to surround himself with, and whom, by extension, the audience should also be eager to embrace. The Duke used himself to span the differences between older members who still enjoyed the types of things the Ducato once sponsored more often (such as poetry readings by local poets) and who may have frequented these new activities with a certain level of suspicion, and the newer members who engaged in different types of activities and initiatives and may have felt more interested in "high culture" offerings. In doing so, he attempted to minimize the risk of losing older members as he strived to appeal to new ones.

These new undertakings for the group, and the attitudes that underlay them, were creating a potential rift within the Ducato. A number of members – who could be called the "old guard" – objected to this change and mourned the loss of what they considered to be the group's basic mission: to promote Bergamasco culture and dialect. They saw the Ducato as the guardian of the local, of all things Bergamasco, and thought that involving themselves in other activities might be to its and their own detriment.

One person's treasured specific past was another's "small, restricted circle." Similar to Maria's explanation to Stefano and me in Chapter 2 about how her mother worked to send her to school outside of her Bergamasco world, so the Ducato worked to open themselves – and by extension Bergamasco culture in general – up to the larger world that included other Italian dialects. They hoped to learn from these different worlds, as well as to strengthen their own position within the Italian situation in which dialects were always subordinate to Italian. The Duke did not, however, aim to challenge this hierarchy. Bergamasco to him was unarguably a dialect, not on the same footing as Italian, and should not be discussed as such. The Duke was also straightforward in his belief that the conditions that supported use of the vernacular had disappeared and that it was approaching obsolescence. His attitude towards Bergamasco was aptly expressed through the local proverb *chiudono la stalla quando i buoi sono fuori* (closing the barn-door once the oxen are out), which he shared with me once while we were discussing the fate of the dialect.

That other members of the Ducato had also essentially given up on Bergamasco was illustrated by their actions if not their public rhetoric. For instance, the language used in interactions among Ducato members followed a telling pattern. Weekly meetings among the group's leaders were conducted nearly entirely in Italian, although side conversations were sometimes in Bergamasco, and Bergamasco exclamations were commonly peppered throughout. Speech at the Ducato's biannual banquets was similar: nearly all official speech was in Italian, while the poems performed as part of the events' entertainment were in Bergamasco, and individual interactions could be in either language. This pattern was particularly striking in the Ducato's yearly writing course, which could have been a space to encourage speaking Bergamasco. Indeed, the years that I participated in it, the few young participants had joined in order to improve their Bergamasco overall. Instead, the course dealt entirely with writing and reading Bergamasco, and was designed to be taught as if participants already spoke and understood it. Younger course members struggled to master written as well as verbal skills. Some opted to take the course repeatedly, for at least it gave them a chance to practice Bergamasco at all.

We must see the dialect for what it is, the Duke maintained, and not try to force it to do things it is not fit for, such as being taught in schools or used in government. Through maintaining such positions, the Ducato sought to carve a role for itself in the future of Bergamasco that overlapped as little as possible with the activities and attitudes of the Northern League.

Integralist Politics: The Value of the Local

The Northern League, indeed, had very different ideas about what local languages such as Bergamasco should be used for and what they mean, even as they shared a commitment to the importance of locality with the Ducato. Northern Leaguers (known as *leghisti* (pl.) or *leghista* (sing.)) cast the national government as a colonizing force, which imposed its foreign language and culture upon the north and tried to erase the sociocultural and linguistic differences that fill the peninsula in order to achieve an artificial unity. As the leghista mayor of a small town on the periphery of Bergamo put it during an interview in 2000, "*Vogliamo essere padroni di casa nostra, come si può dire*" ("We want to be masters of our own house, one could say"). For the League, being master of their own house often focused on ridding this house of unwanted outsiders from elsewhere.

The Northern League had enjoyed widespread support in Bergamo and its province since the early 1990s, when it entered the local, provincial, regional, and national political scenes with a force that upset long-standing power balances (Wild 1996).[9] A part of the so-called Catholic or "white" territory since World War II, the province and town of Bergamo consistently voted for the Christian Democrat Party (*Democrazia Cristiana,* or DC), the Catholic centrist party that controlled power in Italy for most of the post-war period through a series of strategic coalitions and control of numerous important ministerial posts until its near demise in the political scandals of the early 1990s (Ravanelli 1996).[10] Numerous sources, from newspaper articles to academic studies to personal anecdotes, suggest that this was a function of the strong position held by the Catholic Church, and the central role of local priests in particular. When the DC crumbled and lost its place at the forefront of Italian politics in the early 1990s through various political scandals, creating a power vacuum, the largest block of voters in the town and the province switched their votes to the League.[11] Annabella, the retired schoolteacher, put it this way during a conversation with me: "*Prima, tutti con la DC. Tutti in massa con la Democrazia Cristiana, perché il parocco diceva che bisognava votare, o se no si andava in inferno. Passato quella ondata lì, tutti Lega!*" ("First, everyone with the DC. Everyone en masse with the Christian Democrats, because the parish priest said that you had to vote that way, otherwise you'd go to hell. Once that wave was past, everyone to the League!")

Although Annabella personally believed that Bergamaschi's voting for the League was born out of ignorance, others offered reasoned motives for these political choices. For many Bergamaschi, as with other northerners, the League appeared at a moment when the old parties collapsed and initially offered a refreshing critique of the corruption of everyday national politics, as well as validation of a number of locally held concerns: where do my taxes go? Why do I work so hard and receive so little in return from the state? Why are my children now (and/or why was I back in the 1950s, 1960s, or 1970s) punished for speaking Bergamasco, our mother tongue, in school? What does my life here have to do with Rome anyway? (Cento Bull and Corner 1993; D'Amato and Schieder 1997; Levy 1996; Wild 1996). Bergamaschi quickly elected not only a large number of League representatives to Parliament, they also voted a number of leghisti into regional, provincial, and local offices.[12] From 1995 to 1999, members of the League dominated the town council of Bergamo, as well as the provincial council. A number of smaller towns elected leghisti as mayors or onto their town councils.

During this period, local initiatives organized by the League in support of the dialect and Bergamasco culture flowered and multiplied. The province put out a calendar in Bergamasco, elaborated with recipes for local cuisine and proverbs in vernacular, marking traditional festivals and locally important saints' days. Town councils across the province pushed for, and in many places succeeded in, putting up signs announcing town names in Bergamasco.[13] Various town councils attempted with mixed success to make it legal for Bergamasco to be spoken in official contexts, such as when citizens conducted business in town hall, or during town council meetings. A few town councils sponsored courses on Bergamasco and a number sponsored performances of dialect theater, as well as poetry readings in dialect.

Bergamasco leghisti were clear about why they undertook these efforts: they were trying to save what was theirs. As the same mayor explained to me about Bergamasco, "*E` la base, le, le, le nostre radici sono, in pratica. Che vanno conservati*" ("It is the base, our, our, our roots they [the dialects] are, in practice. That should be saved"). This was not a leghista stance, he told me, but rather one of common sense. As an example, he pointed to the administration of another small town in the province of Bergamo. They were not leghisti, but still had put up signs of their town's name in Bergamasco because "*Proba-bilmente sentono anche loro la necessità, eh, superando quegli ignippi politici, stupidi, centralisti – proprio schiavi di Roma, io gli considero – E invece crede che è una cosa ben fatta ricordare le radici, da dove . . . E anche proprio, ancora . . . Cioè, non è solamente il passato, neh? Ma anche il presente, così*" ("Probably they feel as well the necessity of overcoming these annoy-ing politicians, stupid, centralist – really slaves of Rome, I consider them – and instead believe that it is a good thing to remember your roots, from where . . . and even now . . . that is, it's not just the past, right? It's also the present, like that"). The national government pro-vided a point of contrast to the League's local efforts in the mayor's depiction of leghista goals. Local ways of life and values were impor-tant not just because they represented the past and thus one's roots, but also because they help define oneself in the present. Without ties to the local, in this view, one becomes a "slave of Rome" – ignorant and despicable. Over the 1990s, this position evolved to include a strong opposition to the increasing numbers of immigrants who had come to Italy from elsewhere, resulting in an at times xenophobic discourse of "us" versus "them."

Such views were disseminated through political meetings and rallies, as well as through the League's daily newspaper, *La Padania*, and through its radio station, *Radio Libera Padana* (Padanian Free

Radio).[14] Programming such as *Lingue e dialetti* (Languages and dialects), a weekly hour-long show hosted by Giovanni Polli, helped to concretize the connections between northern values and practices and the League. During "Lingue e dialetti," speakers called in to discuss topics pertaining to their own and other dialects; share information about cultural events, such as dialect theater productions; or ask questions about the differences between one dialect and another. This show, and others like it, portrayed speaking local languages as a basic human right, and participants often criticized editorials in newspapers they saw as anti-dialect and officials who did not allow individuals to speak in their own dialects in public spheres, like town council meetings.[15] Callers often claimed that all vernaculars, southern as well as northern, should be protected in some way, connecting speaking local language to the fight against globalization. The formation of a group by supporters of the League that called itself the Padanian Linguistic Association (*Associazione Linguistica Padana*, ALP) underlined the important symbolic role that dialects and their study could play in defining what was specific to and precious about northern culture(s).

In spite of its loud rhetoric in support of Bergamasco and all northern dialects, however, the League's support for these varieties was almost entirely symbolic. At the national level, its efforts to support local languages have been purely rhetorical; local and provincial efforts have been similarly limited. Italian is the language spoken almost exclusively at its rallies, printed in its newspaper, used in the meetings of ALP, and in most interactions I witnessed and participated in among its supporters, though it was often a strongly bivalent Bergamasco-ized Italian, with a Bergamasco accent, and occasional Bergamasco words or phrases thrown in. Similar to how the Ducato's interactions were most often in Italian, this pattern – Bergamasco as the target or object of speech, Italian as the language used to describe it and conduct all other "normal" business – recalls the patterns of language used at poetry readings and play performances. Such a pattern reinforced the dominance of Italian and subordinate position of Bergamasco, even in the name of valorizing Bergamasco.

In addition, the enduring salience of campanilismo meant that loyalty to local place rarely translated into regional orientations, such that ALP and the League were able to do little more than get people to agree that dialects were important in the face of the homogenizing forces of the state and globalization. Indeed, the meetings of ALP that I attended consisted almost entirely of participants (nearly all of whom came from different places across the north, mostly Lombardy) discussing the conditions of their own separate dialects, and their plans for studying it or otherwise supporting it. Northern cultural unity, beyond the shared value of hard work, was similarly hard to construct (Stacul 2003).

League efforts to promote Bergamasco were also often met with protests rooted in the association of the dialect with provincialism. One of the lightning rods for this type of discussion at the end of the 1990s and early 2000s were the signs of town names written in Bergamasco. Driving around in the province of Bergamo in the late 1990s, one was bound to notice the proliferation of these signs posted on the road as one entered a number of towns. In these places, next to the official signs (white writing on a blue background) that indicate the Italian name of the town, there would be another sign (white writing on a brown background). Brown signs usually indicate tourist information, such as if one could find hotels or restaurants in this community. These signs, however, were not aimed at the outsider but rather at various insiders: they gave the name of the town in Bergamasco, complete with Bergamasco spellings and diacritic markings. Next to the blue sign telling one that they had just entered *"Seriate"* was a brown sign, telling them that they were in **"Seriàt"**; along the mountain road that ran through *"Zogno"* was a brown sign announcing **"Zògn."**

These signs were a common topic of conversation in 1999–2000, and Bergamaschi with whom I spoke about them regarded them with mixed feelings. Many felt proud that the "real" names of their local places were finally being officially acknowledged in some fashion. Others thought that these signs were silly and old-fashioned, not to mention potentially confusing for non-Bergamaschi, who might be looking for *"Ranica,"* for example, and find themselves in **"Ranga."** Furthermore, as these signs were seen as the work of the Northern League – specifically, of local town councils dominated by members of the Northern League – a person's political leanings often dictated their views on these signs, such that they were described accordingly as useful and "about time," or embarrassing and overly provincial.

However, during the many conversations I had with Bergamaschi of various political stripes in 1999–2000, few objected to *all* of the League's positions, especially those in favor of increased local autonomy in areas like taxation, education, and infrastructure development, such as local road maintenance. The League's defense of the shared northern values of hard work and close family – especially as it linked them to local ways of speaking and other traditions – made it attractive to many voters who would otherwise have steered clear of such an apparently right-wing reactionist party. Indeed, some scholars assert that the Northern League owed much of its success to this ability to emphasize the value of family and work, as well as to tie these two interests together as "theirs" (Cento Bull and Corner 1993) (see also Cachafeiro 2002; Diamanti 1996). Even Bergamaschi who expressed disgust at the League's stance on immigrants and southerners and bewilderment at its success during elections often commented that its support of local culture, language, and traditions was laudable and made sense. The League's stance against the homogenizing forces of the nation-state and globalization also resonated with many Bergamaschi, even those who violently disagreed with many of its other positions. Since Bergamaschi thought of themselves as distinctive from other Italians, in both positive and negative respects, most wanted to retain at least some of these differences. As one leghista politician who held a city council seat in another small Bergamasco town in 2000 told me, *"Noi ci crediamo in identità, alla cultura, alle nostre tradizioni, alla nostra gente"* ("We believe in identity, in culture, in our traditions, in our people"), an appealing stance to many Bergamaschi.

As Stacul (2001, 2003) has argued, the Northern League provided an alternative to the homogenizing discourse of the state through valuing the local over the national, the traditional over the modern, and the past over the present. At the same time, its support for dialects posed a problem for those who did not support the League but wanted to support their language. There were a number of Bergamaschi who left the League due to differences in opinion on various matters or personality clashes with those higher up in the party hierarchy, but continued to support the League's cultural policies, using a variety of means to support these policies. Some founded their own political parties or organizations, staying in local politics or at least as participants in political conversations.[16] Others took a less political path, perhaps pursuing research on some specific element of Bergamasco language or culture, or on the linguistic or social similarities of different Padanian communities, as was true for many of the participants in ALP. For those who desired even more apparent distance from the League – such as the Ducato, or left-wing individuals – such differentiation was much more difficult.

Since its successes in the 1990s, support for the League on the national, regional, provincial, and local levels has fluctuated. Although many of the League initiatives in support of Bergamasco dialect and culture, such as the calendar mentioned above, were short-lived, others arose in their place. The sentiments that underwrote much of the support for the League – especially those that desired a voice for the local within the homogenizing discourse of the nation – persisted, and became woven into the social aesthetics of language in Bergamo. Speaking Bergamasco, or simply speaking in favor of Bergamasco, gained a potentially political flavor. As northern pride of place came to smack of provincialism and close-mindedness, so did the linguistic practices which index these places come to resonate with leghista attitudes that ranked the value of the local over the interests of the state, initiatives of the EU, and tolerance of new immigrants. Indeed, in the national media, there was a tendency for the appearance of a Bergamasco-sounding accent (or similar) to index a leghista stance, whether in comedy sketches or news clips of citizens reacting to an election (see Cavanaugh 2005 for a more in-depth discussion).

In spite of the Ducato's best efforts to distinguish its goals and work from those of the Northern League, the sentiments that supported both its renewal and the success of the League impelled a number of new participants to join the Ducato's activities. Some of the younger participants in the writing course, as well as numerous audience members of its poetry readings and play performances – though not all – were adherents of the Northern League. In contrast to the Ducato's stance as apolitical advocate of Bergamasco culture, these members were explicit about their political leanings. During the casual social conversation that preceded and followed the course each Friday evening, there was often talk about the value and beauty of Bergamasco, and the worth of local traditions and values of simplicity, hard work, and straightforwardness. Such discussions sometimes took a political turn, for the two young men and one older woman who were members of the Northern League were vocal about their participation in various League events, often comparing notes on a particular rally or updating each other on shared acquaintances. When other class members joined in these conversations, they generally tended to agree with the League's stances on dialects and cultures and even the economy. Many felt, for instance, that Bergamaschi worked too hard to see the taxes they paid get sent away to Rome, where they had no control over what happened to them. They found it self-evident that some support of local vernaculars was desirable, even if it was just an individual commitment to learn it better and speak it more. There was one subject, however, upon which the Northern Leaguers and others tended not to agree – indeed, mentioning it generally led to the topic being shifted altogether in these conversations – and that was the League's ideas about immigrants.

Immigrants in Bergamo

Vanessa Maher has argued that "the imagery evoked by the new [i.e. current] immigration . . . is dissociated from its historical context. A sort of collective amnesia has swallowed up the experience of Italian emigration, of Italian colonialism, of Fascism, the knowledge of the complexity of Italian society itself" (Maher 1996:168). This tended to be as true in Bergamo as it was in Turin, the site of Maher's research. Although there were a number of Bergamasco individuals and organizations that supported immigrants and immigration both materially and ideologically, the prevailing view of immigrants was characterized by reductive stereotypes (the image of the immigrant tends to be male, north African, black, undereducated, and Muslim) and distrust of the unknown. Many Bergamaschi had few personal interactions with immigrants in the course of their everyday lives aside from the most casual, and media representations of immigrants tended to represent them as criminals and prostitutes (Castellanos 2004, 2006). Although the League was the most vocal opponent of immigration, many of the sentiments it expressed, such as fear and distrust of these newcomers, resonated with many Bergamaschi.

It has become impossible to live in Bergamo and not be acutely conscious of the presence of immigrants. In 2003, there were roughly seven immigrants for every 100 people in the province of Bergamo, and immigrants could be found in some numbers in every neighborhood of the city and across the province (Casti 2004). In 1999–2000, however, it was just becoming clear to Bergamaschi – like other Italians – that immigrants were here to stay. Newspapers and television and radio newscasts were filled with stories of arriving boatloads of immigrants from North Africa, as well as a constant barrage of stories about crime attributed to Albanians and Roma. Repeated efforts to count and account for as many legal and illegal immigrants in the city and province as possible filled local newspapers during that period, and personal anecdotes about people's experiences with immigrants, both good and bad, were a frequent feature of conversation.

I had my own experiences to share. Early on in my research, I had to go a number of times to the *questura* (main police station) to obtain the permanent copy of my *permesso di soggiorno* (residence permit). One of these coincided with a period in which legal immigrants were required to go to the police station to register. At the questura in Bergamo at that time, there were two separate areas for different groups of people to interact with the police. One area, for European citizens ("*communitari*" or community members), always had short lines, multiple people working the windows, and applicants for visas, residence permits, etc., were allowed to wait in line inside. The other area for "*extra-communitari*" (non-community members), for everyone else – in other words, the majority of the immigrants in Bergamo at that time – always had longer lines, fewer windows open, and applicants were required to line up and wait outside. Police officers stood at the head of the line outside a small fenced-in area outside the door and checked documents before allowing people inside a few at a time. On earlier visits to the questura, I had gone inside to seek information, not knowing the system. On this day, I read the signs more carefully and realized that as a non-European (I am from the US), I should technically stand in the second line. It was raining and cold, and there were several hundred people waiting, speaking a variety of languages, Italian and Bergamasco among them. During the course of what turned into a four hour wait, many of them asked me what I was doing in that line, and urged me to simply go inside, as surely I was allowed to do. I insisted that, as a non-European, I was in the correct line and stayed put. When I finally approached the head of the line, the officer on duty looked at me and demanded my passport. Upon seeing that I was American, he scolded me for wasting my time in this line and shoo-ed me inside to the shorter line, where I waited only a few minutes before being helped and was told to always return to this area in the future.[17]

For most of the people with whom I waited that morning, this type of bureaucratic treatment was typical of their experience in Bergamo. They were treated like necessary impositions, strangers among people known for being personally reserved and slow to warm to newcomers, guests of hesitant hosts. Subject to the Northern League's screed that they were stealing Italian jobs, threatening the Italian way of life, and imposing upon the already overwhelmed social system, recent immigrants faced numerous obstacles to fitting into life in Bergamo and elsewhere in Italy (Carter 1997; Cole 1997).

The same had been said about earlier waves of immigrants to Bergamo: those who had come from the south a generation or two before, also in search of better jobs.[18] Bergamaschi who had gone to school in the 1950s and 1960s complained to me about how often their school teachers had been from the south and how difficult that had made school for them, since these teachers did not know Bergamasco and often "didn't even really speak Italian" (i.e. spoke a form of Italian influenced by their own dialect of origin). Indeed, Annabella described a former colleague from the south who had experienced moments when she could not communicate with her students since she did not know Bergamasco. By the end of the 1990s, most of those immigrants had been integrated into Bergamasco society, many marrying Bergamaschi. A surprising number of Bergamaschi under the age of 50 with whom I interacted and/or interviewed had at least one parent or grandparent who was southern. Some of Bergamasco's most ardent supporters had southern ancestors, including Daniele, from Chapter 2, who displayed such interest in Bergamasco, and several of the participants in the other Bergamasco course I attended. Many southerners who settled in Bergamo had children and grandchildren who grew up speaking with Bergamasco accents and thinking of Bergamo as their home.

Those who had Bergamasco relatives often thought of themselves as primarily Bergamasco; even those without Bergamasco relatives who may have thought of themselves in different terms were generally indistinguishable from their peers in terms of dress and consumption habits. Certainly not all of them were interested in or spoke any Bergamasco; but then, nor did many Bergamaschi themselves. Once commonly discriminated against and reviled as incomers and strangers, most southerners in Bergamo had for the most part become integrated into Bergamasco society. Sara, for example, who is from Puglia, admitted that she sometimes felt the cultural differences between her home town and Bergamo, although marrying a Bergamasco made her feel that Bergamo was her home now, too. It helped that her brother also lived in Bergamo and worked in Milan, and that their parents visited often, especially after she and Federico had a child.

It was striking to me that Bergamaschi did not seem to consider explicitly how southerners became integrated as a model for how to interact with the new immigrants. Maher found a similar situation in Turin, which was the site of large-scale south–north immigration during the 1960s (1996) (see also Yanagisako 2002 on a similar tendency in Como). Maher observes that although the negative aspects of that period of migration – such as the illegal exploitation of southern workers at extremely low wages – are often referred to in discussions of current immigration, the positive aspects of it – such as the speed with which these southerners have been integrated into Turinese society, or the necessity of the labor the southerners provided to a booming economy – are rarely included. Likewise, in Bergamo, although I often heard about those troublesome southern school teachers from the 1950s and 1960, there was virtually no comparison between what had happened to those school teachers and other southerners (i.e. most had stayed and become part of Bergamasco society) and what might happen with current immigrants given a generation or two. The gulf between themselves and the newcomers was seen as too large to overcome easily, despite the fact that Bergamaschi increasingly lived and worked alongside immigrants. The League's hyperbolized rhetoric (Fader 2007), which portrayed all immigrants as Muslims, thereby emphasizing the insurmountable differences between Muslim immigrant culture and Catholic Italian culture, surely played a large role in this.

There were signs, however, that a certain level of integration was happening in spite of these perceived differences. During the course of my research in 1999–2000, Bergamaschi often told me about an immigrant they knew or had heard about who spoke Bergamasco. In fact, it became a predictable and familiar topic whenever I got into a conversation with someone about Bergamo and Bergamasco and the subject of immigrants came up, as it so often did. For instance, during a group interview with high school students, one female student said, "*Ho sentito parlare non so, forse un marocchino, che parlava in bergamasco, sembrava strano perché . . . magari non sanno l'italiano però sentendo tante persone che parlano in dialetto imparano . . .*" ("I've heard speak, I don't know, maybe a Moroccan, who spoke in Bergamasco. It seemed strange because . . . I think maybe they don't know Italian, however, hearing lots of people who speak in dialect, they learn . . ."). Most often, this Bergamasco-speaking immigrant was encountered in the workplace. "There is an immigrant who speaks Bergamasco at my work" – or "my husband's work" or "my parents' work" – I heard several times. He (always a male) spoke it just like everyone else does. People often marveled at how good the immigrant's accent was, as well as how strange it sounded to have someone who looked so different speak something so familiar. Sometimes this anecdote was offered as proof that Bergamasco was not being lost and would persevere. Sometimes it was presented as a marvel, as an exception to the rule of how hard Bergamasco is to learn. Sometimes it was told as a way to fill out the image of how Bergamaschi value hard work, such that those who come here and act like us, by working hard and speaking like us, will be accepted, will become part of our social landscape. In speaking about his own printing business, the Duke asserted that such hard workers, like the Pakistani who worked for him, were generally trying to save up to go home, making them perhaps less of a threat to Bergamasco society.

The fact that I heard this story so often (although was never able to meet such an immigrant, although I did overhear immigrants speaking Bergamasco a few times) seemed to me to be evidence of several things. First, it helped demonstrate that Bergamasco itself was alive and well in certain contexts, work being one of the most vibrant, in spite of ongoing protestations about its imminent loss.

Second, I saw it as proof that the cultural differences that leghisti and others emphasized so heavily in their arguments for limiting immigration or immigrants' rights to certain services or privileges were just one limited version of how Italians and Bergamaschi were adjusting to being the site of immigration. The conversations I had with some immigrants there seemed to attest to the work-in-progress nature of Bergamaschi's dealings with immigrants. "Don't you find them [Bergamaschi] closed (*'chiusi'*)?" I was asked several times. "But then they warm up as you get to know them." Other immigrants seemed resigned to being treated as outsiders, and remained oriented toward fellow immigrants – most often from the same place – in their social networks and employment choices whenever possible. For instance, businesses that primarily served immigrants, such as phone and Internet centers, grocery stores with food from abroad, and restaurants serving non-Italian food (few and far between in 2000, and only slightly more numerous by 2007), tended to be grouped together and run by immigrants.

European Belonging Against the Other

This Bergamasco-speaking immigrant I heard about so often was also a material and symbolic link between this community and the rest of western Europe, where efforts to deal with non-European and eastern European immigrants are currently one of the biggest challenges (Auslander 2000; Berdahl 1999; Beriss 1990; Bowen 2004; Bunzl 2005; Campani 1993; Grillo 1985). The Bergamasco-speaking immigrant, whether fictional or actual, was an international element made sense of through everyday experience.

Especially in the post-9/11 world, the struggle to overcome cultural differences between Christian host countries and Muslim immigrant communities – which has often been portrayed in the US and in Europe as a "clash of civilizations" – could seem nearly overwhelming when viewed as a large-scale, national problem in need of national policy choices. The League constantly played up, for instance, the differences between the presumed Catholicism of most Italians with the more recently arrived waves of Muslim immigrants, helping to concretize the contrast between how Catholics and Muslims live. These differences, which ignore the largely secular nature of modern Italy (Catholic church participation has been decreasing since World War II (Duggan 2007; Mack Smith 1997)), were offered as evidence that the newcomers' differences would prevent them from participating in community life in predictable and suitable ways. *Questa gente* (these people) was a common way for leghisti to begin conversations about the differences between themselves and immigrants, usually neighbors or groups encountered in public spaces. In one conversation, *questa gente* was an Egyptian family who lived above my leghista interlocutors; the unfamiliar smells of their cooking, the frequency with which they hosted gatherings with other Egyptians, and the relatively large size of the family itself were complained about at length, making it seem impossible that there could be any common ground between the newcomers and the Bergamaschi who spoke to me.

As Stolcke, among others, has argued, "the entry and settlement of immigrants in Europe poses again the question of what constitutes the modern nation-state, and what are conceived as the prerequisites for access to nationality and citizenship" (1999:29). Language skills are an easy emblem of and access to civic participation (Blommaert and Verschueren 1998); in the national and local media as well as casual conversations, immigrants' lack of Italian competence was often held up as an example of their lack of integration into Italian society. This was especially true of immigrant children, who were often portrayed as clogging the educational system with their lack of Italian competence when they were placed in age-appropriate grade levels. Immigrant children's difficulties in Italian schools, however, were indicative not just of their own linguistic abilities, but also of the Italian educational system's slow response to their needs.

Rising immigration rates have coincided with increasing European integration, such that immigration has provoked discussion of regional, national, and European identifications (ÖzyÜrek 2005, Paasi 2001, Pettigrew 1998). Describing the place of Turks in Berlin after the fall of the Wall, for instance, White argues that increasing the unity of Europe (such as with Maastricht Treaties) "encouraged a reevaluation not only of national identity, but also of identities of encapsulated groups" (1996:16) (see also M. Feldman 2001). Shore

(2001) and others have argued that increasing Europeanization has required the formation of a non-European Other, most potently imagined as a Muslim immigrant who does not share European ideals, values, and practices (Boyer 2005; Borneman and Fowler 1997). And while in Italy the political Right in general and Northern League in particular are most commonly portrayed as hostile to immigrants and their integration, Però has argued that the Left has also been complicit in "their unwillingness to consider immigrants part of their 'imagined communities'" (2005:834).[19] Indeed, the success of integralist parties across Europe has been built on their successfully linking local ethnic identities to national protectionist policies/positions, such that immigrants cannot be integrated into these places specifically due to their perceived and elaborated cultural differences. Political success by a Swiss integralist party in 2007 national elections, for instance, relied on continued reference to "our" versus "their" traditions, selectively focusing on ethnic traditions that immigrants could not share, much to the dismay of their political opponents. Likewise, the uproar in Italy in late 2007 over a pair of murders of Italians by Romanians heavily emphasized inherent cultural differences between Italians and Romanians, and stressed their incompatibility.[20] In Bergamo, media frequently blamed crimes on foreigners (particularly Albanians) in terms that appeared blatantly xenophobic by American standards of political correctness.

In such contexts, speaking Italian – or not – potentially indexed these cultural divides, but may also be read as an orientation toward integration. Immigrants speaking Italian indicated a desire to become Italian and embrace Italian society and its values; speaking Bergamasco seemed to display shared attitudes about the value of hard work, the importance of personal reserve, the weight of honesty. In the small details of everyday life, where workers literally spoke the same language, learning to live together seemed possible, even probable. This appeared to me especially promising at a time when Bergamaschi were getting used to the idea that immigrants were there to stay, bringing their labor to become a part of the hardworking industrial Bergamasco economy, their children to join Bergamasco children in school,[21] and their sociocultural practices to contrast with how Bergamaschi and Italians lived, at least for the moment. What it meant for the social aesthetics of language in

Bergamo remains to be seen, although it does suggest a reinforcement of the association of Bergamasco with locally prized values, if not a speaker's immediate connection to these values through a shared, emplaced history.

Conclusion

By the 1980s and 1990s, with most Bergamaschi now safely a generation or two away from the difficulties of poverty, hard manual labor, and under-education, some began to worry about their rush to modernity and prosperity. Annabella, the recently retired schoolteacher, likened these shifts to throwing out old family heirlooms in favor of new, modern furniture. She opined that "people, at least a lot of people, have renounced the dialect with the same spirit with which they threw away the old things because of this desire for everything new, everything – afterwards sure, now yes, they are realizing that they were stupid" ("*la gente, tanta gente almeno, abbia rinunciato il dialetto con lo stesso spirito con cui buttava via le cose vecchie perché questa voglia di tutto nuovo, tutto – dopo, certo, adesso sì, stanno accorgendo che sono stati stupidi*"). Hers was a commonly voiced view in Bergamo that shortsighted socioeconomic aspirations have led to hasty social and linguistic changes; later, people see the mistakes that they made and regret them, lamenting that buying back the family heirlooms will prove costly indeed.

The Ducato di Piazza Pontida and the Northern League appointed themselves the collectors and keepers of these cultural heirlooms. Both asserted the value of the vernacular and other local practices; both contributed in various ways to the complicated position in which these practices found themselves in the early 2000s. Since its birth, the Ducato has claimed to be acting against the loss of the dialect; in doing so, it has perhaps helped make such loss come about. The Northern League's role as champion of all northern local cultures has lent these cultures their political sheen, making sounding Bergamasco potentially equivalent to sounding pro-Northern League. These factors made up just one part of the social aesthetics of language in Bergamo, but they may be thought of as persistent undercurrents in what speaking in Bergamo meant, one element of the indexical background against which everyday speaking and special cultural events took place. By perhaps unintentionally reinforcing the already strong associations between speaking Bergamasco and sounding old-fashioned (i.e. displaying an orientation toward the past) and close-minded (i.e. displaying an orientation toward provincialism), the Ducato and the Northern League redrew the restricted circle that many Bergamaschi had sought to escape. That so much of their own interaction occurred in Italian underlined how removed Bergamasco was from their daily practices.

In such a context, the meaning of being local became highly charged and dynamic. Some scholars of Europe have noted that strong connections to local places need not interfere with attachments to the nation or EU, and may even reinforce them (Cohen 1996; Eidson 2005; Galbraith 2004; Nadel-Klein 1991; Ruzza 2000). Anti-leghista rhetoric generally portrayed the League's attachment to local identities and ways of life as anachronistic and anti-modern, implicitly promoting the nation-state as the proper vehicle for modern advancement. In such discussion, a straight line of progress was often drawn from the archaic provincialism of the past (to which the League allegedly wants to return) to the modern nationalism of the present toward the process of integration into the EU and global economy. The Ducato and the League, however, shared the idea that a commitment to the local was the only way to approach such large-scale political and economic integrations. In a rare optimistic moment, the Duke once speculated that perhaps in 50 years there would be only English and Bergamasco left to speak. The leghista mayor of Seriate saw supporting local culture as a tactic to fight globalization, saying "*Io dico, ogni nazione, ogni posto ha la sua traditione, è bello andar a visitare, perché vedi là la loro tradizione, e quindi noi dobbiamo mantenere la nostra. Non globalizzare il mondo! Ostrega! . . . Dobbiamo invece salvaguardare questo proprio. Se no, brutto mondo si presentarà domani, mettendo tutto piatto*" ("I say, every nation, every place has its own tradition. It's nice to go to visit, in order to see there their traditions, and therefore we must maintain our own. Don't globalize the world! Heavens! We must instead really save this. If not, what an ugly world we will see tomorrow, with everything flattened out").

The fact that such rhetoric in favor of the value of all local –
which he calls here "national" – traditions was often used as a
strategy for saying that immigrants should return to their homes
does not diminish the potential to use this quote to peek at one
vital dimension of what it felt like to be Bergamasco. Indeed, we
can see how it parallels Giorgio's comments in Chapter 2 about
why Bergamasco is valuable: "*il dialetto è un qualchecosa di nostro, che
abbiamo sentito da quando* **a m' séra s-cècc e che nóter, nóter e
i nóter <u>poeti</u>, töcc chei chi scrif,** *e* anche **chei <u>chi la parla</u>**
cerchiamo di manterlo vivo" ("the dialect is something of ours, that
we have heard (lit. 'felt') from when we were children, and that
we, we and our poets, all those who write and also those who speak
it, we try to keep it alive"). In a time of obvious social transformation, making sense of the broader world started with making sense
of one's own place, its history, and its language(s) vis-à-vis one's
neighbors, both near and far.

7

Conclusion

In June of 2001, Paolo Frér passed away in his home. A few months later, Stefano, the architect, followed him, and Bergamo had lost two important citizens and champions. Long time friends, neighbors in the Città Alta, and occasional professional collaborators, Paolo and Stefano lived very different lives, although they shared a number of passions and interests about local practices, places, and values. Both had dedicated themselves to preserving what they saw as the best about Bergamo, practicing what they preached, as it were. Paolo's work as a poet provided textual representations of a shared past that had been lived in Bergamasco; his performances of those poems enacted a traditional practice whose pleasures were becoming increasingly rare. Paolo's lifetime in the butiga passed down to him from his father and grandfather was a material testament to the value of hard, careful work, and his expansive collections of Bergamasco objects – puppets, keys, iron-working tools – were concrete representations of Bergamasco work and leisure in the past. Stefano's long-term project to make the Città Alta the place of beauty he imagined it should be, as well as his daily efforts to make it a more livable place, were key in making the Città Alta what it is today. As a continuation of the work begun by his father, Stefano's efforts provided an unbroken link to Bergamo's past, bridging how it used to be and what it has become. Through his many contributions to the artistic life of Bergamo – in addition to architecture, Stefano designed avant-garde theater sets and published a number of books of his drawings – Stefano emphasized the importance of visual aesthetics in everyday life. Both left indelible marks on the shape of modern Bergamo through their engagement with traditional practices.

That summer day at the restored cassina in the mountains, Paolo and Stefano sat at opposite ends of the long convivial table, Stefano raising his glass to toast Paolo's poems, Paolo listening attentively to Stefano's stories about projects he had done in India, Oman, and Spain. In their work together, Stefano had often designed the iron-work that Paolo produced. Both deferred to the other's expert knowledge. Others frequently pointed to one or the other or both as important to Bergamo, and the Città Alta in particular. Repre-sentatives of the elite and working class of Bergamo respectively, Stefano and Paolo had approached their work and advocacy for Bergamasco culture from different perspectives. In a conversation with me, Stefano recalled the courtly, mellifluous Bergamasco his mother used to speak, a variety he said no one – including himself – could speak at all any more. His extensive education, upper-class background, and professional successes put him in a privileged posi-tion vis-à-vis other Bergamaschi, although he brought his worldli-ness to bear on his commitment to Bergamo. Paolo's workshop and stories were full of evidence of his father and grandfather's prowess as ironsmiths; his own hands and feet, gnarled and painful, were testament to the embodied effort he had expended to follow them. When praised for his poetry, Paolo often demurred that he was a man of little education and simple tastes. Those who knew him recognized him as a *un poeta vero, un bergamasco vero* – a real poet, a true Bergamasco.

What does it mean to Bergamo, and to its language and culture in particular, to have lost these two individuals? There were other champions of Bergamo and Bergamasco who would continue to tell their stories, read what they wrote, practice the skills they honed, and cherish the place they called home. But with their deaths, the past that they worked so hard to keep present recedes a little further onto the horizon. This past – of the pòer bortulì and polenta, of share-cropping and crowded palazzi, of wooden clogs and poets at the head of the table – was a world lived within the intimate circle of Bergamasco. That circle has long since become a restraint, a "lin-guistic ghetto" (De Mauro 1972), and the way out and up was Italian. Bergamasco need not have been left entirely behind in this flight – and perhaps it will still persevere – but the heralds of its death are loud and forceful.

Worrying and Celebrating in the New Millennium

We began this book in a classroom with Bergamaschi worried that their dialect might be dying, worried enough to dedicate an evening a week to it. Those dozen people were, like Paolo and Stefano, invested in the value of their language. This value was constructed through Bergamasco's multiple indexical associations to the multivalent past, to certain characteristics and ethics, to an idea of self as grounded in a place. They came to this orientation toward their language, and hence this class, from different origins: through a desire to join the ranks of local poets; through the goal to read more easily – and thus better perform – dialect play scripts; through a curiosity about lining up orthographic rules and speaking practices; through the ambition to speak better to one's grandmother, father, infant daughter; through a politically shaped wish to avoid sounding like a slave to Rome; through the simple aspiration to appreciate more thoroughly their Bergamasco.

In reflecting on the social aesthetics of language in Bergamo, I find it hard not to compare this group with the people who surrounded us on New Year's Eve as we waited for the new millennium to begin. My *moroso* and I had joined the enormous public festivities in the center of the Lower City, where a DJ played Italian and English-language pop songs, fireworks whizzed dangerously close to the crowd (it seemed to us), and thousands of revelers danced and sang. The crowd included groups of young people, couples, and families with strollers and grandparents – it seemed most of Bergamo was packed into the *Sentierone*, the center square in the Lower City. Just before the countdown to midnight began, the DJ played John Lennon's "Imagine." Everyone tried to sing along at the top of their lungs, stumbling over the English except during the central lines: "Imagine all the people, living for today ..." Once midnight struck and the campanile bells all over town began to sound, the crowd began to disperse, as many people began to walk up to the Città Alta, capping their evenings with a social stroll up and down the *corsaröla* and perhaps around the Mura, enjoying the view on this crisp, clear, historic night. The Italian media had just the preceding week started to print stories wondering about Y2K and the potential technological mishaps the new year might bring, often focusing in particular on how cellphone service would surely be the first to go if there were any computer catastrophes. As we were swept up in the surge to the Città Alta, it seemed everyone was on his or her cellphone. During the walk, again and again we heard: "*Pronto? Ci sei? Funziona!*" ("Hello? Are you there? It's working!"). The chorus continued until the wee hours, as we lay listening to the crowds pass under our window in Via Porta Dipinta as we tried (and failed) to sleep through the continuing revelry. The birreria beneath us overflowed with happy customers who spilled out to join the hordes of passers-by in the streets.

We did not hear much Bergamasco that night, neither as part of the public entertainment nor in the individual conversations that surrounded us. Occasionally a Bergamasco exclamation or curse or "pòta!" would follow a joke or story, and we heard older people address one another and their loved ones in Bergamasco. The accents around us ran the gamut from barely discernible to extremely stretto. Like the John Lennon song we sang along to during the festivities, it seemed most of these revelers were indeed "living for today" – for the Italian modernity represented in cellphones, for the technological conveniences that allowed these brief phone connections, for the globalization that brought music from all over the world to be enjoyed, and for the comfort of modern prosperity obvious in the *bella figura* displayed in nice clothes, expensive watches, elaborate strollers. The Bergamasco future, not the past, was the focus that night – and probably most of the time – for those out celebrating; the linguistic dominance of Italian was obvious that night.

I have often reflected on these other Bergamaschi, the ones who did not attend poetry recitals or play performances; who did not join the Ducato's writing course or other activities, and who may never have heard of the group at all; who did not know Paolo or Stefano, or their work; who considered the Città Alta a site of recreation, not lived history. I imagine that, like many of the high school students I interviewed, when they thought of Bergamasco at all, they thought of it as something their grandparents spoke, something that had nothing to do with them. They grew up in and inhabited a world of Italian.

Indeed, as many of the young 20- and 30-somethings who sprayed the crowd with *prosecco* on New Year's went to work, perhaps for Hewlett-Packard and Italcementi, two of the largest employers in the area, their professional experiences probably involved frequent interaction with fellow workers across Italy, Europe, and around the world, via email, on the phone or through travel. Their leisure time may have been spent as far a field as the Maldives, the Caribbean, or Finland, as the small local airport (now referred to as Milan's third) had become a busy hub in the growth of low-cost European airlines in the early 2000s. Tourists from all over Europe who flew in on these same low fares may have joined them in their strolls around the Città Alta or while shopping at the ipermercati that dotted Bergamo's industrial periphery. Their hobbies may have included bike riding on Sunday mornings or following auto racing on television. These activities would have been conducted in Italian or other national languages, probably not Bergamasco.

My tone is speculative because my research did not bring me into close contact with many of these "others." Most of the speakers in these pages were focused on their dialect in some way; this was not true for all Bergamaschi, even for many who spoke it extensively everyday. For many young, educated women especially, the dialect was not even a force to be struggled against. It was just something one's grandparents spoke; something occasionally seen on shop signs or signs for certain towns; intermittently overheard in the piazza or shouted in political rallies. My interest in studying Bergamasco seemed to them quaint and folklorish.

Casual conversation with these "others," however, demonstrated that Bergamasco informed their speech in important ways. High school students could and did describe what their own Bergamasco accents sounded like; some – especially young men – admitted when pressed to speaking it with parents, grandparents, even friends, occasionally. Young people in their twenties and thirties had older relatives who spoke it; chances were good they understood – and perhaps even spoke – more than they let on. Outside of Bergamo, the shape of their vowels or structure of their syntax would have connected them to their place, indexing the Bergamasco stereotype of hard work, personal reserve, paucity of education, and provoked a sneaking suspicion of Northern League leanings. The póer bortulì were never too far away.

Alongside these more immediately obvious others in that New Year's crowd, there was another group of Bergamaschi whose lives more resembled Marco's – they lived in the same small Bergamasco town in the valleys or plains of the province or even neighborhood of the city where they grew up, where their extended family lived and had lived for generations. They may have left school early in order to start work quickly, or have gone to a technical high school to gain skills to help them in the family business, like Roberto. Their workdays may have been spent speaking Bergamasco to their co-workers (who perhaps included immigrants from the south or abroad), and Italian to their supervisors, while their socializing with friends may have spanned the continuum between Bergamasco and Italian. Like Ella and Rina, their grandparents and parents may have continued to speak Bergamasco; they may or may not have answered them in kind. These were the people for whom the association of Bergamasco with men and Italian with women may have mattered the most, as young women may have found their linguistic respon-sibilities to their families weighted heavily in favor of Italian, even when they may have used Bergamasco ways of speaking without reflection or censure in other contexts.

These differences were clearly shaped by class, but also an orienta-tion toward place and one's location in time. Age mattered, too, as did political orientation, although both were more complicated than at first glance. Older people certainly spoke more Bergamasco, but the types of campanilistic activities that included a focus on the dialect may have been more associated with a particular stage of life – being retired and in pursuit of appropriate leisure-time activities – than with a particular generation. Members of the Northern League were explicit about their political stances and support of the dialect, but there were many Bergamaschi who agreed with only a few of the League's positions, linking the importance of local culture and language to concerns like local political autonomy or taxation.

The Social Aesthetics of Language

Together, these aspects composed the social aesthetics of language in Bergamo, the feel of language when hierarchy and sentiment met in the everyday rhythm of speech. This "tense intersection" between power and emotion overlapped with another intersection: between good Italian and real Bergamasco. Good Italian was Italian with no trace of Bergamasco; real Bergamasco was similarly absent of any interference from Italian. These varieties were mirages, ideals that persisted in spite of their impossibility in practice. The Italian spoken in Bergamo was full of vowel sounds, calques, and lexical choices that made it "speaking in a Bergamasco way." The Bergamasco used in the early 2000s contained words like "**forchéta**" and "**televissiù**," with a perceived paucity of colorful terms such as "**malfàt**." As interactions like the discussion about clogs or the argument over cards in Chapter 2 demonstrate, much everyday interaction occurred on a continuum between the two languages, with different speakers drawing on Italian and Bergamasco to differing degrees throughout an interaction. Despite language ideologies that drew a bright line between the two varieties and evaluated them differently, much speech involved, to use Carla's felicitous phrase, "**mesciando sö** 'l **bergamàsch e** *italiano*" ("mixing up Bergamasco and Italian").

In the heteroglossic unfolding of day-to-day conversation, such mixing drew on the linguistic and symbolic resources of both languages, constantly impacting and reshaping the indexical background. Using Bergamasco words or phrases indexed shared values of speaking simply in order to be "one of us," though the use of Bergamasco syntactic structures may have sounded old-fashioned or ignorant, "typically Bergamasco," to some. Tapping into the semantic treasure trove of Bergamasco through using linguistic heirlooms like **malfàt** reminded listeners of how acutely and immediately Bergamasco signified what was important about Bergamasco culture. Such terms did double duty: referentially valuable, as well as indexically loaded, pointing to the past where such characteristics and values were common and shared by all. Even those who talked about the dialect as being precious or important most often associated it with the stereotype of the Bergamasco contadino: hard work, straightforwardness, honesty, and a roughness, all of which seem iconically evidenced in the very sound of spoken Bergamasco. It seems a difficult if not unlikely task to polish these heirlooms so that they no longer reflect the roughness of the past, but only its desired values.

The ideology of purism that supports the evaluation of terms like **malfàt** as worth more than other words helped to make contemporary Bergamasco-speaking practices as "not the real thing" in contrast.[1] These perceptions about and indexical associations involved in dividing good from bad language were prescriptive rather than descriptive, helping create the very divides they purported to depict (Milroy and Milroy 1985). Such evaluations were experienced as aesthetic judgments, immediately felt to be true. This feel of and for language was anchored in the affective ties between speakers and their languages, as well as the emotions they claimed while reflecting on those languages: desire, fear, shame, anxiety, satisfaction. Nostalgic sentiments colored efforts to "save" Bergamasco, while Italian felt "normal" in its role as the language in which much of everyday public life is conducted.

Linguistic cultural production – including poets' voices, poetic turns of phrase, play rehearsals and performances, staged poetry readings with expert commentary – made up an essential cornerstone of the social aesthetics of language in Bergamo, playing important parts in what Bergamasco and Italian meant. Ruminations on the value of old words, intuitions that "mixed" phrases like **smistà fò** cannot be the "real thing," and grandmothers who confirm this intuition and supply the true form (**desmescià fò**) – all of these metalinguistic judgments helped support the purified, often archaic Bergamasco in which plays and poetry were written. The purified Bergamasco in these cultural productions portrayed a world lived entirely in Bergamasco, one that was often located squarely in an unspecified but local past, when personal sentiment, honesty, perseverance and a Giopì-inspired wit could be used to overcome the toughest obstacles. The Italian that surrounded these performances and texts served to underline how very different everyday life is now, linguistic contrasts that indexed and reinforced social, economic, even technological disparities between past and present. Moving up on the socioeconomic ladder meant leaving behind "traditional" practices which, though once associated with one group of Bergamaschi – i.e. pre-Economic Boom rural agriculturalists and manual laborers – had been generalized to be "authentic" Bergamasco culture. A peasant past, however, was easy to long for nostalgically when it was securely in the past, when the deprivations and difficulties that characterized so much of everyday life were safely distant, present only on the page or the stage. This uneasy tension between the idealized solidarity of the Bergamasco past with the difficulties of living entirely within the restricted circle of Bergamasco was displayed, for instance, in stories about **póer bortulì** and insurance men, and partially resolved through humorous re-tellings that "said bread for bread, and wine for wine."

One need not ever have attended a poetry reading, opened a volume of poetry, or attended a play performance in order to have known that the value of Bergamasco was closely bound up with these activities, or that the language used in them was distinctive from everyday life. For instance, in describing why it was so difficult for young people like him to understand Bergamasco poetry, a male high school student observed that in poetry, *"ci sono dei termini che proprio non stanno ne in cielo ne in terra rispetto all'italiano"* ("there are terms that really don't exist either in heaven or on earth in respect to Italian"). One person's linguistic heirlooms were another's inaccessible anachronisms. It is difficult to imagine this youth and his peers becoming the next generation of participants in either of these genres; the archaic Bergamasco prized by others stood as a barrier between these youths' linguistic habits and preferences and their participation in these genres that were seen as helping to save Bergamasco (see Hill 2002 for a similar situation with Mexicano).

There were other ways as well in which dialect poetry and theater potentially contributed to the loss of Bergamasco, although many Bergamaschi viewed them as antidotes to this loss. Early efforts by elites to simultaneously characterize the language and practices of their coevals as belonging to the past and to celebrate particular activities as essential signifiers of these practices, while portrayed as efforts to "save" these things, may have helped put in motion the very changes they lamented. In addition, an ongoing shift toward weighing the value of written forms as equally important to or more important than oral forms seems to have been occurring, through the growing importance of published works, poetry contests, and having poetry published in Giopì. Given how difficult and inaccessible the written form of Bergamasco was for most people – as evidenced not only in the existence of courses dedicated to teaching how to write and read it, but also by the fact that participants may take such courses several times in order to master the current complicated orthographic system – prioritizing these forms may mean that Bergamasco comes to live more often on bookshelves than on speakers' tongues. Coupled with the diminution in frequency of the most traditional form of poetry performance – among friends and family around the table – Bergamasco poetry seems multiply removed from most people's everyday lives, a tool with little practical application, like the iron-working utensils from the past that decorated the walls of Paolo's butiga.

As with scholars of aesthetics, some of the central and ongoing challenges for scholars of language in use have been to describe and analyze the relationships between subject and object, practices and beliefs. Paradigms like language ideology have been efforts to connect various levels of inquiry, bringing together analysis of beliefs about language, linguistic practices, and cultural norms, ideals, and judgments. The concept of the social aesthetics of language, which uses indexicality to track and ground the heteroglossic use of language across various spheres of interaction and cultural domains, allows just such a perspective. Through focusing on how people feel about their own and other people's language use – the emotions they express about and through language, the affective practices that allow such expression, the sentiments that "bridge the dichotomy between emotion and thought" (Yanagisako 2002:10) – analysts can look two ways at once: toward the cultural notions, social valences, and political economic structures within which people speak as well as toward the linguistic practices that they use to put their understandings of these into action.

Such a perspective also provides a vantage point that encompasses both shared orientations and individual choices. Aesthetics provide common orientations for those who share them, but cannot be reduced to singular viewpoints; one may agree that a particular object is a piece of art, while disagreeing on whether one enjoys it or thinks that it is "good." Similarly, a social aesthetics of language allows for both shared orientations across speakers, as well as individual variation in terms practices and opinions. Through adopting such a focus, I have sought to depict the complex texture of everyday life, in which language use is informed by national policies and neighborly interactions; humorous punch-lines and treacherous stereotypes; ideas of right and wrong as well as standards of beauty and vulgarity. Like most people, Bergamaschi only occasionally pause to think about what and how they speak. Nonetheless, their choices about language are intimately linked to their ideas of desirable selves, located within particular times and places.

The Politics of Language and Linguistic Choice

In the spring of 2007, the politics of language in Italy enjoyed a new iteration when Parliament approved a constitutional amendment declaring Italian the official language of the Republic. Like English-only legislation recently passed in the US (Crawford 2000), this legislation passed on the strength of being presented as apparently unobjectionable, as simply describing an already-existing linguistic reality. Italian is the de facto language of the Republic already, such implacable logic goes, so why not make it official? Although the measure passed resoundingly with 371 votes in favor, 75 members of the parliament voted against it and 28 abstained. Those who voted against it predictably included several members of the Northern League, one of whom, Federico Bricolo, protested that his language was not Italian but Venetian, speaking in Venetian until his microphone was switched off due to an Italian-only rule in Parliament. Other opponents included deputies from the left, who proclaimed that the measure recalled oppressive Fascist policies, which enforced national unity over all else.[2]

Although the measure has been dismissed as simply symbolic, it rehearsed several of the familiar tensions central to contemporary iterations of the *questione della lingua*. In addition, it changed nothing for either the minority languages with special constitutional status, such as German in Trentino-Alto Adige and Franco-Provençal in Val D'Aosta, or the Italo-Romance varieties – dialects – that so many Italians continue to speak.[3] Dialects like Bergamasco remain essentially and officially invisible in the sociopolitical linguistic landscape, not worthy of protection or recognition, no longer vital enough to be worried about or legislated against.

Language minority groups across Europe have pursued various political or academic paths towards revitalization and against obsolescence (Drysdale 2001; Urla 1993a, 1993b). Some have turned to the European Bureau for Lesser Used Languages (EBLUL) for aid in terms of political recognition, legal protections, and financial support (Di Giacomo 1999, 2001; Jaffe 2001; McEwan-Fujita 2003, 2005; O'Reilly 2001). Others have joined forces with language activists in different communities. Language such as Welsh, Scottish Gaelic, and Basque have profited from such revitalization activities, aligning themselves with language activists across Europe (Williams 2005). Groups such as Mercator, which publishes a regular email newsletter concerning the work of its three centers – Mercator Legislation, located at the CIEMEN foundation in Barcelona; Mercator Media at the University of Wales in Aberystwyth; and the Mercator European Research Centre on Multilingualism and Language Learning (the Mercator Research Centre for short) at the Fryske Akademy in Ljouwert/Leeuwarden – advocate for European minority languages, and provide focus points for research and information dissemination. Conferences such as the Tenth International Conference on Minority Languages that took place in 2005 in Trieste provide a forum for discussing the political, social, and cultural roles and fates of minority languages in Italy and Europe.

Tullio De Mauro, respected linguist, author of the highly influential volume, *Storia Linguistica dell'Italia Unita* (Linguistic History of United Italy; 1972), and past Italian Minister of Public Education, was one of the plenary speakers at this conference. He began his talk, "Crisis of the linguistic monolithism and aspects of the situations of the more or less spread languages," asserting that he was going to speak in Italian, since he was more comfortable in it than English, the language of most of the other presentations. Of course, he observed, he would have been most comfortable speaking the variety of Neapolitan that was his true mother tongue, his most intimate code of communication, sentiment, and thought. He lamented – in Italian – the impossibility of such an address, blaming it on what he called the ideology of monolithism, which valorizes national languages and excludes minority languages.

As of 2007, De Mauro's beloved Neapolitan, like other Italian dialects, had no legal recourse to challenge its current invisible status. In order to pursue EU protections, minority languages need to have been recognized as such by the nation-states in which they reside. Since Italian dialects had received no such recognition, these possibilities were closed to them. Indeed, Italian dialects were absent from official lists of European minority languages maintained by EBLUL, as well as invisible on the maps produced by Eurominority, another pan-European advocacy group. Perhaps most importantly, in addition to being invisible to outsiders, to my knowledge no dialect groups have so far attempted to assert their status and be listed and mapped as minority languages. As with the Duke of the Ducato di Piazza Pontida, these vernaculars continue to be regarded as "just dialects." The politics of the Northern League have not changed this.

The terms of the modern conversation about language in Italy, which concerned how close the dialects were to being lost – and not, for instance, why these language varieties appeared to be persisting, albeit in different forms, in spite of repeated assertions of their loss over the last several generations – were established at the national and international level. Within this conversation, when dialects were mentioned at all, they were seen as throwbacks to a more backward era, not worthy of conducting the modern life for which national languages were more appropriate. The Northern League brought dialects onto the national political stage in the 1990s, but simultaneously colored them with a political tint that made widespread support complicated, even for those who cared about their dialect. This valence of Bergamasco as sounding *leghista* made it all the harder for some younger speakers to want to claim Bergamasco as their own or see speaking it as pleasurable or desirable. Older people who may have otherwise felt inclined to embrace activities such as poetry and dialect theater may have also felt repelled by this political sting.

Living Memory: Does Bergamasco Have a Future?

What did it mean to be living memory in Bergamo at the beginning of the new millennium, for those who cared about Bergamasco as well as those who did not? As Krause argues, "history provides people with moorings for orienting themselves in their social world. Hence, memories are socially situated" (2005:594). I have argued here that social memory is reflected and enacted in language use. In Bergamo, memory was present in the broad vowels and syntactic contours of speech that recalled a peasant past, in the cultural productions that placed the past on the stage or in the pages of a book, and in the physical geography of a treasured site, all demonstrating the "embeddedness of representations of the past in social situations in which particular actors, audiences, precedents, intentions, conventions, and strategies – which are never the only possible ones – come into play" (Eidson 2005:567). Living memory need not be a conscious orientation towards the past. Instead the past was part of the texture of everyday life where choices about language indexically associated life experiences and their value. Hierarchies structured the relationship between the past, present, and future, which were in turn linked to linguistic rankings. Sentimental attachments to people, places, objects, and practices oriented speakers towards the linguistic resources available to them.

This social aesthetics of language had implications for Bergamasco and its perceived impending loss, but while there were multiple shifts in action, loss was not as yet a foregone conclusion. The heteroglossic nature of everyday language use in Bergamo, in which both languages are in tense and dynamic play, makes it hard to make predictions about the potential futures of Bergamasco in some form. Clearly, the archaic Bergamasco featured in poetry and referred to in laments comparing the use of **forchèta** over **pirù** was quickly becoming a practice of the past and the stage. Indeed, the viewpoint of most Bergamaschi – including many prominent members of the Ducato di Piazza Pontida – was that Bergamasco was irrevocably in decline. In this, they were in accord with many language scholars, who have been predicting the death of the dialects for decades. The viewpoint expressed by Sanga (1992:1) illustrates a common view:

Nella storia linguistica italiana il dialetto assai spesso è stato associato ad immagini negative di subalternità, marginalità, rozzezza, dalle satire medievali ad improperio del dialetto (o dei vilani) alla repressione sistematica dei dialetti operata dalla scuola fino a non molto tempo addietro. La situazione oggi non è mutata, forse è peggiorata: se vi è maggiore comprensione e tolleranza e anche simpatia per il dialetto, questa è la simpatia che si tributa al vinto alla specie in via di estinzione.

In Italian linguistic history, the dialect has rather often been associated with negative images of subalternity, marginality, roughness, from Medieval satires of dialectal insults (or dialectal villains) to the systematic repression of the dialect operated by school until not long ago. The situation today is not changed, and may even be worse; if there is better comprehension and tolerance and even sympathy for the dialect, this is the sympathy that comes with the victory over a species that is on its way to extinction.

It is common to regard minority languages in this fashion. As Timm has observed about one minority language in France, "now that the long-term survival of Breton is in question, it is perhaps easier to feel affection and nostalgia for it" (2001:124). Breton was no longer essential to Breton identity, even as formerly negative attitudes about Breton language that earlier generations expressed are largely gone. Will this be the fate of Bergamasco, its use becoming less important to being Bergamasco, its symbolic value all that remains? Indeed, very few monolingual speakers of Bergamasco remained in the early 2000s, one of the various indicators that Sanga points to in making his prediction of the impending extinction of dialect.

There are others who see the changes that have affected the dialects in a different light. Benucci, for instance, asserts that "*italiano e dialetto si intersecano e vengano sempre più avvertiti come registri diversi della stessa lingua di cui rappresentano alternative pragmatiche*" ("Italian and dialect intersect and come to be known increasingly as different registers of the same language, which represent pragmatic alternatives") (1999:15). For the majority of the 347 speakers from across the peninsula in Benucci's interview survey who were asked "*che cosa è secondo Lei il dialetto?*" ("what is the dialect to you?"), dialect is just a regional language, connected to where you are from, which is often used with intimates instead of Italian.[4] Vizmuller-Zocco further observes that "*[s]e è vero che l'uso del dialetto sta diminuendo fra i giovani, è anche vero che hanno una competenza passiva che pure avrà una sua funzione del mantenimento di certi tratti linguistici*" ("if it is true that use of dialect is diminishing among youth, it is also true that they have a passive competence that indeed will have its own function in the maintenance of certain linguistic features") (1999:477). Such predictions are built as much on attitudes (speakers', researchers') as they are on data; loss and its possibility or probability are central to each.

The idea of loss was similarly strong for many Bergamaschi, many of whom looked ahead and saw a modern Italian future, with no room for the weight of the Bergamasco past. There were others, however, for whom the idea of loss was simply that: an idea. In an interview at her workplace in a valley above Bergamo, Serena, a 23-year-old office worker, at first insisted that she really could not speak Bergamasco that well, and used it mostly for humor – "*per fare le battute*" ("to make jokes"). Later, however, after the discussion turned to families she knew who claimed to speak only Italian at home, she became emotional, saying, "*Non, non ci credo! Cioè è impossibile che in una famiglia non si parli il dialetto. Secondo me. E' impossibile*" ("No, no I don't believe it! That is, it's impossible that in a family dialect isn't spoken. To my way of thinking. It's impossible"). In the face of these families, who, we speculated, were perhaps embarrassed by the "*brutto*" (as she had described it) dialect, she declared, "*Io non mi vergogno a dire che lo parlo, perché comunque sono – bergamasca sono e bergamasca resto*" ("I am not embarrassed to say that I speak it, because in any case I am – Bergamasco I am, and Bergamasco I'll stay"). Serena was in many ways a perfect candidate to be a young mother trying not to *fare una brutta figura* (look bad) by her children speaking anything but Italian, and indeed, her earlier claim to use Bergamasco only while joking seemed to adhere to this image of the linguistically responsible mother. It appeared to me, however, that at this later point in the conversation she was speaking plainly, bread to bread and wine to wine: she is Bergamasco, and will stay Bergamasco. Both require that she and her future family not only speak Bergamasco, but are proud to do so. As Serena's *moroso* was a *muratore* (construction worker), it seemed likely to her that they would speak Bergamasco at home.

Kulick (1992) and others have argued that without linguistic input and the social need to speak a language, novices such as children will not learn it. As Hoffman has recently argued (2006, 2008), revitalization efforts that ignore the role of language socialization within the home and family – more specifically, the important role of women in language maintenance – may miss the mark all together. Indeed, as we have seen, Bergamasco revitalization efforts, being largely the responsibility of men, did not seem to have resulted in Bergamasco being spoken more. Serena and others like them were perhaps swimming against the tide. However, such choices made up part of the dynamic texture of language in use in Bergamo; perhaps the values that Serena saw in the dialect – as part and parcel of what it means to be a family in Bergamo – will color the aesthetic judgments of others as they relate to their language, making "good Bergamasco" something new – a thing of the future, not just the past.

Notes

Constructing Transcripts

1. Bergamasco is an adjective that refers to the language and people from Bergamo. It is also an adjective implying linked to this place, as in "a Bergamasco house." I use this Anglicized adjective form here, except when referring to people, in which case I follow Italian norms and modify it for gender and number.
2. All names are pseudonyms.
3. The Italian "*laurea*" requires minimally five years and writing a thesis to complete.
4. When I undertook this research, I intended to enlist transcribers who had been involved in the interactions they transcribed. As this did not prove to be uniformly possible once research was underway, due to a number of reasons, I opted for uniformity in social distance between transcribers and people I recorded, hoping for a perspective that perhaps would have been lacking in the first scenario.
5. Silverstein has noted that speakers tend to be more aware of lexical issues than other types of linguistic phenomena (1981).
6. Drawn from Bernini and Sanga 1987; Berruto 1987; Blondeau 1996; Giannelli and Cravens 1997; Maiden 1995; Maiden and Parry 1997; Mora 1966, 1972; Sanga 1984, 1987, 1997; as well as my own research.
7. An example of this was Eduardo Olmi's film, *L'Albero degli Zoccoli* (*The Tree of the Wooden Shoes*), which featured amateur Bergamasco actors exclusively. After its release, numerous viewers claimed to not understand the dialog and the film was consequently subtitled in Italian.

Chapter 1   Introduction

1. Statistics from 2006, available online via Bergamo's website, www.comune. bergamo.it/servizi/notizie/notizie_fase02.aspx?ID=3156

2. By "language form" I mean everything from which language was being used (Italian, Bergamasco or the expansive continuum between the two) to word choice, shape of grammatical structures, and phonological contours.

3. As a Romance language, Bergamasco has T and V forms of address, which correspond, respectively, to informality and solidarity, and formality and social distance.

4. It has been relatively common in Italian language scholarship (sociolinguistic and dialectological) to try to capture the variety of the Italian linguistic landscape using a number of different terms (see Cavanaugh 1997 for discussion).

5. As Ivanov argues, "In a single utterance different speech attitudes may appear simultaneously" (2000:101).

6. I am indebted to Woolard's suggestion that the concept of indexicality is one possible route for putting heteroglossia and voice into action (2004).

7. For discussions of indexicality, see Ochs 1992 and Silverstein 1976, 2003 among others.

8. Analysts have demonstrated how the relationships between language and emotions can be multiplex and extremely varied cross-culturally (see, for instance, Abu-Lughod and Lutz 1990; Ahearn 2004; Irvine 1990; Kockelman 2004; Lutz 1986, 1988; Milton and Svašek 2005; Rosaldo 1984; Shoaps 2002; Wilce 2009).

9. Scholars often point to the shared language spoken by soldiers in the trenches in WWI as one of these (Bertacchi 1981).

10. Although there is regional variation in how Italian and local languages are used across communities and regions in Italy, there are also similarities across the board. Generally, Italian is the language of the state and its institutions, while the local language is used to varying degrees in more informal interactional spheres and contexts (Dal Negro 2005; Ruzza 2000; Sobrero 1993; Stacul 2001; Strassoldo 1996; Vizmuller-Zocco 1999). More dialect was spoken in certain areas (such as most southern regions, and the Veneto in the northeast) than others, although regional accents and ways of speaking associated with dialects remained strong. In most Italian communities, the local language and Italian were still each used for specific contexts, activities, and with and among particular speakers (generally older speakers). All Italians spoke with some trace of where they came from except for newscasters, and even that was shifting.

11. See preface.

12. The organization's name, which translates literally as "the Duchy of Pontida Square," is entirely ironic. The duchy itself is fictional, a play on the populist orientation of the organization; the Duke (*Duca*) who heads the organization is elected by a vote of the membership every three years. See Chapters 3, 4, 5, and 6 for discussions of the *Ducato*.

13. See Cardona 1990 for a discussion of the concept of *koinè*.

14. For instance, with the high school students, I asked them about the television show "Big Brother" (*Grande Fratello*), which was extremely popular at the time. Their responses often focused on the regional differences between show

participants, affording a valuable perspective on the persistence of regional loyalties and prejudices.

Chapter 2 Bergamasco in Use: The Feel of Everyday Speaking

1. Giacalone Ramat has described similarly bivalent occurrences between Italian and dialect as neutral moments in which speakers suspend oppositions between the two codes (1995). Following Woolard (1999), I see such occurrences as drawing on both languages and their symbolic associations.

2. The linguistic term "interference" has been used to describe the penetration of one language into a speaker's use of another (as with an accent), making speakers sound like they are at the mercy of their languages, and do not and/or cannot make choices about how they speak.

3. The difference in Daniele's translation from line 1 '*poco agevole da fare,*' to line 3 '*poco agevole da farsi,*' reflects a very slight change in meaning, changing '*fare*' into a transitive verb.

4. **Malfàt** can also simply be translated as "difficult," a translation that would not support either Daniele's argument here, nor the widespread conceptualization of Bergamasco as semantically rich in this particular fashion. It is perhaps not surprising, then, that it does not appear here. I'm grateful to Guy Lanoue for pointing this out.

5. See Sobrero 1997 on this process across Italian dialects.

6. **Pirù** and *forchetta* are referred to in a well-known Bergamasco folk song, **Nóter de Berghem**, that describes how different Bergamasco and Italian are by comparing a series of nouns in both languages. It includes, as well, the words for window: *finestra* and **balcù**.

7. Architect is used as a formal address term in Italy, similar to how in American English one addresses an MD as "doctor."

8. This pattern was common across Italy. Before World War II, roughly 50 percent of employed Italians worked in agriculture, mostly subsistence agriculture, a rate which fell to about three to five percent by the 1990s (Counihan 2004; Krause 2005).

9. Bergamo's university, founded in 1968, which draws primarily local students, has been slowly expanding. See Carra 2000 for further discussion.

10. Bergamaschi who were born before WWII sometimes talk about growing up in houses with no electricity or running water (even in the city), conveniences that they see their grandchildren taking for granted as necessities.

11. See Alfonzetti 1998, Berruto 1997, Fellìn 2003, Giacalone Ramat 1995, Jacquemet 1992, Sobrero 1988, and Trumper 1989 for discussions of code-switching between Italian and other dialects.

12. I always imagined the tight narrow mountain passes where this perhaps imaginary variety of Bergamasco was spoken as being similarly difficult to navigate.

13. Italian intransitive verbs, however, require prepositions, for example, *andare a* (to go + to).

14. See Berruto 1987 for a more complete discussion of this phenomenon.

15. See Haney 2003 and Jaffe 2000 for discussions of the use of minority and standard languages in humor.

16. It is only an interesting coincidence that two of the instances of this type of calque that I ran into while transcribing had to do with the word for "to mix" (see earlier discussion of "**smistàa fò**").

17. It was common for me, until the final months of the first period of my research, to have speakers translate even the most simple Bergamasco phrases into Italian. This was in keeping with the ideology of Bergamasco being a *"duro"* (hard) and *"stretto"* (narrow, strict) language, difficult for outsiders to understand and speak.

18. I was often told that I should really study **Gaì**, the secret language of transhumant shepherds in the mountains, which was held up as the most *stretto* Bergamasco of all.

19. Discourse markers are particles used to focus on or organize discourse structure (Schiffrin 1987).

Chapter 3 Gendering Language

1. There is a relative high percentage of Bergamaschi who leave school after middle school (Cavanaugh 2004). For discussions of the uneven economic development of Italy, see Bagnasco 1977, Blim 1990, Duggan 2007, and Schneider 1998, among others.

2. See Rogers 1987 on how the concept of peasant has been utilized toward various ends in France.

3. The search for the "real culture" of Bergamo and its neighbors within that of the peasants and working classes was an academic as well as layperson's pursuit. For instance, *Mondo Popolare in Lombardia: Bergamasco e il suo territorio* (*Popular World of Lombardy: Bergamo and its territory*) was a collection of scholarly work that *"ha messo in luce, contro molte opinioni correnti, l'esistenza di un forte tessuto di cultura popolare in tutto il territorio regionale"* ("brought to light, against many current opinions, the existence of a strong fabric of popular culture across the whole regional territory") (Leydi 1977, from back cover).

4. Bauer 1992 describes a similar situation for the inhabitants of the Spanish village of Sierra del Caurel, who have used outsider descriptions of themselves as "rough" and "backward" peasants – based on cultural elements like their crude dialect, a poor traditional diet of chestnuts and rye, and their engagement with agriculture – in order to further their own goals, such as appealing to ruling institutions for aid.

5. See Ochs 1992 on how gender and language are connected through such indirect indexicality.

6. This is the opposite of the well-known Italian concept "*fare una bella figura*" which is "to burnish the image of self for the consumption of others" (Pitkin 1993:98).

7. The collocation of negation markers posterior to the verb is attested to in many northern Italian dialects including Bergamasco (Maiden 1995:242; Sanga 1984, 1997), and has been documented as typical of what Berruto 1987 calls Regional Bergamasco Italian (*Italiano Regionale Bergamasco*).

8. I am grateful to Alessandro Duranti for supplying this example (personal communication).

9. See Hill and Hill 1986 for a similar situation with Mexicano.

10. See Echevarria 2003, Fader 2007, Hoffman 2006, and LeMaster 2006 for discussions of how the gendering of language can be linked to language shift and revitalization in varied and complex ways.

Chapter 4   Bergamasco on Stage: Poetry and Theater

1. The **cassina** (*cascina* in Italian) is a particularly Bergamasco type of rural building, found from the mountains down to the plains. Traditionally, they have space for both humans and animals in the same or connected buildings, and are often large enough to house more than one family and their animals, as they worked lands together, often under the local *mezzadria* (share-cropping) system.

2. **Frér** (blacksmith in Bergamasco) was Paolo's poetic nickname (**scotöm**). It is very common practice for Bergamasco poets to have nicknames by which their work is known, and indeed, nicknaming was once a common practice for Bergamaschi in general.

3. The form of the poem you see here is taken from a transcription of my tape-recording from that day compared with a printed copy of the poem, which Paolo gave me at a later date. The English translation is my own, with help from Paolo by way of Italian.

4. Carla Fracci, born and trained in Milan, is considered one of the best contemporary classical ballet dancers.

5. Trosset describes how Welsh poetry is perceived as an essential part of language activism, connected to beliefs that to be truly Welsh is to speak Welsh as much as possible in everyday life as well as in poetry (1993).

6. Official historiography of the *Ducato* holds that a group of friends who were artists and poets led an impromptu procession on a New Year's Eve mission from the Piazza Pontida (where this group usually met to socialize, drink, play music, recite poetry, and so on) to the center of town to dedicate a newly built city monument, a dedication long postponed by the local Fascist government. During the improvised ceremony, an unknown voice from the back of the crowd called out to praise the leader of the troupe: "*Viva il Duca di Piazza Pontida!*" (Long live the Duke of Piazza Pontida!).

7. See Chapter 6 for a discussion of this renewal and its causes.

8. Paraphrase and translation of comment by Franco Brevini, personal communication.

9. Similarly, Ngugi wa Thiongo (1986), discussing African poetry, stresses its roots in oral traditions and thus the absolute centrality of it being composed and recited in a local African language, not a colonial European language.

10. *Menabò*, an Italian word, translates roughly as a model or mock-up.

11. An annual national Italian-language poetry competition held in San Pellegrino, in the Province of Bergamo.

12. For a discussion of why elites would want to save populist cultural practices like the dialect, see Cavanaugh 2004.

13. *Borgo* is neighborhood (**bòrgh**, in Bergamasco). Borgo Santa Caterina is one of the oldest *borghi* (pl.) in the Lower City, and its history is nearly as long as that of the Città Alta, although it was once technically outside of the city limits. Many of Bergamo's poets, playwrights, and local leaders have hailed from Borgo Santa Caterina.

14. Through its enactment of a common dynamic in Bergamasco life, this play helps to support Ngugi wa Thiongo's assertion about political theater in vernacular that "drama is closer to the dialectics of life than poetry or the fiction" (1986:54).

15. This is similar to the discourse of nostalgia that Hill (1998) analyzes in the Mexicano situation.

16. Of course, the fact that I flubbed one of my two lines that evening (calling Rosina the wrong name) was taken as evidence that I had not yet become properly *Bergamaschizzata* (Bergamasco-ized). Some of the cast also politely suggested that I not quit my day job.

17. The Italian of the love note does call into question the association of Bergamasco with more private domains of expression, at least making the link between Bergamasco and personal sentiment (so key to Bergamasco's role as a poetic language) appear questionable. However, when the note is seen in light of the use of both languages throughout the play, it appears that the link between home, family, memory and Bergamasco is reinforced, while the possibility of Italian expression to be alienated from what speakers say, feel, and mean and what intended and unintended addressees comprehend is demonstrated.

18. Lemon is referring to Frantz Fanon's *Black Skin, White Masks* (1967) in making this observation.

Chapter 5 Modern *Campanilismo*: The Value of Place

1. *Palazzo* (sing.) in Italian means both "palace" and simply "large building."

2. *Campanilismo* has long historical roots in the sociopolitical development of Italy, as individual cities and town were often separate political entities such as

"city-states," sharply differentiated from their neighbors (Duggan 2007; Galli della Loggia 1998; Sciolla 1997). As the work of Galt (1991), Kertzer (1980), and Silverman (1975), among others, makes clear, however, conceptualizations of local identity are as varied as those sociopolitical histories across the peninsula. The meaning and effects of locality have been anthropological topics of discussion at least since Banfield introduced the concept of "amoral familism" in the 1950s to describe how inhabitants in one southern town related to one another and their civic responsibilities (1958).

3. See also Gupta and Ferguson's (1992, 1997a, and b) and Clifford's (1997) arguments in favor of anthropological attention to borderlands and people on the margins, which maintain that in traditional ethnography, "space functions as a central organizing principle … at the same time that it disappears from analytical purview" (Gupta and Ferguson 1992: 7).

4. See, among others, Horn (1994), Krause (2000) and Schneider and Schneider (1996) on this demographic shift across Italy, and Ravanelli (1996) and Rumi et al (1997) in Bergamo.

5. Unfortunately, I was never able to arrive at a satisfactory way to record these interactions in terms of both ethics and technology, so cannot comment extensively on them.

6. "*Case chiuse*" (closed houses), as bordellos were known, were not illegal until 1958, and could be found in all types of neighborhoods.

7. "*Il risanamento di Bergamo Alta è stato oggetto di indagini, di dibattiti e di interventi dalla metà dell'ottocento ad oggi, come in pochissime, forse nessun'altra città italiana*" ("The renovation of Upper Bergamo have been the object of investigations, debates and interventions/studies from the middle of the nineteenth century until today as in few, perhaps no other Italian cities") (Angelini 1989:72).

8. While I can only speculate here as to the links between this image and the gendered nature of linguistic practice and ideology that emerged later in Bergamo, it is seems telling that the Città Alta is depicted as an older female, presumably long past her reproductive years.

9. According to *Il Sole 24 Ore*, though, it was not in the top 10 in terms of livability (Ravanelli 1996:396).

10. Exemplary of this type of resident during the time I spent in Bergamo was the television anchorwoman, Cristina Parodi, who lived in the Città Alta with her husband, a television producer, and their young son. The studios and offices of the network for which they worked were located in Milan. The head of that studio, Silvio Berlusconi, was widely reported to have been interested in purchasing one of the more famous *palazzi* in the Città Alta in 2000, though this never came to fruition (*Bergamo Sette*, September 8, 2000).

11. In 2007, the University counted 15,000 students, its most numerous student body yet (*L'Eco di Bergamo*, December 14, 2007).

12. See, for instance, the letter entitled, "*Città Alta sempre più invivibile*" ("Città Alta always more unlivable") *L'Eco di Bergamo*, June 30, 2000.

13. See Pagliai 2003 for a discussion of how place and identity are closely linked in Tuscan contrasto poetry.

14. From the volume of poems entitled, **Sentér, Zét e Cansù de la Mé Tèra** (*Paths, People, and Songs of My Land*) (1980). Villa d'Almé (BG): Artigrafiche Mariani e Monti.

15. For example, Tak notes how essential campanilismo's linguistic dimensions are, even from one small village to its neighbor, mere kilometers away (1990:90). Also, see Galli de' Paratesi 1977 and 1985 for discussions of matched guise tests revealing what certain local accents mean across Italy.

16. Mock describes a similar process of transformation of Hikone's castle and grounds in Japan, potent symbols of the place, into tourist destinations after a long period of deterioration (1993).

Chapter 6 Bergamo, Italy, Europe: Speaking Contextualized

1. See, for instance, Bauman and Briggs 2003, Eisenlohr 2006, Hoffman 2008, Inoue 2006, Makihara 2004, and Tsitsipis 1998.

2. See Cavanaugh 2008 for a more complete discussion of the language question in Bergamo.

3. For example, Klein outlines an October 1923 Fascist decree that established Italian as the only language for public signs throughout Trento (1986:92).

4. This text is taken verbatim from Giopì, and thus differs orthographically from how it would be written today.

5. Bergamo's middle class was less than 5% at the time, and did not expand significantly until the 1960s and 1970s (Belotti 1989; Della Valentina 1984; Rumi et al. 1997).

6. See, for example, the issue from November 17, 1935, p. 1.

7. In the 1960s and 1970s, there were a few regionalist political parties, but these were generally in support of populations that depicted themselves as *not* Italian (German, Franco-Provençal, Ladin, Friulian, etc.).

8. The League selected it for its symbolic significance as the site where a pan-northern military accord was forged in the 12th century.

9. Wild asserts that the province of Bergamo was in fact the province where the League found the most widespread support. In the elections of 1996, for instance, the League took 43.23% of the province (1996:27–28).

10. Historically there have been other political parties that have enjoyed some local prominence, but since World War II, Bergamo and its province have voted primarily for the DC (Wild 1996). See Cento Bull (2000) and Mack Smith (1997) on the predominance of the DC in Italian politics since the Second World War.

11. Bergamo is typical of the type of community that has supported the League throughout the 1990s, in being smaller, slightly peripheral, and heavily industrial (Cachafeiro 2002; Cento Bull 1993, 1996). See also Agnew (2002) for an analysis of this phenomenon across northern Italy.

12. In 1992, the *Lega Lombarda* won 20% of the local vote and 11 seats on the city council (the DC took 35% and 20 seats, the PCI (Communist party) took 9% and 5 seats, with a few other parties gaining 2 seats or fewer). In 1994, the Northern League took 21.96% of the local votes, ahead of *Forza Italia* by 700 votes, and far ahead of all other parties (Wild 1996).

13. See Landry and Bourhis (1997) for a discussion of signs and their functional and symbolic values in the linguistic landscape of multilingual areas.

14. Padania is the *leghista* name for the areas north of the Po River (see Biorcio 1997).

15. *Leghisti* consider themselves for the most part shut out of the mainstream mass media, and discriminated against when they are covered.

16. One of these was **Tera Insubria** (Insubrian Land, another name for the area around Bergamo), which had representatives in several small town administrations in the northern parts of the province in the early 2000s.

17. See J. Feldman (2001) on a similar account about who belongs to the category of *extra-communitari*.

18. The causes and effects of the widespread phenomenon of south-to-north migration have been examined in everything from movies (e.g. *Rocco and His Brothers*, directed by Visconti) to academic accounts (see, for example, Di Scala 1995; Duggan 2007; Galt 1991; Ginsborg 1990; Pitkin 1985; Schneider 1998).

19. Indeed, immigrants in Italy are often identified as "*delinquenti*" (delinquents or criminals) (Angel-Ajani 2002).

20. See *New York Times* article, "Romanian Premier Tries to Calm Italy After A Killing," from November 7, 2007.

21. According to the *Centro Servizi Amministrativi di Bergamo* (Center for Administrative Services of Bergamo), as of the 2001–2002 school year, foreigners accounted for 3% of the school population, most in elementary school (Casti 2004:114).

Chapter 7   Conclusion

1. See Dorian 1994, Hill 1998, Hill and Hill 1986, Hoffman 2008, and Kroskrity 1993 for discussions of the effects of ideologies of purism in different ethnographic contexts.

2. From *L'Eco di Bergamo* and Reuters online, March 30, 2007.

3. See Dal Negro 2005, Iannaccaro and Dell'Aquila 2005, and Orioles 2002, among others, on the legal and sociolinguistic status of various Italian minority languages.

4. Berruto concurs, stating that "*il dialetto nei primi anni novanta si stia avviando a perdere il valore negativo di collocazione sociale bassa e svantaggiata, di discriminazione di prestigio ecc., e stia diventando da questo punto di vista assai più neutro*" ("the dialect in the beginning of the 1990s is starting to lose its negative, socially low and disadvantaged associations, etc., and is becoming from this point of view much more neutral") (1994:23). See also Dal Negro 2005, Fellìn 2003, Orioles 2002, Strassoldo 1996 for more nuanced views on the fates of Italian vernaculars.

References

Abu-Lughod, Lila 1999 Veiled Sentiments: Honor and Poetry in a Bedouin Society. Berkeley: University of California Press.

Abu-Lughod, Lila and Catherine A. Lutz 1990 Introduction: Emotion, Discourse, and the Politics of Everyday Life. *In* Language and the Politics of Emotion. Catherine Lutz and Lila Abu-Lughod, eds. pp. 1–23. Cambridge: Cambridge University Press.

Agha, Asif 1998 Stereotypes and Registers of Honorific Language. Language in Society 27:151–193.

Agnew, John A. 2002 Place and Politics in Modern Italy. Chicago: University of Chicago Press.

Ahearn, Laura M. 2004 Invitations to Love: Literacy, Love Letters, and Social Change in Nepal. Ann Arbor: University of Michigan Press.

Alfonzetti, Giovanna 1998 The Conversational Dimension in Code-Switching Between Italian and Dialect in Sicily. *In* Code-Switching in Conversation. Peter Auer, ed. pp. 180–211. London: Routledge.

Alighieri, Dante 1996 De Vulgari Eloquentia. Steven Botterill, ed. and trans. Cambridge: Cambridge University Press.

Anderson, Benedict 1991 Imagined Communities. New York: Verso.

Angel-Ajani, Asale 2002 Diasporic Conditions: Mapping Race and Criminality in Italy. Transforming Anthropology 11(1):36–46.

Angelini, Sandro, ed. 1989 Bergamo: Città Alta. Una Vicenda Urbana. Bergamo: Edizione del Comune di Bergamo.

Arno, Andrew 2003 Aesthetics, Intuition, and Reference in Fijian Ritual Communication: Modularity in and out of Language. American Anthropologist 105(4):807–819.

Auer, J. C. P. and A. di Luzio, eds. 1988 Variation and Convergence: Studies in Social Dialectology. Berlin: Walter de Gruyter.

Auslander, Leora 2000 Bavarian Crucifixes and French Headscarves: Religious Signs and the Postmodern European State. Cultural Dynamics 12(3):283–309.

Bagnasco, A. 1977 Tre Italie. La Problematica Territoriale dello Sviluppo Italiano. Bologna: Il Mulino.

Bakhtin, M. M. 1981 The Dialogic Imagination: Four Essays. M. Holquist, ed. C. Emerson and M. Holquist, trans. Austin: University of Texas Press.

Bakhtin, M. M. and P. N. Medvedev 1985 The Formal Method in Literary Scholarship: A Critical Introduction to Sociological Poetics. Albert J. Wehrle, trans. Cambridge, MA: Harvard University Press.

Banfield, Edward 1958 The Moral Basis of a Backward Society. New York: Free Press.

Banti, Giorgio and Francesco Giannattasio 2004 Poetry. *In* A Companion to Linguistic Anthropology. Alessandro Duranti, ed. pp. 291–320. Malden, MA: Blackwell Publishing.

Barbieri, Francesco 1996 Prefazione. *In* Tra sògn e realtà: Composizioni dialettali bergamasche, pp. 2–8. Bergamo: Stefanoni.

Basso, Keith 1996 Wisdom Sits in Places: Notes on a Western Apache Landscape. *In* Senses of Place. Steven Feld and Keith Basso, eds. pp. 53–90. Santa Fe, NM: School of American Research Press.

Basso, Keith 1999 Wisdom Sits in Places. Santa Fe, NM: School of American Research Press.

Bauer, Ranier Lutz 1992 Changing Representations of Place, Community, and Character in the Spanish Sierra del Caurel. American Ethnologist 19(3):571–588.

Bauman, Richard 1983 Let Your Words Be Few. Symbolism of Speaking and Silence among Seventeenth-century Quakers. Prospect Heights, IL: Waveland Press.

Bauman, Richard 2000 Genre. Journal of Linguistic Anthropology 9(1): 84–87.

Bauman, Richard 2004 A World of Others' Words: Cross-Cultural Perspectives on Intertextuality. Malden, MA: Blackwell Publishers.

Bauman, Richard and Charles Briggs 1990 Poetics and Performance as Critical Perspectives on Language and Social Life. Annual Review of Anthropology 19:59–88.

Bauman, Richard and Charles Briggs 2003 Voices of Modernity. Language Ideologies and the Politics of Inequality. Cambridge: Cambridge University Press.

Belotti, Bortolo 1989 Storia di Bergamo and dei Bergamaschi. Bergamo: Edizioni Bolis, Banca Popolare di Bergamo.

Benucci, Antonella 1999 Che cosa è secondo Lei il dialetto? Supporto Informativo e Notizario Accademico. Siena: Università per Stranieri di Siena 4(2):15.

Berdahl, Daphne 1999 Where the World Ended: Reunification and Identity in the German Borderland. Berkeley: University of California Press.

Beretta, Claudio 1998 Grammatica del Milanese Contemporanea. Milan: Libreria Milanese.

Beriss, David 1990 Scarves, Schools, and Segregation: The *Foulard* Affair. French Politics and Society 8(1):1–13.

Bernini, Giuliano and Glauco Sanga 1987 Fonologia del dialetto di Bergamo. *In* Lingua e Dialetti di Bergamo e delle Valli. Glauco Sanga, ed. pp. 65–81. Bergamo: Pierluigi Lubrina Editore.

Berruto, Gaetano 1978 Uso di Italiano e Dialetto a Bergamo. Alcuni Dati. Rivista Italiana di Dialettologia. Scuola, Società, Territorio 1:45–77.

Berruto, Gaetano 1987 L'italiano regionale Bergamasco. *In* Lingua e Dialetti di Bergamo e delle Valli. Glauco Sanga, ed., pp. 499–592. Bergamo: Pierluigi Lubrina Editore.

Berruto, Gaetano 1989 Main Topics and Findings in Italian Sociolinguistics. International Journal of the Sociology of Language 76:1–30.

Berruto, Gaetano 1990 Sociolinguistica dell'Italiano Contemporaneo. Roma: La Nuova Italia Scientifica.

Berruto, Gaetano 1994 Come si parlerà domani: italiano e dialetto. *In* Come Parlano gli Italiani. Tullio De Mauro, ed. pp. 15–24. Florence: La Nuova Italia Editrice.

Berruto, Gaetano 1997 Code-switching and Code-mixing. *In* The Dialects of Italy, Martin Maiden and Mair Parry, eds. pp. 394–400. London: Routledge.

Bertacchi, Giuliana 1981 La Domanda di Storia e il 'Caso di Bergamo': Ipotesi di Lavoro. *In* Il Movimento Operaio e Contadino Bergamasco dall'Unità al Secondo Dopoguerra. pp. 11–24. Bergamo: La Porta, Centro Studi e Documentazione.

Bertacchi, Giuliana 2000 Ricordi di Scuola. *In* Da Collere a Colere: Una Communità Alpina, Storie e Immagini. Angela Bendotti, ed. pp. 219–240. Bergamo: Associazione Editoriale Il Filo di Arianna.

Besana, Claudio 1997 La Riconstruzione e il Miracolo Economico. *In* Bergamo e il Suo Territorio. Giorgio Rumi, Gianni Mezzanotte and Alberto Cova, eds. pp. 391–412. Milan: Cassa di Risparmio della Provincie Lombarde, S.p.a. (Cariplo).

Besnier, Niko 1990 Language and Affect. Annual Review of Anthropology 19:419–451.

Biorcio, Roberto 1997 La Padania Promessa: La Storia, le Idee, e la Logica d'Azione della Lega Nord. Milano: Il Saggiatore.

Blim, Michael L. 1990 Made in Italy: Small-Scale Industrialization and Its Consequences. New York: Praeger.

Blommaert, J. 1994 The Metaphors of Development and Modernization in Tanzanian Language Policy and Research. *In* African Languages, Development and the State. R. Fardon and G. Furniss, eds. pp. 213–226. London: Routledge.

Blommaert, J. and J. Verschueren 1998 The Role of Language in European Nationalist Ideologies. *In* Language Ideologies: Practice and Theory. Bambi B. Schieffelin, Kathryn A. Woolard and Paul V. Kroskrity, eds. pp. 189–210. New York: Oxford University Press.

Blondeau, Philippe 1996 Les Dialectes e la Conscience Linguistique dans la Province de Bergame, Lombardie. These sous la direction d'Alvero Rochetti. Université de la Sorbonne Nouvelle, Paris III.

Blu, Karen 1996 "Where Do You Stay At?": Homeplace and Community among the Lumbee. *In* Senses of Place. Steve Feld and Keith Basso, eds. pp. 197–228. Santa Fe, NM: School of American Research Press.

Borneman, John and Nick Fowler 1997 Europeanization. Annual Review of Anthropology 26:487–514.

Bourdieu, Pierre 1984 Distinction: A Social Critique of the Judgment of Taste. Cambridge, MA: Harvard University Press.

Bourdieu, Pierre 1991 Language and Symbolic Power. John B. Thompson, ed. Cambridge, MA: Harvard University Press.

Bourdieu, Pierre and Jean-Claude Passeron 1977 Reproduction in Education, Society and Culture. London: Sage.

Bowen, John R. 2004 Does French Islam Have Borders? Dilemmas of Domestication in a Global Religious Field. American Anthropologist 106(1):43–55.

Boyer, Dominic 2005 Welcome to the New Europe. American Ethnologist 32(4):521–523.

Brenneis, Donald 1987 Performing Passions: Aesthetics and Politics in an Occasionally Egalitarian Community. American Ethnologist 14(2): 236–250.

Brevini, Franco, ed. 1999 La Poesia in Dialetto. Storie e Testi dalle Origini al Novecento. Milan: Arnoldo Mondadori Editore.

Brevini, Franco 2000 Alla Scoperta di Bergamo: Un Tesoro in Lombardia. TuttoTurismo. Giugno, pp. 86–101.

Briggs, Charles and Richard Bauman 1995 Genre, Intertextuality, and Social Power. *In* Language, Culture, and Society. Ben G. Blount, ed. pp. 567–608. Prospect Heights, IL: Waveland Press.

Brown, Roger and Albert Gilman 1972 The Pronouns of Power and Solidarity. *In* Language and Social Context. P. P. Giglioli, ed. pp. 252–282. New York: Penguin.

Brusco, D. 1986 Small Firms and Industrial Districts: The Experience of Italy. *In* New Firms and Regional Developments in Europe. D. Keeble and E. Wever, eds. London: Croom Helm.

Bunzl, Matti 2005 Between Anti-Semitism and Islamophobia: Some Thoughts on the New Europe. American Ethnologist 32(4):499–508.

Burke, Peter 1987 The Uses of Literacy in Early Modern Italy. *In* The Social History of Language. Peter Burke and Roy Porter, eds. pp. 21–42. Cambridge: Cambridge University Press.

Cachafeiro, Margarita Gómez-Reino 2002 Ethnicity and Nationalism in Italian Politics. Inventing the Padania: Lega Nord and the Northern Question. Burlington, VT: Ashgate.

Cameron, Deborah 1995 Verbal Hygiene. London: Routledge.

Campani, G. 1993 Immigration and Racism in Southern Europe: The Italian Case. Ethnic and Racial Studies 16:507–35.

Capellini, Pino 1989 Città Alta dal 1763–1924. *In* Bergamo: Città Alta. Una Vicenda Urbana. Sandro Angelini, ed. Bergamo: Edizione del Comune di Bergamo.

Cardona, Giorgio Raimondo 1990 Il Concetto di Koinè in Linguistica. *In* Koinè in Italia dalle Origini al Cinquecento. Glauco Sanga, ed. pp. 25–34. Bergamo: Pierluigi Lubrina Editore.

Carra, Natale 2000 "Educazione e Industria, Artigianato, Commercio, Agricoltura tra Passato e Futuro." Presentation at "Economia e Territorio," Part 6 in series of conferences on 20th century sponsored by Ateneo, Bergamo.

Carter, Donald M. 1997 States of Grace: Senegalese in Italy and the New European Immigration. Minneapolis: University of Minnesota Press.

Castellanos, Erick 2004 Alarming Hoards and Ideological Masses: The Impact of Immigrants on the Definition of Community and Society in Bergamo, Italy. Ph.D. Dissertation. Department of Anthropology, Brown University.

Castellanos, Erick 2006 Migrant Mirrors: The Replication and Reinterpretation of Local and National Ideologies as Strategies of Adaptation by Foreigner Immigrants in Bergamo, Italy. American Behavioral Scientist 50(1):27–47.

Casti, Emmanuela, ed. 2004 Atlante dell'Immigrazione a Bergamo. L'Africa di Casa Nostra. BG: Bergamo University Press, Edizioni Sestante.

Caton, Steven C. 1990 "Peaks of Yemen I Summon:" Poetry as Cultural Practice in a North Yemeni Tribe. Berkeley: University of California Press.

Cavanaugh, Jillian R. 1997 Italian Language Ideologies: A Meta-level Exploration of Academic Discourse. Unpublished Master's Thesis. Department of Anthropology, New York University.

Cavanaugh, Jillian R. 2004. Remembering and Forgetting: Ideologies of Language Loss in a Northern Italian Town. Journal of Linguistic Anthropology 14(1):24–38.

Cavanaugh, Jillian R. 2005 Accent Matters: Material Consequences of Sounding Local in Northern Italy. Language and Communication 25:127–148.

Cavanaugh, Jillian R. 2006 Little Women and Vital Champions: Gendered Language Shift in a Northern Italian Town. Journal of Linguistic Anthropology 16(2):194–210.

Cavanaugh, Jillian R. 2008 A Modern *Questione della Lingua*: The Incomplete Standardization of Italian in a Northern Italian Town. Journal of the Society for the Anthropology of Europe 8(1):18–31.

Cento Bull, Anna 1981 L'Industria nel Periodo Fascista. *In* Il Movimento Operaio e Contadino Bergamasco dall'Unità al Secondo Dopoguerra, pp.123–140. Bergamo: La Porta, Centro Studi e Documentazione.

Cento Bull, Anna 1993 Industrializzazione Diffusa e Rappresentanza Politica in Lombardia: Dalla Democrazia Cristiana alla Lega Lombarda. Studi e Ricerche di Storia Contemporanea 39:7–20.

Cento Bull, Anna 1996 Ethnicity, Racism and the Northern League. *In* Italian Regionalism: History, Identity and Politics. Carl Levy, ed. pp. 170–187. Washington, DC: Berg.

Cento Bull, Anna 2000 Social Identities and Political Cultures in Italy: Catholic, Communist and 'Leghist' Communities Between Civicness and Localism. New York: Berghahn Books.

Cento Bull, Anna and Paul Corner 1993 From Peasants to Entrepreneurs: The Survival of the Family Economy in Italy. Oxford: Berg.

Cento Bull, Anna, Martyn Pitt, and Joseph Szarka 1993 Entrepreneurial Textile Communities. A Comparative Study of Small Textile and Clothing Firms. London: Chapman & Hall.

Clancy, Patricia 1999 The Socialization of Affect in Japanese Mother–Child Conversation. Journal of Pragmatics 31(11):1397–1421.

Clifford, James 1988 The Predicament of Culture. Cambridge, MA: Harvard University Press.

Clifford, James 1997 Routes: Travel and Translation in the Late Twentieth Century. Cambridge, MA: Harvard University Press.

Cofini, Stefano 2000 "Sistema: Industria, Artigianato, Commercio, Agricoltura tra Passato e Futuro." Presentation at "Economia e Territorio," Part 6 in series of conferences on 20th century sponsored by the Ateneo, Bergamo.

Cohen, Anthony P. 1996 Personal Nationalism: A Scottish View of Some Rights, Rites and Wrongs. American Ethnologist 23(4):802–815.

Cole, Jeffrey 1997 The New Racism in Europe: A Sicilian Ethnography. New York: Cambridge University Press.

Coote, Jeremy 1992 'Marvels of Everyday Vision': The Anthropology of Aesthetics and Cattle-keeping Among the Nilotes. *In* Anthropology,

Art, and Aesthetics. Jeremy Coote and Anthony Shelton, eds, pp. 245–273. Oxford: Clarendon Press.

Cortelazzo, Manlio 1977 Introduzione alla Sezione Secondo: Quale Italiano? *In* La Lingua Italiana Oggi: Un Problema Scolastico e Sociale. Lorenzo Renzi and Manlio Cortelazzo, eds. pp. 107–112. Bologna: La Società Editrice il Mulino.

Counihan, Carole 2004 Around the Tuscan Table: Food, Family, and Gender in Twentieth Century Florence. New York: Routledge.

Coupland, Nikolas 2001 Dialect Stylization in Radio Talk. Language in Society 30(3):345–375.

Crawford, James 2000 At War with Diversity: U.S. Language Policy in an Age of Diversity. Buffalo, NY: Multilingual Matters.

Crowley, Tony 1996 Language in History. Theories and Texts. London: Routledge.

Dal Negro, Silvia 2005 Minority Languages between Nationalism and New Localism: The Case of Italy. International Journal for the Sociology of Language 174:113–124.

D'Amato, Gianni and Siegfried Schieder 1997 Italy's Northern League: Between Ethnic Citizenship and a Federal State. *In* Rethinking Nationalism and Ethnicity: The Struggle for Meaning and Order in Europe. Hans-Rudolf Wicker, ed. pp. 273–286. Oxford: Berg.

De Bernardi, Alberto 1998 Il Fascismo e le Sue Interpretazioni. *In* Il Fascismo. Dizionario di Storia, Personaggi, Cultura, Economia, Fonti e Dibattato Storiografico. Alberto De Bernardi and Scipione Guarracino, eds. pp. 3–135. Milano: Edizioni Bruno Mondadori.

De Grazia, Victoria 1981 The Culture of Consent. Mass Organization of Leisure in Fascist Italy. New York: Cambridge University Press.

De Grazia, Victoria 1992 How Fascism Ruled Women: Italy 1922–45. Berkeley: University of California Press.

Della Valentina, Gianluigi 1984 Terra, Lavoro e Società. Fonti per la Storia del Bergamasco in Età Contemporanea. Bergamo: Associazione Editoriale Il Filo di Ariana.

De Mauro, Tullio 1972 Storia Linguistica dell'Italia Unita. Bari: Edizioni Laterza.

De Mauro, Tullio, ed. 1994 Come Parlano gli Italiani. Florence: La Nuova Italia.

Diamanti, Ilvo 1996 Il Male del Nord. Lega, Localismo, Secessione. Roma: Donzelli.

Di Giacomo, Susan M. 1999 Language Ideological Debates in an Olympic City: Barcelona, 1992–1996. *In* Language Ideological Debates. Jan Blommaert, ed. pp. 105–42. Berlin: Mouton de Gruyter.

Di Giacomo, Susan M. 2001 'Catalan is Everyone's Thing': Normalizing the Nation. *In* Language, Ethnicity and the State. Volume 1: Minority Languages in the European Union. Camille C. O'Reilly, ed. pp. 56–77. New York: Palgrave Macmillan.

Di Scala, S. 1995 Italy: From Revolution to Republic 1700 to the Present. Boulder, CO: Westview Press.

Dorian, Nancy C. 1981 Language Death. The Life Cycle of a Scottish Gaelic Dialect. Philadelphia, PA: University of Pennsylvania Press.

Dorian, Nancy C. 1982 Defining the Speech Community to Include Its Working Margins. *In* Sociolinguistic Variation in Speech Communities. S. Romaine, ed. pp. 25–33. London: Edward Arnold.

Dorian, Nancy C. 1994 Purism vs. Compromise in Language Revitalization and Language Revival. Language in Society 23:479–494.

Drysdale, Helen 2001 Silenced or Liberated: Endangered Languages within the European Union. 'Endangered Languages and the Media'. *In* The Proceedings of the Fifth Foundation for Endangered Languages Conference. C. Mosely, N. Ostler, H. Ouzzate, eds. pp. 124–130. Bath: Foundation for Endangered Languages.

Duggan, Christopher 2007 The Force of Destiny: A History of Italy Since 1796. New York: Allen Lane.

Duranti, Alessandro and Charles Goodwin, eds. 1992 Rethinking Context: Language as Interactive Phenomenon. New York: Cambridge University Press.

Eagleton, Terry 1990 The Ideology of the Aesthetic. Oxford: Blackwell Publishers.

Echevarria, Begoña 2003 Language Ideologies in (En)gendering the Basque Nation. Language in Society 32(3):383–414.

Eckert, Penelope 1980 Diglossia: Separate and Unequal. Linguistics 18:56–64.

Eckert, Penelope 1996 Vowels and Nail Polish: The Emergence of Linguistic Style in the Preadolescent Heterosexual Marketplace. *In* Gender and Belief Systems. Jocelyn Ahlers et al., eds. Berkeley: Berkeley Women and Language Group.

Edwards, Jane A. 1989 Transcription in Discourse. *In* Oxford International Encyclopedia of Linguistics. Oxford: Oxford University Press.

Eidson, John R. 2005 Between Heritage and Countermemory: Varieties of Historical Representation in a West German Community. American Ethnologist 32(4):556–575.

Eisenlohr, Patrick 2006 Little India: Diaspora, Time, and Ethnolinguistic Belonging in Hindu Mauritius. Berkeley: University of California Press.

Fader Ayala 2000 Morality, Gender, and Language: Socialization Practices in a Hasidic Community. Ph.D. thesis. Department of Anthropology, New York University.

Fader Ayala 2001 Literacy, Bilingualism and Gender in a Hasidic Community. *Linguistic Education* 12(3):261–83

Fader Ayala 2007 Reclaiming Sacred Sparks: Linguistic Syncretism and Gendered Language Shift among Hasidic Jews in New York. *Journal of Linguistic Anthropology* 17(1):1–22.

Fanon, Frantz 1967 Black Skin, White Masks. Charles Lam Markmann, trans. New York: Grove Press.

Feld, Steven 1988 Aesthetics as Iconicity of Style, or 'Lift-Up-Over Sounding': Getting into the Kaluli Groove. Yearbook for Traditional Music 108:74–113.

Feld, Steven 1990 Sound and Sentiment: Birds, Weeping, Poetics, and Song in Kaluli Expression, 2nd edition. Philadelphia: University of Pennsylvania Press.

Feldman, Jeffrey D. 2001 Ghetto Association: Jewish Heritage, Heroin, and Racism in Bologna. Identities 8(2):247–282.

Feldman, Merje 2001 European Integration and the Discourse of National Identity in Estonia. National Identities 3(1):5–21.

Fellìn, Luciana 2003 Language Ideologies, Language Socialization, and Language Revival in an Italian Alpine Community. Austin: Texas Linguistic Forum, Vol. 45. Inger Mey, Ginger Pizer, Hsi-Yao Su, Susan Szmania, eds.

Fenigsen, Janina 1999 "A Broke-Up Mirror": Representing Bajan in Print. Cultural Anthropology 14(1):61–87.

Ferguson, Charles, A. 1959 Diglossia. Word 15:325–340.

Foresti, Fabio 1978 Proposte Interpretive e di Ricerca su Lingua e Fascismo: La "Politica Linguistica". *In* La Lingua Italiana e il Fascismo. Leso, Erasmo, Michele A. Cortelazzo, Ivano Paccagnella, and Fabio Foresti, eds. Bologna: Consorzio Provinciale Pubblica Lettura.

Forlani, Mimma 1998 Sandro Angelini e Città Alta. Bergamo: Comune di Bergamo, Terza Circoscrizione Città Alta e Colli, Civica Biblioteca A. Mai.

Friedland, Roger and Dierdre Boden 1994 NowHere: An Introduction to Space, Time, and Modernity. *In* NowHere: Space, Time, and Modernity. Roger Friedland and Dierdre Boden, eds. pp. 1–60. Berkeley: University of California Press.

Gal, Susan 1978 Peasant Men Can't Get Wives: Language Change and Sex Roles in a Bilingual Community. Language in Society 7(1):1–16.

Gal, Susan 1979 Language Shift. Social Determinants of Linguistic Change in Bilingual Austria. New York: Academic Press.

Gal, Susan 1989 Language and Political Economy. Annual Review of Anthropology 18:345–367.

Gal, Susan 1995 Lost in a Slavic Sea: Linguistic Theories and Expert Knowledge in 19th Century Hungary. Pragmatics 5(2):155–166.

Gal, Susan 2007 Circulation in the "New" Economy: Clasps and Copies. Paper presented at the 106th AAA Annual Meeting, Washington, DC.

Gal, Susan and Kathryn A. Woolard 1995 Constructing Languages and Publics: Authority and Representation. Pragmatics 5(2):129–138.

Galbraith, Marysia H. 2004 Between East and West: Geographic Metaphors of Identity in Poland. Ethos 32(1):51–81.

Galli della Loggia, Ernesto 1998 L'Identità Italiana. Bologna: il Mulino.

Galli de' Paratesi, Nora 1977 Opinioni Linguistiche e Prestigio delle Principali Varietà Regionali di Italiano. *In* Italiano D'Oggi: Linguistica Nazionale e Varietà Regionali. Centro per lo Studio dell'Insegnamento all'Estero dell'Italiano, pp. 145–197. Trieste: Edizioni LINT.

Galli de' Paratesi, Nora 1985 Lingua Toscana in Bocca Ambrosiana. Tendenze verso l'Italiano Standard: Un'Inchiesta Sociolinguistica. Bologna: il Mulino.

Galt, Anthony H. 1991 Far from the Church Bells: Settlement and Society in an Apulian Town. New York: Cambridge University Press.

Garrett, Paul 2005 What Language Is Good For: Language Socialization, Language Shift and the Persistence of Code-specific Genres in St. Lucia. Language in Society 34(3):327–361.

Garrett, Paul B. and Patricia Baquedano-López 2002 Language Socialization: Reproduction and Continuity, Transformation and Change. Annual Review of Anthropology 31:339–361.

Giacalone Ramat, Anna 1995 Code-Switching in the Context of Dialect/ Standard Language Relations. *In* One Speaker, Two Languages: Cross-Disciplinary Perspectives on Code-Switching. L. Milroy and P. Muysken, eds. pp. 45–67. Cambridge: Cambridge University Press.

Giannelli, Luciano and Thomas D. Cravens 1997 Consonantal Weakening. *In* The Dialects of Italy, pp. 32–40. London: Routledge.

Giddens, Anthony 1979 Central Problems in Social Theory: Action, Structure and Contradiction in Social Analysis. Berkeley: University of California Press.

Giddens, Anthony 1994 Foreword. *In* NowHere: Space, Time and Modernity. Roger Friedland and Dierdre Boden, eds. pp. xi–xiii. Berkeley: University of California Press.

Gieryn, Thomas F. 2000 A Space for Place in Sociology. Annual Review of Sociology 26:463–496.

Ginsborg, Paul 1990 A History of Contemporary Italy. Society and Politics 1943–1988. London: Penguin.

Grasseni, Cristina 2000 Developing Skill, Developing Vision: Locality and Identity in Rural Northern Italy. Ph.D. Dissertation. Department of Anthropology, University of Manchester.

Grillo, Ralph D. 1985 Ideologies and Institutions in Urban France: The Representation of Immigrants. Cambridge: Cambridge University Press.

Grillo, Ralph D. 1989 Dominant Languages. New York: Cambridge University Press.

Gross, Joan 1987 Transformations of a Popular Culture Form in Northern France and Belgium. Anthropology Quarterly 60(2):71–76.

Gumperz, John 1982 Discourse Strategies. Cambridge: Cambridge University Press.

Gupta, Akhil and James Ferguson 1992 Beyond "Culture": Space, Identity, and the Politics of Difference. Cultural Anthropology 7(1):6–23.

Gupta, Akhil and James Ferguson, eds. 1997a Anthropological Locations: Boundaries and Grounds of a Field Science. Berkeley: University of California Press.

Gupta, Akhil and James Ferguson, eds. 1997b Culture, Power, Place: Explorations in Critical Anthropology. Durham: Duke University Press.

Haney, Peter 2003 Bilingual Humor, Verbal Hygiene, and the Gendered Contradictions of Cultural Citizenship in Early Mexican American Comedy. Journal of Linguistic Anthropology 13(2):163–188.

Haugen, Einar 1966 Dialect, Language, Nation. American Anthropologist 68(4):922–935.

Haviland, John 1996 Text from Talk in Tzotzil. In Natural Histories of Discourse. Michael Silverstein and Greg Urban, eds. pp. 45–78. Chicago: University of Chicago Press.

Heatherington, Tracey 2005 'As if someone dear to me had died': Intimate Landscapes, Political Subjectivity, and the Problem of a Park in Sardinia. In Mixed Emotions: Anthropological Studies of Feeling. Kay Milton and Maruška Svašek, eds. pp. 145–162. Oxford: Berg.

Heller, Monica 1994 Crosswords: Language, Education and Ethnicity in French Ontario. New York: Mouton de Gruyter.

Heller, Monica 1995 Code-Switching and the Politics of Language. In One Speaker, Two Languages: Cross-Disciplinary Perspectives on Code-Switching. L. Milroy and P. Muysken, eds. pp. 158–174. Cambridge: Cambridge University Press.

Herzfeld, Michael 1991 A Place in History. Social and Monumental Time in a Cretan Town. Princeton, NJ: Princeton University Press.

Herzfeld, Michael 2005 Cultural Intimacy: Social Poetics in the Nation-State, 2nd edition. New York: Routledge.

Hill, Jane H. 1987 Women's Speech in Modern Mexicano. *In* Language, Gender and Sex in Comparative Perspective. Susan U. Philips, S. Steele and C. Tanz, eds. pp. 121–160. New York: Cambridge University Press.

Hill, Jane H. 1998 "Today There Is No Respect": Nostalgia, "Respect," and Oppositional Discourse in Mexicano (Nahautl) Language Ideology. *In* Language Ideologies: Practice and Theory. Bambi B. Schieffelin, Kathryn A. Woolard and Paul V. Kroskrity, eds. pp. 68–86. New York: Oxford University Press.

Hill, Jane H. 2002 "Expert Rhetorics" in Advocacy for Endangered Languages: Who Is Listening and What Do They Hear? Journal of Linguistic Anthropology 12(2):119–133.

Hill, Jane H. and Kenneth C. Hill 1986 Speaking Mexicano. Dynamics of Syncretic Language in Central Mexico. Tucson: University of Arizona Press.

Hoffman, Katherine E. 2006 Berber Language Ideologies, Maintenance, and Contraction: Gendered Variation in the Indigenous Margins of Morocco. Language and Communication 26(2):144–167.

Hoffman, Katherine E. 2008 We Share Walls: Language, Land, and Gender in Berber Morocco. Malden, MA: Blackwell Publishing.

Holmes, Douglas 2000 Integral Europe: Fast-Capitalism, Multiculturalism, Neofascism. Princeton: Princeton University Press.

Horn, David G. 1994 Social Bodies: Science, Reproduction, and Italian Modernity. Princeton, NJ: Princeton University Press.

Iannaccaro, Gabriele and Vittorio Dell'Aquila 2005 From Sociolinguistic Studies to Language Planning Actions: Experiences in the Ladin Speaking Region of the Dolomites. Paper presented at the Tenth International Conference on Minority Languages, Trieste, Italy.

Inglehart, R. F. and M. Woodward 1972 Language Conflicts and Political Community. *In* Language and Social Context. P. P. Giglioli, ed. pp. 358–377. New York: Penguin.

Inoue, Miyako 2006 Vicarious Language: Gender and Linguistic Modernity in Japan. Berkeley: University of California Press.

Irace, Fulvio 1997 Le Due Città: Piacentini e Angelini. *In* Bergamo e il Suo Territorio. Giorgio Rumi, Gianni Mezzanotte and Alberto Cova, eds. pp. 161–197. Milan: Cassa di Risparmio delle Provincie Lombarda S.p.A (Cariplo).

Irvine, Judith T. 1989 When Talk Isn't Cheap: Language and Political Economy. American Ethnologist 16(2):248–267.

Irvine, Judith T. 1990 Registering Affect: Heteroglossia in the Linguistic Expression of Emotion. *In* Language and the Politics of Emotion. C. Lutz and L. Abu-Lughod, eds. pp. 126–161. New York: Cambridge University Press.

Irvine, Judith T. and Susan Gal 2000 Language Ideology and Linguistic Differentiation. *In* Regimes of Language. Paul V. Kroskrity, ed. Santa Fe, NM: School of American Research Press.

Istituto Nazionale di Statistico (ISTAT) 1997 Note Rapide: Lingua Italiana e Dialetti. Rome.

Istituto Nazionale di Statistico (ISTAT) 2007 La lingua italiana, i dialetti e le lingue straniere. Statistiche in breve. Famiglia e Società. Rome.

Ivanov, Vyacheslav 2000 Heteroglossia. Journal of Linguistic Anthropology 9(1–2):100–102.

Jacquemet, Marco 1992 'If he speaks Italian it's better': Metapragmatics in Court. Pragmatics 2(2):111–126.

Jaffe, Alexandra 1996 The Second Annual Corsican Spelling Contest: Orthography and Ideology. American Ethnologist 23(4):816–835.

Jaffe, Alexandra 1999 Ideologies in Action. Language Politics in Corsica. New York: Mouton de Gruyter.

Jaffe, Alexandra 2000 Comic Performance and the Articulation of Hybrid Identity. Pragmatics 10(1):39–59.

Jaffe, Alexandra 2001 State Language Ideology and the Shifting Nature of Minority Language Planning on Corsica. *In* Language, Ethnicity and the State. Volume 1: Minority Languages in the European Union. Camille C. O'Reilly, ed. pp. 40–55. New York: Palgrave Macmillan.

Jakobson, Roman 1960 Closing Statement: Linguistics and Poetics. *In* Style in Language. Thomas A. Sebeok, ed. pp. 350–377. Cambridge, MA: MIT Press.

Joseph, John E. and Talbot J. Taylor, eds. 1990 Ideologies of Language. New York: Routledge.

Judge, Anne 2007 Linguistic Policies and the Survival of Regional Languages in France and Britain. New York: Palgrave Macmillan.

Kabatek, Johannes 1997 Strengthening Identity: Differentiation and Change in Contemporary Galician. *In* Taming the Vernacular: From Dialect to Written Standard Language. Jenny Cheshire and Dieter Stein, eds. pp. 185–199. London: Longman.

Kahn, Miriam 1996 Your Place and Mine: Sharing Emotional Landscapes in Wamira, Papua New Guinea. *In* Senses of Place. Steven Feld and Keith Basso, eds. pp. 167–196. Santa Fe, NM: School of American Research Press.

Keane, Webb 2007 Christian Moderns: Freedom and Fetish in the Mission Encounter. Berkeley: University of California Press.

Kertzer, David I. 1980 Comrades and Christians: Religion and Political Struggle in Communist Italy. Cambridge: Cambridge University Press.

Klein, Gabriella 1986 La Politica Linguistica del Fascismo. Bologna: il Mulino.

Kockelman, Paul 2004 Stance and Subjectivity. Journal of Linguistic Anthropology 14(2):127–150.

Kramer, Johannes 1983 Language Planning in Italy. *In* Language Reform: History and Future, Vol. VII. Istavan Fodor and Claude Hagège, eds. pp. 301–316. Belgium: Buske.

Krause, Elizabeth L. 2000 "Empty Cradles" and the Quiet Revolution: Demographic Discourse and Cultural Struggles of Gender, Race, and Class in Italy. Cultural Anthropology 16(4):576–611.

Krause, Elizabeth L. 2005 Encounters with the 'Peasant': Memory work, masculinity, and low fertility in Italy. American Ethnologist 32(4): 593–617.

Kroskrity, Paul V. 1993 Language, History and Identity: Ethnolinguistics of the Arizona Tewa. Tucson: University of Arizona Press.

Kroskrity, Paul V., ed. 2000 Regimes of Language. Ideologies, Politics, and Identities. Santa Fe, NM: School of American Research Press.

Kulick, Don 1992 Language Shift and Cultural Reproduction: Socialization, Self and Syncretism in a Papua New Guinea Village. Cambridge: Cambridge University Press.

Kulick, Don 1993 Speaking as a Woman: Structure and Gender in Domestic Arguments in a New Guinean Village. Cultural Anthropology 8(4): 510–541.

Kulick, Don 1998 Anger, Gender, Language Shift, and the Politics of Revelation in a Papua New Guinean Village. *In* Language Ideology: Practice and Theory. Bambi B. Schieffelin, Kathryn A. Woolard and Paul V. Kroskrity, eds. pp. 87–102. Oxford: Oxford University Press.

Kulick, Don and Bambi B. Schieffelin 2004 Language Socialization. *In* A Companion to Linguistic Anthropology. Alessandro Duranti, ed. Malden, MA: Blackwell Publishing.

Kuter, Lois 1989 Breton vs. French: Language and the Opposition of Political, Economic, Social and Cultural Values. *In* Investigating Obsolescence: Studies in Language Contraction and Death. N. Dorian, ed. pp. 75–90. New York: Cambridge University Press.

Labov, William 1966a The Social Stratification of English in New York City. Washington: Center for Applied Linguistics.

Labov, William 1966b Hypercorrection by the Lower Middle Class as a Factor in Linguistic Change. *In* Sociolinguistics. William Bright, ed. pp. 84–113. The Hague: Mouton.

Landry, Rodrigue and Richard Y. Bourhis 1997 Linguistic landscape and ethnolinguistic vitality: an empirical study. Journal of Language and Social Psychology 16(1):23–49.

LeMaster, Barbara 2006 Language Contraction, Revitalization, and Irish Women. Journal of Linguistic Anthropology 16(2):211–228.

Lemon, Alaina Maria 2002 "Form" and "Function" in Soviet Stage Romani: Modeling Metapragmatics through Performance Institutions. Language in Society 31(1):29–64.

Leoni, Federico Albano, ed. 1980 I Dialetti e Le Lingue delle Minoranze di Fronte all'Italiano. Società di Linguistica Italiana. Rome: Bulzoni.

Lepschy, Anna L., Giulio Lepschy and Miriam Voghera 1996 Linguistic Variety in Italy. *In* Italian Regionalism: History, Identity, and Politics. Carlo Levy, ed. pp. 69–80. Oxford: Berg.

Leso, Erasmo, Michele A. Cortelazzo, Ivano Paccagnella, and Fabio Foresti 1978 La Lingua Italian e il Fascismo. Bologna: Consorzio Provinciale Pubblica Lettura.

Levy, Carl, ed. 1996 Italian Regionalism: History, Identity and Politics. Washington, DC: Berg.

Leydi, Roberto, ed. 1977 Mondo popolare in Lombardia: Bergamo e il suo territorio. Milano: Silvana Editoriale d'Arte.

Leydi, Roberto 1996 Guida alla Musica Popolare in Italia. Lucca: Libreria Musicale Italiana.

Lutz, Catherine 1986 Emotion, Thought, and Estrangement: Emotion as a Cultural Category. Cultural Anthropology 1:405–436.

Lutz, Catherine 1988 Unnatural Emotions: Everyday Sentiments on a Micronesian Atoll and Their Challenge to Western Theory. Chicago: University of Chicago Press.

Mack Smith, Denis 1988 The Making of Italy: 1796–1866. London: Holmes & Meier.

Mack Smith, Denis 1997 Modern Italy. A Political History. Ann Arbor: University of Michigan Press.

Maher, Vanessa 1996 Immigration and Social Identities. *In* Italian Cultural Studies: An Introduction. David Forgacs and Robert Lumley, eds. pp. 160–177. New York: Oxford University Press.

Maiden, Martin 1995 A Linguistic History of Italian. New York: Longman.

Maiden, Martin and Mair Parry, eds. 1997 The Dialects of Italy. London: Routledge.

Makihara, Miki 2004 Linguistic Syncretism and Language Ideologies: Transforming Sociolinguistic Hierarchy on Rapa Nui (Easter Island). American Anthropologist 106(3):529–540.

Martinelli, Alberto, Antonio M. Chiesi, and Sonia Stefanizzi 1999 Recent Social Trends in Italy 1960–1995. Montreal: McGill-Queen's University Press.

McEwan-Fujita, Emily 2003 Gaelic in Scotland, Scotland in Europe: Minority Language Revitalization in the Age of Neo-Liberalism. Ph.D. Dissertation. Department of Anthropology, University of Chicago.

McEwan-Fujita, Emily 2005 Neoliberalism and Minority Language Planning in the Highlands and Islands of Scotland. International Journal of the Sociology of Language 171:155–171.

Migliorini, Bruno and T. Gwynfor Griffith 1984 [1960] The Italian Language. London: Faber & Faber.

Milesi, Sereno Locatelli 1932 Maschere Bergamasche (Arlecchino e Giopì), con prefazione in versi di Giacinto Gambirasio. Bergamo: Ducato di Piazza Pontida.

Milroy, James and Leslie Milroy 1985 Authority in Language: Investigating Language Prescription and Standardization. London: Routledge & Kegan Paul.

Milroy, Leslie 1987 Language and Social Networks. Baltimore, MD: University Park.

Milton, Kay and Maruška Svašek, eds. 2005 Mixed Emotions: Anthropological Studies of Feeling. Oxford: Berg.

Mock, John 1993 We Have Always Lived Under the Castle: Historical Symbols and the Maintenance of Meaning. *In* The Cultural Meaning of Urban Space. Robert Rotenberg and Gary McDonogh, eds. pp. 63–74. Westport, CT: Bergin & Garvey.

Mora, Vittorio 1966 Note di Grammatica del Dialetto Bergamasco. Bergamo: Edizioni Orobiche.

Mora, Vittorio 1972 Per un'Atlante Linguistico Bergamasco (Temi e Problemi). Bergomum: Bollettino della Civica Biblioteca de Bergamo, No. 1.

Mora, Vittorio 1975 Rilevazione sulla conoscenza del dialetto e sulla situazione socio-economica culturale degli iscritti ai Licei Scientifici ed agli Istituti Tecnici Industriali della Provincia di Bergamo. [Unpublished study of dialect use in several high schools in Bergamo.]

Mora, Vittorio 1982 Questionnari vari. [Unpublished questionnaires.]

Mora, Vittorio 1983 Questionnari vari a Redona. [Unpublished questionnaires at Redona.]

Mora, Vittorio 1984 Contributi per una storia del teatro dialettale Bergamasco. Bergamo: Ducato di Piazza Pontida.

Morford, Janet 1997 Social Indexicality in French Pronomial Address. Journal of Linguistic Anthropology 7(1):3–37.

Myers, Fred R. 1994 Culture-Making: Performing Aboriginality at the Asia Society Gallery. American Ethnologist 21(4):679–699.

Myers, Fred R. 2002 Painting Culture: the Making of an Aboriginal High Art. Durham: University of North Carolina.

Nadel-Klein, Jane 1991 Reweaving the Fringe: Localism, Tradition, and Representation in British Ethnography. American Ethnologist 18(3):500–517.

Nencioni, Giovanni 1994 Introduzione. *In* Come Parlano gli Italiani. Tullio De Mauro, ed. pp. xxvii–xxxiv. Firenze: La Nuova Italia.

Ngugi wa Thiongo 1986 Decolonizing the Mind. New York: Heineman.

Ochs, Elinor 1979 Transcription as Theory. *In* Developmental Pragmatics. Elinor Ochs and Bambi B. Schieffelin, eds. pp. 43–72. New York: Academic Press.

Ochs, Elinor 1992 Indexing Gender. *In* Rethinking Context: Language as Interactive Phenomenon. Alessandro Duranti and Charles Goodwin, eds. pp. 335–358. Cambridge: Cambridge University Press.

Ochs, Elinor and Bambi B. Schieffelin 1984 Language Acquisition and Socialization: Three Developmental Stories and Their Implications. *In* Culture Theory: Essays on Mind, Self, and Emotion. R. Shweder and R. LeVine, eds. pp. 276–320. New York: Cambridge University Press.

O'Reilly, Camille, ed. 2001 Language, Ethnicity and the State. Volume 1: Minority Languages in the European Union. New York: Palgrave Macmillan.

Orioles, V., ed. 2002 La legislazione nazionale sulle minoranze linguistiche. Problemi, applicazioni, prospettive [special issue of Plurilinguismo: contatti di lingue e culture 9]. Udine: Centro Internazionale del Plurilinguismo.

ÖzyÜrek, Esra 2005 The Politics of Cultural Unification, Secularism, and the Place of Islam in the New Europe. American Ethnologist 32(4):509–512.

Paasi, Aansi 2001 Europe as a Social Process and Discourse: Considerations of Place Boundaries and Identity. European Urban and Regional Studies 8(7):7–28.

Pagliai, Valentina 2000 Through Veils of Words: Performing Politics, Gender and Identity in the Tuscan Contrasto. Ph.D. Dissertation. University of California Los Angeles.

Pagliai, Valentina 2003 Lands I Came to Sing: Negotiating Identities and Places. *In* Sociolinguistics: The Essential Readings. Christina Bratt Paulston and G. Richard Tucker, eds. pp. 48–69. Malden, MA: Blackwell Publishing.

Paugh, Amy L. 2001 'Creole is every day': Language Socialization, Shift, and Ideologies in Dominica, West Indies. Ph.D. thesis. New York University.

Pei, Mario 1941 The Italian Language. New York: Columbia University Press.

Però, Davide 2005 Left-wing Politics, Civil Society, and Immigration in Italy: The Case of Bologna. Ethnic and Racial Studies. 28(5): 832–858.

Pettigrew, Thomas F. 1998 Reactions Towards the New Minorities of Western Europe. Annual Review of Sociology 24:77–103.

Philips, Susan U. 2000 Constructing a Tongan Nation State through Language Ideology in the Courtroom. *In* Regimes of Language. Paul V. Kroskrity, ed. pp. 229–257. Santa Fe, NM: School of American Research Press.

Pitkin, Donald S. 1985 The House that Giacomo Built: History of an Italian Family, 1898–1978. Cambridge: Cambridge University Press.

Pitkin, Donald S. 1993 Italian Urbanscape: Intersection of Private and Public. *In* The Cultural Meaning of Urban Space. Robert Rotenberg and Gary McDonogh, eds. pp. 95–101. Westport, CT: Bergin & Garvey.

Puccini, Sandra and Massimo Squillacciotti 1980 Per una prima ricostruzione critico-bibliografica degli studi demo-etno-antropologici italiani nel periodo tra le Due Guerre. *In* Studi antropologici italiani e rapporti di classe: Dal positivismo a dibattito attuale. Quaderni di Problemi del Socialismo, 14, pp. 67–93, 201–239. Milan: F. Angeli.

Ravanelli, Renato 1996 La Storia di Bergamo, three volumes. Bergamo: Grafica e Arte.

Rogers, Susan C. 1987 Good to Think: The "Peasant" in Contemporary France. Anthropology Quarterly 60(2):56–63.

Rosaldo, Michelle Z. 1984 Toward an Anthropology of Self and Feelings. *In* Culture Theory: Essays on Mind, Self, and Emotion. R. Shweder and R. LeVine, eds. pp. 137–157. New York: Cambridge University Press.

Rumi, Giorgio, Gianni Mezzanotte and Alberto Cova, eds. 1997 Bergamo e il Suo Territorio. Milan: Cassa di Risparmio delle Provincie Lombarda S.p.A (Cariplo).

Ruzza, Carlo 2000 Language and Nationalism in Italy: Language as a Weak Marker of Identity. *In* Language and Nationalism in Europe. Stephen Barbour and Cathie Carmichael, eds. pp. 168–182. Oxford: Oxford University Press.

Sanga, Glauco 1984 Dialettologia Lombarda. Lingue e culture popolari. Pavia: Aurora.

Sanga, Glauco 1992 Per la Storia Linguistica dell'Italia Medievale. Milan: Edizioni.

Sanga, Glauco 1997 Lombardy. *In* The Dialects of Italy. Martin Maiden and Mair Parry, eds. pp. 253–259. London: Routledge.

Sanga, Glauco, ed. 1987 Lingua e Dialetti di Bergamo e delle Valli. Bergamo: Pierluigi Lubrina Editore.

Sapir, Edward 1949[1927] The Unconscious Patterning of Behavior in Society. *In* Selected Writings of Edward Sapir in Language, Culture and Society. D. G. Mandelbaum, ed. pp. 544–559. Berkeley: University of California Press.

Saunders, George 1984 Italian Cultural Anthropology. American Review of Anthropology, 13:447–466.

Saussure, Ferdinand 1986 Course in General Linguistics. Open Court.

Scheper-Hughes, Nancy 1985 Culture, Scarcity and Maternal Thinking: Maternal Detachment and Infant Survival in a Brazilian Shantytown. Ethos 13:291–317.

Scheper-Hughes, Nancy 1992 Death Without Weeping: The Violence of Everyday Life in Brazil. Berkeley: University of California Press.

Schieffelin, Bambi B. 1990 The Give and Take of Everyday Life: Language Socialization of Kaluli Children. Cambridge: Cambridge University Press.

Schieffelin, Bambi B. 2000 Introducing Kaluli Literacy: A Chronology of Influences. *In* Regimes of Language. Ideologies, Politics, and Identities. Kroskrity, Paul V., ed. pp. 293–327. Santa Fe, NM: School of American Research Press.

Schieffelin, Bambi B., Kathryn A. Woolard and Paul V. Kroskrity, eds. 1998 Language Ideologies: Practice and Theory. New York: Oxford.

Schiffrin, Deborah 1987 Discourse Markers. Cambridge: Cambridge University Press.

Schneider, Jane C., ed. 1998 Italy's 'Southern Question': Orientalism in One Country. Oxford: Berg.

Schneider, Jane C. and Peter T. Schneider 1996 Festival of the Poor. Fertility Decline and The Ideology of Class in Sicily, 1860–1980. Tucson: University of Arizona Press.

Sciolla, Loredana 1997 Italiani. Stereotipi di Casa Nostra. Bologna: il Mulino.

Sharman, Russell Leigh 2006 Re/Making La Negrita: Culture as an Aesthetic System in Costa Rica. American Anthropologist 108(4): 842–853.

Shoaps, Robin 2002 "Pray Earnestly": The Textual Construction of Personal Involvement in Pentecostal Prayer and Song. Journal of Linguistic Anthropology 12(1):34–71.

Shore, Cris 2001 The Cultural Politics of European Integration. New York: Routledge.

Shusterman, Richard 2000 Pragmatist Aesthetics: Living Beauty, Rethinking Art, 2nd edition. Boston: Rowman & Littlefield Publishers, Inc.

Silverman, Sydel 1975 Three Bells of Civilization: The Life of an Italian Hill Town. New York: Columbia University Press.

Silverstein, Michael 1976 Shifters, Linguistic Categories, and Cultural Description. *In* Meaning in Anthropology. Keith Basso and H. Selby, eds. pp. 11–55. Albuquerque: School of American Research, University of New Mexico Press.

Silverstein, Michael 1981 The Limits of Awareness. Working Papers in Sociolinguistics 84. Austin, TX: South West Educational Development Laboratory.

Silverstein, Michael 2003 Indexical Order and the Dialectics of Sociolinguistic Life. Language and Communication 23:193-229.

Sobrero, Alberto 1988 Conversational Microconvergences Between Dialect and Language. *In* Variation and Convergence: Studies in Social Dialectology. P. Auer and A. Di Luzio, eds. pp. 194–215. Berlin: Walter de Gruyter.

Sobrero, Alberto, ed. 1993 Introduzione all'Italiano Contemporaneo. La Variazione e gli Usi. Bari: Editori Laterza.

Sobrero, Alberto 1997 Italianization of the Dialects. *In* The Dialects of Italy. Martin Maiden and Mair Parry, eds. pp. 253–259. London: Routledge.

Stacul, Jaro 2001 When Language Does Not Matter: Regional Identity Formation in Northern Italy. *In* Language, Ethnicity and the State. Volume 1: Minority Languages in the European Union. Camille C. O'Reilly, ed. pp. 128–146. New York: Palgrave Macmillan.

Stacul, Jaro 2003 The Privatisation of Locality. Integralist Political Engagements in Northern Italy at the Turn of the Millennium. Cambridge Anthropology 23(2):36–53.

Stacul, Jaro 2005 Natural Time, Political Time: Contested Histories in Northern Italy. The Journal of the Royal Anthropological Institute 11(4):819–836.

Steinberg, Jonathan 1987 The historian and the 'questione della lingua'. *In* The Social History of Language. Peter Burke and Roy Porter, eds. pp. 198–209. Cambridge: Cambridge University Press.

Stewart, Kathleen 2007 Ordinary Affects. Durham: Duke University Press.

Stolcke, Verena 1999 New rhetorics of exclusion in Europe. International Social Science Journal 51(1):25–35.

Strassoldo, Raimondo 1996 Lingua, Identità, Autonomia: Ricerche e Riflessioni Sociologiche sulla Questione Friuliana. Campoformido; Udine: Ribis.

Swiggers, Pierre 1990 Ideology and the 'Clarity' of French. *In* J. Joseph and T. Taylor, eds. Ideologies of Language. New York: Routledge.

Tak, Herman 1990 Longing for Local Identity: Intervillage Relations in an Italian Mountain Area. Anthropological Quarterly 63(2):90–100.

Thompson, Doug 1991 State Control in Fascist Italy. Culture and Conformity, 1925–43. Manchester: Manchester University Press.

Tilley, Christopher 1993 Space, Place, Landscape and Perception: Phenomenological Perspectives. In A Phenomenology of Landscape Places, Paths and Monuments. pp. 7–35. Oxford: Berg.

Timm, Lenora 2001 Ethnic Identity and Minority Language Survival in Brittany. In Language, Ethnicity and the State. Volume 1: Minority Languages in the European Union. Camille C. O'Reilly, ed. pp.104–127. New York: Palgrave Macmillan.

Trosset, Carol 1993 Welshness Performed: Welsh Concepts of Person and Society. Tucson: University of Arizona Press.

Trudgill, Peter 1972 Sex, Covert Prestige, and Linguistic Change. Language in Society 1(2):179–196.

Trumper, John 1989 Observations on Sociolinguistic Behavior in Two Italian Regions. International Journal of the Sociology of Language 76:31–62.

Tsitsipis, Lukas D. 1998 A Linguistic Anthropology of Praxis and Language Shift. Arvanítika (Albanian) and Greek in Contact. Oxford: Clarendon Press.

Tullio-Altan, Carlos 1995 Ethnos e Civiltà: Identità Etniche e Valori Democratici. Milano: Feltrinelli.

Urciuoli, Bonnie 1995 Exposing Prejudice: Puerto Rican Experiences of Language, Race, and Class. Boulder, CO: Westview Press.

Urla, Jacqueline 1993a Contesting Modernities: Language Standardization and the Production of an Ancient/Modern Basque Culture. Cultural Anthropology 13(2):101–118.

Urla, Jacqueline 1993b Cultural Politics in an Age of Statistics: Numbers, Nation and the Making of Basque Identity. American Ethnologist 20(4):818–843.

Vitali, Gabriele 2000 Prefazione: Spunti per una presentazione. In Menabò: Poesie in dialetto bergamasco, pp. 9–10. Bergamo: Edizioni Grafital.

Vizmuller-Zocco, Jana 1999 Il Sostrato Dialetto nella Deriva dell'Italiano Neo-Standard. Italica. Linguistics and Pedagogy 76(4):469–479.

Weber, Eugen 1976 Peasants into Frenchmen: The Modernization of Rural France, 1870–1914. Stanford: Stanford University Press.

White, Jenny B. 1996 Belonging to a Place: Turks in Unified Berlin. City & Society 8(1):15–28.

Wilce, James M. 2009 Language and Emotion. New York: Cambridge University Press.

Wild, Sarah 1996 Distretti Industriali, Regionalismo e la Lega Lombardo: Il Caso di Bergamo. *In* Studi e Ricerche di Storia Contemporarea, 46:27–40.

Williams, Glyn 2005 Sustaining Language Diversity in Europe: Evidence from the Euromosaic Project. New York: Palgrave Macmillan.

Willis, Paul E. 1981 Learning to Labor. How Working Class Kids Get Working Class Jobs. New York: Columbia University Press.

Wolf, Richard K. 2006 The Poetics of "Sufi" Practice: Drumming, Dancing, and Complex Agency at Madho Lāl Husain (and beyond). American Ethnologist 33(2): 246–268.

Woolard, Kathryn A. 1989 Double Talk: Bilingualism and the Politics of Ethnicity in Catalonia. Stanford: Stanford University Press.

Woolard, Kathryn A. 1994 Gendered Peer Groups and the Bilingual Repertoire in Catalonia. Austin: University of Texas, SALSA II.

Woolard, Kathryn A. 1998 Introduction: Language Ideology as a Field of Inquiry. *In* Language Ideologies: Practice and Theory. Bambi B. Schieffelin, Kathryn A. Woolard and Paul V. Kroskrity, eds. pp. 3–47. New York: Oxford University Press.

Woolard, Kathryn A. 1999 Simultaneity and Bivalency as Strategies in Bilingualism. Journal of Linguistic Anthropology 8(1):3–29.

Woolard, Kathryn A. 2004 Codeswitching. *In* A Companion to Linguistic Anthropology. Alessandro Duranti, ed. pp. 73–94. Malden, MA: Blackwell Publishing.

Yanagisako, Sylvia Junko 2002 Producing Culture and Capital. Family Firms in Italy. Princeton: Princeton University Press.

Zanetti, Umberto 1966 Sonetti in Dialetto Bergamasco. Bergamo: Edizioni Orobiche.

Zanetti, Umberto 1969 Poesie in Dialetto Bergamasco. Bergamo: Edizioni Orobiche.

Zanetti, Umberto 1978 La Letteratura Dialettale Bergamasca del Novecento: Saggio di Bibliografia. Bergamo: Tipografia Editrice Secomandi.

Zentella, Ana C. 1987 Language and Female Identity in the Puerto Rican Community. *In* Women and Language in Transition. J. Penfield, ed. Albany, NY: SUNY Press.

Zentella, Ana C. 1997 Growing Up Bilingual: Puerto Rican Children in New York. Oxford: Blackwell Publishers.

Zuanelli Sonino, Elisabetta 1989 A Sociolinguistic Perspective of Language-education Problems in Italy. The International Journal of the Sociology of Language 76:87–107.

Index

Note: "n." after a page reference indicates the number of a note on that page.